Issues in Religion and

3

The Interpretation of Matthew

Titles in the series include:

Issues in Religion and Theology 3

The Interpretation of Matthew

Edited with an introduction by

GRAHAM STANTON

FORTRESS PRESS | SPCK
Philadelphia | London

First published in Great Britain 1983
SPCK
Holy Trinity Church
Marylebone Road
London NW1 4DU

First published in the USA 1983
Fortress Press
2900 Queen Lane
Philadelphia
Pennsylvania 19129

Library of Congress Cataloging in Publication Data
Main entry under title:

The Interpretation of Matthew

(Issues in religion and theology; 3)
Bibliographu: p.
Includes index.
1. Bible. N.T. Matthew—Criticism, interpretation, etc.—Addresses,
essays,
lectures. I. Stanton, Graham. II. Series.
BS2575.2.157   1983   226′.206   83–5508
ISBN0–8006–1766–5

British Library Cataloguing in Publication Data

The Interpretation of Matthew.—(Issues in religion and theology; 3)
1. Bible. N.T. Matthew—Commentaries
I. Stanton, Graham   II. Series
226′.206   BS2575.3

ISBN 0–281–04058–3

Filmset in Monophoto Times by Northumberland Press Ltd, Gateshead
Printed in Great Britain by Richard Clay (The Chaucer Press) Ltd,
Bungay, Suffolk

Contents

Acknowledgements

Ernst von Dobschütz, "Matthew as Rabbi and Catechist" was first published as "Matthäus als Rabbi und Katechet" in *Zeitschrift für die neutestamentliche Wissenschaft* 27 (1928) 338–48.

Otto Michel, "The Conclusion of Matthew's Gospel: a Contribution to the History of the Easter Message" was first published as "Der Abschluss des Matthäusevangeliums" in *Evangelische Theologie* 10 (1950–1) 16–26. It is reprinted by permission of the author. Copyright © Otto Michel 1950.

Nils Alstrup Dahl, "The Passion Narrative in Matthew" is reprinted by permission from *Jesus in the Memory of the Early Church* (Minneapolis: Augsburg, 1976) 37–51. Copyright © Augsburg Publishing House 1976.

Krister Stendahl, "Quis et Unde? An Analysis of Matthew 1–2" is reprinted by permission of the author from *Judentum, Urchristentum: Kirche*, ed. W. Eltester (Berlin: Topelmann, 1960) 94–105. Copyright © Krister Stendahl 1960.

Georg Strecker, "The Concept of History in Matthew" is reprinted by permission of the author and the *Journal of the American Academy of Religion*. Original publication (in German) in *Evangelische Theologie* 26 (1966) 57–74, in part translated and reprinted in the *Journal of the American Academy of Religion* 35 (1967) 219–30. Copyright © American Academy of Religion 1967.

Günther Bornkamm, "The Authority to 'Bind' and 'Loose' in the Church in Matthew's Gospel: the Problem of Sources in Matthew's Gospel" is reprinted by permission from *Jesus and Man's Hope*, ed. Donald G. Miller (Pittsburgh: Pittsburgh Theological Seminary, 1970) 1:37–50. Copyright © Pittsburgh Theological Seminary, 1970.

Ulrich Luz, "The Disciples in the Gospel according to Matthew" is reprinted by permission of the author. Original publication as "Die Junger im Matthäusevangelium" in *Zeitschrift für die neutestamentliche Wissenschaft* 62 (1971) 141–71. Copyright © Ulrich Luz 1971.

Eduard Schweizer, "Matthew's Church" is reprinted by permission from *Matthäus und seine Gemeinde* (Stuttgart: Verlag Katholisches Bibelwerk, 1974) 138–70. Copyright © Verlag Katholisches Bibelwerk 1974.

The editor and the publishers gratefully acknowledge the help of Robert Morgan in translating (from German) Chapters 1, 2, 7, 8 and part of Chapter 5 of this book.

The Contributors

GRAHAM STANTON is Professor of New Testament Studies in the University of London, King's College. *Jesus of Nazareth in New Testament Preaching* was published in 1974, and he has recently published several articles on Matthew's Gospel. He is the Associate Editor of *New Testament Studies*.

ERNST VON DOBSCHÜTZ (1870–1934) held a Chair of New Testament Studies at Halle from 1913 to 1934. He wrote a commentary on 1 and 2 Thessalonians in the Meyer series and made a number of major contributions to textual criticism. Four of his books were translated into English between 1904 and 1914.

OTTO MICHEL spent most of his career as Professor of New Testament Studies and Director of the Institutum Judaicum at the University of Tübingen. His major commentaries on Hebrews and Romans are part of the Meyer series. *Paulus und seine Bibel* was published in 1929. His four-volume edition (with German translation and notes) of Josephus' *De Bello Judaico* is a standard work.

NILS ALSTRUP DAHL is Emeritus Professor of New Testament at the Yale University Divinity School. His *Das Volk Gottes* was published in 1941. Three volumes of his essays have now been translated into English: *The Crucified Messiah* (1974), *Jesus in the Memory of the Early Church* (1976) and *Studies in Paul* (1977).

KRISTER STENDAHL was ordained in the Church of Sweden in 1944. In 1954 he took up an appointment at Harvard Divinity School, where he has been the Frothingham Professor of Biblical Studies since 1963. His published works include *The School of St Matthew* (1954) and *Paul among Jews and Gentiles* (1976).

GEORG STRECKER is Professor of New Testament Studies at the University of Göttingen. His study of Matthew's Gospel, *Der Weg der Gerechtigkeit* (1962) has been influential, and he has recently published several major essays on Matthew. Other works include *Das Judenchristentum in den Pseudoklementinen* (1958) and a volume of essays, *Eschaton und Historie* (1979).

GÜNTHER BORNKAMM held a Chair of New Testament Studies at

the University of Heidelberg for thirty years. Translations of his *Jesus of Nazareth* (1960) and *Paul* (1971) have reached a wide readership, as has *Tradition and Interpretation in Matthew* (1963), which he wrote together with G. Barth and H. J. Held. Essays from the first two of four volumes of his collected essays have been published in English in *Early Christian Experience* (1969).

ULRICH LUZ is Professor of New Testament Studies at the University of Berne. After a period as *Assistent* to Eduard Schweizer in Zürich, he held a Chair at the University of Göttingen for several years. His *Das Geschichtsverständnis des Paulus* was published in 1968, and a major commentary on Matthew is forthcoming.

EDUARD SCHWEIZER was Professor of New Testament Theology and Exegesis at the University of Zürich from 1949 to 1978. A number of his books have been translated, including his commentaries *The Good News according to Mark* (1971), *The Good News according to Matthew* (1976) and *The Letter to the Colossians* (1982). A volume of essays, *Matthäus und seine Gemeinde*, was published in 1974.

Series Foreword

The "Issues in Religion and Theology" series intends to encompass a variety of topics within the general diciplines of religious and theological studies. Subjects are drawn from any of the component fields, such as biblical studies, systematic theology, ethics, history of Christian thought, and history of religion. The issues have all proved to be highly significant for their respective areas, and they are of similar interest to students, teachers, clergy, and general readers.

The series aims to address these issues by collecting and reproducing key studies, all previously published, which have contributed significantly to our present understandings. In each case, the volume editor introduces the discussion with an original essay which describes the subject and its treatment in religious and theological studies. To this editor has also fallen the responsibility of selecting items for inclusion – no easy task when one considers the vast number of possibilities. Together the essays are intended to present a balanced overview of the problem and various approaches to it. Each piece is important in the current debate, and any older publication included normally stands as a "classical" or seminal work which is still worth careful study. Readers unfamiliar with the issue should find that these discussions provide a good entrée, while more advanced students will appreciate having studies by some of the best specialists on the subject gathered together in one volume. The editor has, of course, faced certain constraints: analyses too lengthy or too technical could not be included, except perhaps in excerpt form; the bibliography is not exhaustive; and the volumes in this series are being kept to a reasonable, uniform length. On the other hand, the editor is able to overcome the real problem of inaccessibility. Much of the best literature on a subject is often not readily available to readers, whether because it was first published in journals or books not widely circulated or because it was originally written in a language not read by all who would benefit from it. By bringing these and other studies together in this series, we hope to contribute to the general understanding of these key topics.

The series editors and the publishers wish to express their gratitude to the authors and their original publishers whose works are reprinted or translated here, often with corrections from living authors. We are also conscious of our debt to members of the editorial advisory board. They have shared our belief that the series will be useful on a wide scale, and they have therefore been prepared to spare much time and thought for the project.

DOUGLAS A. KNIGHT
ROBERT MORGAN

Abbreviations

BFCT	Beiträge zur Förderung christlicher Theologie
BZ	*Biblische Zeitschrift*
CBC	Cambridge Bible Commentaries
CBQ	Catholic Biblical Quarterly
Exp Tim	*Expository Times*
HTR	*Harvard Theological Review*
JAAR	*Journal of the American Academy of Religion*
JBL	*Journal of Biblical Literature*
JTS	*Journal of Theological Studies*
KEK	Kritisch-exegetischer Kommentar über das Neue Testament
NovT	*Novum Testamentum*
NTD	Das Neue Testament Deutsch
NTS	*New Testament Studies*
RB	*Revue biblique*
RE	*Realencyklopädie für protestantische Theologie und Kirche*
SJT	*Scottish Journal of Theology*
TDNT	G. Kittel and G. Friedrich (ed.), *Theological Dictionary of the New Testament*
TLZ	*Theologische Literaturzeitung*
TU	Texte und Untersuchungen
TWNT	G. Kittel and G. Friedrich (ed.), *Theologisches Wörterbuch zum Neuen Testament*
TZ	*Theologische Zeitschrift*
ZNW	*Zeitschrift für die neutestamentliche Wissenschaft*
ZTK	*Zeitschrift für Theologie und Kirche*

Introduction: Matthew's Gospel

A New Storm Centre

GRAHAM STANTON

In 1966 Luke-Acts was described by W. C. van Unnik as a storm centre in contemporary scholarship.[1] At that time it would hardly have been appropriate to refer to Matthew in this way. Although several major books had appeared between 1945 and 1965, there was a measure of scholarly agreement on many of the central issues in Matthean scholarship.[2]

Since 1965 discussion of Matthew has been much more intense: over forty books and an enormous number of articles have been published. Several issues long regarded as settled have been re-opened. Today debate is keener than ever. So many of the distinctive features of this Gospel continue to fascinate and to puzzle scholars that it is no exaggeration to suggest that Matthew is a new storm centre in contemporary scholarship.[3]

Here are some of the questions which have been debated over the last twenty years or so. Was the evangelist himself a Jew or a Gentile? Were his Christian readers mainly Jews or Gentiles? Was Matthew's community still under strong pressures from neighbouring Jewish synagogues? Or was Jewish persecution of Christians a matter of past history for the evangelist's community?

On what theological principles did Matthew rearrange and reinterpret his sources? Did he intend to set out his five lengthy discourses and related narrative sections as a counterpart to the Pentateuch? Is the evangelist primarily concerned with Christology or with ecclesiology? Is this Gospel a record of the life and teaching of Jesus as the central period in salvation history – a period of past time which has now been replaced by "the time of the Church"? Or is Matthew using his account of the actions and words of Jesus to address directly Christian readers in his own day? Does Matthew have a distinctive understanding of the significance of Jesus?

1

Can this Gospel be criticized as a retrogression from the teaching of Jesus or of Paul – or, for that matter, of Mark? Do some parts of the evangelist's "anti-Jewish" teaching have to be rejected by Christians today as profoundly un-Christian? What criteria can the Christian theologian use in deciding which aspects of this Gospel to accept, which aspects to reject and which to neglect? If Matthew's Gospel was originally written to meet quite specific pastoral or historical circumstances towards the end of the first century, how can it still speak to Christians today?

It will readily be apparent that some of these questions – and more could easily have been added to the list – are of special interest to the historian of first-century Judaism and Christianity; some of them are exegetical questions and some are hermeneutical questions of interest to the Christian theologian.

Most of these questions are discussed or at least touched on in the essays which have been included in this volume. The essays have been chosen partly because they are among the most perceptive and influential contributions to Matthean scholarship, and partly because they are not readily accessible to most English-speaking readers.

In this introductory essay attention is drawn to some of the points raised in the chosen essays which have been at the centre of more recent debate. We shall then examine briefly some features of Matthew which are not prominent in the essays which have been included.

Although the opening essay by Ernst von Dobschütz was written before the numerous redaction critical studies which began to appear in ever increasing numbers after 1945, most of his observations and assumptions are now widely accepted. All of the scholars whose essays are included here follow von Dobschütz's lead and accept as axiomatic that Matthew is heavily dependent on Mark. The essays by Dahl and Bornkamm provide valuable examples of the fruitfulness of careful source critical work.

Several attempts have recently been made to challenge Marcan priority. Supporters of the view that Matthew is closely dependent on Mark and on Q have been forced to reconsider some of the arguments which have been used in the past to support this hypothesis. A few of these arguments have now been shown to be untenable, while others have been shown to be reversible and to offer some support for a rival hypothesis. But in my view – and this is a view which is widely shared – none of the alternative explanations of the literary relationships between Matthew, Mark and Luke offers a more plausible and coherent account of the ways in which the evangelists have handled their sources than the traditional view. If we accept that Matthew is rearranging and reinterpreting Mark, Q and some oral traditions to which he alone among the evangelists had access, then we can give a reasonably clear and consistent account of his methods. This cannot be done on the basis of any of the other source critical hypotheses. Marcan priority and the Q hypothesis are not without some difficulties, but these are minimal in comparison with those raised by rival hypotheses.[4]

While von Dobschütz's arguments against Luke's use of Matthew (a view which still has a few supporters) are well worth careful consideration, his own claim that Matthew has used Luke's Gospel (if only in a secondary way) is probably the only point in this essay which would now generally be regarded as implausible.

Discussion of von Dobschütz's view that the evangelist was a converted rabbi is still very much alive. Many of his points have been taken further by M. D. Goulder in the opening chapters of his *Midrash and Lection in Matthew* (1974). According to Goulder, the evidence is weighty that von Dobschütz was "on the right lines: not quite that Matthew was a converted rabbi, but that he was a scribe, a provincial schoolmaster" (5). A very different view has been taken by K. W. Clark (1947), P. Nepper-Christensen (1958) and G. Strecker (1962) among others. They have been so impressed by the evangelist's apparent ignorance of Jewish customs and teaching and by his emphasis on "preaching the gospel of the kingdom throughout the whole world as a testimony *to all nations*" (Matt. 24:14) that they are convinced that the evangelist himself must have been a Gentile. They do, however, acknowledge that the evangelist has used Jewish-Christian traditions.

I am not sure that we yet know enough about all the currents of first-century Judaism to be able to pronounce confidently on Matthew's ignorance. In any case some of the phrases which clearly come from the evangelist's own hand (and which are not found elsewhere in the Gospels) do recall phrases and motifs which are prominent in the Jewish apocalypses which are roughly contemporary with Matthew's Gospel.

Otto Michel's 1950 study of the closing verses of the Gospel was one of the first modern studies to concentrate on the distinctive theological emphases of the evangelist. In 1948 G. Bornkamm had claimed that Matthew's reinterpretation of the Marcan account of the stilling of the storm offered "proof of definite theological intentions" (57); "the Marcan miracle story is reinterpreted with reference to discipleship and to 'the little ship of the church'" (55).

These two essays, along with G. D. Kilpatrick's book (1946), sparked off a whole series of studies of the distinctive features of Matthew. Close attention was given to Matthew's revision and re-arrangement of his sources. This general approach, known as redaction criticism, has been adopted by almost all recent writers on Matthew.

Michel's statement that Matt. 28:18–20 is the key to the understanding of the whole book has been quoted frequently. His claim that these words are a christological reshaping of Dan. 7:13–14 has been accepted by many writers, but it has been strongly challenged by A. Vögtle (1964). In a fine detailed study of this passage Vögtle insists that the perspective in Daniel is totally different from that in Matthew.

In another important essay on Matt. 28:18–20 G. Bornkamm accepts most of O. Michel's points, though he does note that in spite of the echoes of Dan. 7, the Son of Man title should not be imported too readily into Matt. 28, for that would imply the concept of the parousia which is absent from these verses. Bornkamm notes, surely correctly, that Matt. 28:18–20 is a summary of the evangelist's distinctive themes which is based firmly on traditional material. He concludes that "the Exalted Jesus who sets forth with authority the commands of the earthly Jesus for the church until the end of the world, and who makes them obligatory, gives to that church the pledge of his presence (28:20b), so that the gospel ends with the 'Immanuel' with which it began (1:23)."[5]

Two monographs have been devoted to the final five verses of the Gospel. Both studies advance our understanding of the background of this passage and of the evangelist's intention, but both abandon (unnecessarily in my view) Bornkamm's judicious and balanced assessment of the relationship between tradition and redaction in this passage. J. Lange (1973) argues that the whole pericope is a Matthean creation so closely modelled on Matt. 11:27/Luke 10: 22 (Q) that it can be called a "new edition" of this logion (488).

B. J. Hubbard (1974) concentrates on the literary form of these verses. He claims that many of the features which recur in narratives of commissionings of patriarchs and prophets in the OT can be readily discerned in Matt. 28:18–20. Behind these verses and the parallel material in John 20:19–23 and Luke 24:36–53 there is a "primitive apostolic commissioning" which has been redacted by the evangelist to bring it into closer correspondence with the form and language of the OT commissionings. J. Meier (1977) asks, rightly, whether there is any special commissioning "form" over against the general "form" of a theophany or angelophany; he believes that the form of the closing verses of Matthew is unique and is a combination of tradition and redaction.

While there is general agreement that these verses are crucial for Matthean Christology, views differ widely on their precise christological focus. J. Kingsbury ("Matthew 28" 1974) rejects the view of earlier scholars who have interpreted this passage either in terms of a Kyrios or of a Son of Man Christology. He claims that they are throughout the composition of the evangelist and that they have been informed by a Son of God Christology. Unless one accepts Kingsbury's view that the title Son of God is the central christological title in Matthew, this seems to be a lop-sided interpretation of the closing verses. Surely it is more plausible to see a cluster of related Matthean themes in this passage.

Nils Dahl's study of Matthew's passion narrative is a characteristically careful and thorough study of the evangelist's redactional methods. Not all redaction critics have heeded his warning that any attempt to set out Matthew's theology must beware of the danger of over-interpretation, for not all deviations from Mark are determined by a theological tendency.

Dahl observes that Matt. 21:43, a Matthean redactional verse ("the kingdom of God will be taken away from you and given to a nation producing the fruits of it") might be seen as the theme of the passion narratives, but he does not develop this point. This verse is certainly one of the most significant in the whole Gospel, for it seems to confirm that Matthew's Christian community has parted company with Judaism. We shall return to Matthew's relationship with contemporary Judaism below (see pp. 12ff).

A major monograph on Matthew's passion narratives has now been published by D. P. Senior (1975). He takes the same starting point as Dahl: four fifths of Matt. 26 and 27 is identical in vocabulary and content with its Marcan counterpart; there are no significant changes of order or omission of Marcan material. Senior believes that Matthew modifies his tradition in three main ways:

(i) There is a heightened christological portrait; many other writers have drawn attention to this feature of Matthew, with reference to a wide range of passages.

(ii) The responsibility of the Jews for the death of Jesus is emphasized. But Matthew's interest is not drawn towards the Jewish leaders' hostility *for its own sake*. It serves rather as an effective foil to the majesty and dignity of Jesus.

(iii) The evangelist is particularly aware of the moral value of the characters and events within the passion narrative as an inspiration and counter-example for his community. These observations seem to be correct. Matthew's passion narrative is perhaps the only section of the whole Gospel on which there is fairly general scholarly agreement at present.

In sharp contrast, however, Matthew's infancy narratives have been approached in very different ways. But most scholars would accept K. Stendahl's claim in the essay included here that once we stop reading Matt. 1 and 2 in the light of Luke's infancy narratives, the evangelist's methods and emphases can be seen clearly in these chapters.

In this essay Stendahl says very little about the striking ways OT passages are cited and used in these two chapters, a topic to which a monograph has now been devoted by G. Soares Prabhu (1976). Stendahl had earlier made a notable contribution to discussion of Matthew's use of the OT in his *The School of Matthew* (1954). We shall return to this theme below (see pp. 14f).

The mention of four women, Tamar, Rahab, Ruth and Bathsheba, in the genealogy has frequently fascinated scholars. Stendahl notes that this is unexpected and suggests that their "common denominator" is that they all represent an "irregularity" in the Davidic line, an irregularity by which the action of God and his Spirit is made manifest. Of the other explanations which have been canvassed more recently,[6] perhaps the most plausible is H. Stegemann's claim (which is supported by a detailed discussion of the relevant Jewish evidence) that the four women would have been readily recognized in first-century Jewish circles as *foreigners*.[7] If Matthew is emphasizing that Jesus is related by ancestry to Gentiles, the genealogy may form part of the evangelist's argument with some conservative Jewish Christians in his own day who were still reluctant to accept Gentiles into full membership of the Christian community.

Stendahl's central thesis that Matt. 1 answers the question "Who (*Quis*) is Jesus?", while Matt. 2 answers the question "Whence (*Unde*)?" has been welcomed and adapted by R. Brown (1979). In his analysis of these two chapters Brown suggests that 1:1–17 discusses the "Who?" of Jesus' identity and 1:18–25 the "How

(*Quomodo*)?"; 2:1–12, the "Where (*Ubi*)?" of Jesus' birth at Bethlehem, underlines his identity as Son of David, while in 2:13–23 the "Whence?" of Jesus' destiny is set in motion by the hostile reaction of Herod and the Jewish authorities. But as Brown himself recognizes, no single outline can do justice to the intertwined motifs.

In his final sentences Stendahl stresses that there is nothing which can be called the Matthean "Birth Narrative", for it is only in chap. 3 that the evangelist begins to set out a narrative account of the events of the life of Jesus. B. Nolan (1979) draws attention to the artificial distinction which Stendahl makes between Matt. 1 and 2 and the rest of the Gospel. Nolan shows, with little difficulty, that there are several aspects of these chapters which stamp them as narrative. In his monograph on Matt. 1 and 2 Nolan attempts to show that Matthew expounds "a Christology shaped by the covenant with Saint David" (243). Davidic motifs are prominent in Matthew's infancy narratives (and elsewhere in the Gospel), but Nolan uses phrases such as "Davidic mysticism" and "Davidic mystique" loosely and associates rather too many Matthean themes with the "royal, Davidic theology" which, he claims, integrates the evangelist's Christology.

G. Strecker's essay in this volume is a valuable summary of his influential monograph which was first published in 1962 and which still stimulates scholarly work on this Gospel. According to Strecker the evangelist has "historicized" his traditions because he sees history as a sequence of periods. The central epoch of salvation history is "the time of Jesus"; it is preceded by a "time of preparation" and is followed by "the time of the church", the time of world mission which lasts until the eschaton breaks in. This analysis is reminiscent of H. Conzelmann's exposition of Luke's "salvation history" in his *The Theology of Saint Luke* (ET 1960). Indeed, Strecker has been criticized for reading Matthew through *Lucan* spectacles.

His observations have been supported and taken further by R. Walker (1967) who believes that according to Matthew's schema the mission to Israel continues up to A.D. 70, after which the mission to the Gentiles begins and the mission to Israel ceases. This view, however, fails to do justice to Matt. 28:18–20 which links the mission to the Gentiles closely to the resurrection.[8]

A rather different explanation is offered by J. D. Kingsbury (1976) who claims that Matthew divides the history of salvation history into two (not three) epochs: the "time of Israel" (OT) and "the time of Jesus (earthly-exalted)". Although Kingsbury does not refer to Ulrich Luz's essay which is included in this volume, Luz's argument does support his general approach to Matthew. Both scholars insist that Matthew makes the disciples the representatives of the Christians of his church and both note that in Matthew (unlike Mark) the disciples do come to understand the teaching of Jesus.

In Strecker's view the evangelist is primarily concerned with the *past*, with the life of Jesus as the central epoch of salvation history. The corollary of this view is that in this Gospel Christology is dominant and Matthew's understanding of the Church is not expressed at all. At this point, at least, Strecker and Kingsbury are in agreement, but W. Trilling (1961) and E. Schweizer (1974) have set out the more traditional view that Matthew's main concerns are ecclesiological rather than christological. Surely this is an unnecessary debate: both themes are important for the evangelist; they are intertwined, as 1:21–3 and 28:18–20, for example, confirm.

G. Strecker insists that "righteousness", which Matthew adds to his sources in several places, does not imply the thought of a righteousness given to God (as in Pauline theology) but a righteousness realized by men.[9] In a fresh discussion of this Matthean theme B. Przybylski (1980) also protests against the tendency to read Matthew in terms of Paul. He goes on to show (convincingly, I think) that Matthew *does* teach that salvation is the gift of God (1:21); 26:28) but that this idea is expressed without reference to the concept of righteousness: Strecker has overstated the importance of the concept of righteousness in Matthew.[10]

Günther Bornkamm's first essay on Matthew was published in 1948, his most recent essay appeared in 1978. No scholar has had a greater influence on modern Matthean scholarship. Bornkamm's essay in this volume shows clearly that the whole of Matt. 18 is carefully composed by the evangelist as a unity – as, indeed, are the other Matthean discourses. Matt. 18 has also been examined by W. Pesch (1966) who suggests that the discourses should be seen as "sermons". Although Jesus is addressing his disciples, they are, as it were, ignored, and in their place we find Matthew addressing Christians in his own day with words of Jesus; the same conclusion is reached, with special reference to the discourse in chap. 10, by Ulrich Luz in his essay in this volume.

A monograph has been devoted to Matt. 18 by W. G. Thompson (1970). He also accepts that this section of the Gospel is a "unified and artistic composition" (267); it is designed to help the members of his congregation confront the problem of internal dissension, for scandal and sin were dividing the community. The dominant tone is proverbial rather than legal or prescriptive; the evangelist is giving advice rather than setting out a "community rule".

In the final section of his essay Bornkamm notes that in 18:15–18 the same authority is conferred on the congregation as is given to Peter alone in 16:17–19. These passages, which are the only two places in the Gospels where the term "church" is used, are discussed further by U. Luz and E. Schweizer in this volume and in a fine study of the portrait of Peter in Matthew by J. D. Kingsbury (1979). Kingsbury rejects Bornkamm's view that in Matthew Peter is the "supreme rabbi" whom Jesus has invested with the authority of teaching, and on whom Jesus has therefore built his Church. Kingsbury also rejects G. Strecker's view (1962, 205) that Peter is simply a "typical" disciple who provides the individual member of Matthew's church with an example of what it means, both positively and negatively, to be a Christian. According to Kingsbury, Peter's place is within the circle of disciples, but he does have a "salvation-historical primacy": Peter is the "rock", not because he has been elevated to an office above, or apart from, the other disciples, but by reason of the fact that he was the "first" of the disciples whom Jesus called to follow him. He stresses, surely correctly, that exegetical decisions concerning individual passages have to be made in the light of what one holds to be the overall structure of Matthew's thought.

This is perhaps the greatest single difficulty which confronts students of Matthew. Discussion of many of the evangelist's themes has been given greater precision by the development of redaction criticism. But this method cannot by itself settle some of the most keenly debated topics such as the role given to Peter by Matthew. The exegete is caught in a hermeneutical circle: since it is so difficult to grasp the overall structure of the evangelist's thought, we cannot always be certain that we have understood his intentions in particular passages.

Ulrich Luz's essay in the present volume takes discussion of Matthew's presentation of the disciples a good deal further. In the final verse of the Gospel the disciples are told by the risen and exalted Lord that they are to teach "all nations" to observe all that the disciples have been commanded. This finale underlines just how important the teaching of Jesus is for Matthew. In the main body of the Gospel some of that teaching is given to the disciples, some to the crowds and some, apparently, to both groups.

9

If, as Luz suggests, behind the disciples stands Matthew's community, what role do the crowds play? Quite independently of Luz, P. S. Minear (1974) examines the disciples and the crowds in Matthew. He concludes that the crowds (*ochloi*) correspond to the "laymen" of the evangelist's day. "When, therefore, the modern reader finds Jesus speaking to the crowds, he may usually assume that Matthew was speaking to contemporary laymen. When he finds Jesus teaching the disciples, he may usually suppose that Matthew had in mind the vocation of contemporary leaders as stewards of Christ's household" (41).

This conclusion probably outruns the evidence: as Luz notes, it is not always clear that behind the disciples we are to see the *leaders* in Matthew's community. But Minear has shown that the evangelist has a special interest in the crowds and refers to them in a fairly consistent way.

Minear starts his essay by noting that whereas the Revised Standard Version always translates *mathētai* by disciples, the translation of *ochloi* is varied: "crowd", "multitude", "throng", "people". "This practice reflects the assumption that the *ochloi* are heterogeneous and anonymous bystanders, with a casual and shifting constituency. These translations encourage readers to suppose that the relation of the *ochloi* to Jesus was transient and peripheral, and that any continuing relation they may have had to the *mathētai* was incidental, even accidental" (28f).

This is well observed. It underlines once again that translation of the Greek text is not – as students are so often taught – the first step in exegesis, but its *goal*. The second edition of the *New English Bible* (1970) provides a further illustration of this point. In the first edition (1961) "in fulfilment of" was used to translate *plēroō* at Matt. 4:14; 12:17, and 21:4; at 8:17 and 13:35 "to make good" translates the same verb. In one of the relatively few major revisions in the 1970 edition *all* these verses are brought into line with the other passages in Matthew where "to fulfil" is used to translate *plēroō* in introductions to citations of the OT. In this way the revised edition of the NEB brings out much more clearly the "formula" character of Matthew's introductions to his OT citations.

But back to Luz's essay for a moment. In his final pages he compares and contrasts Matthew's development of the discipleship theme with other strands of early Christianity. This approach is surely correct. A good deal of recent redaction critical work on Matthew (and on the other Gospels) has become much too "inward looking". The distinctive features of each Gospel are examined solely on the basis of each evangelist's redaction of the sources at his disposal: they can be brought into much sharper relief if they are set in the wider context of late first-century Christianity and Judaism. In this way it is possible to sketch the "map" of early Christianity and to trace (in however tentative a way) its development.

This is one of the most helpful and stimulating features of the final essay in this volume. In sections 2 and 8 Eduard Schweizer sets Matthew's references to Christian prophecy (and false prophecy) in the context of early Christianity. He also traces some of the features of Matthean Christianity in the recently discovered Nag Hammadi *Apocalypse of Peter* as well as in the *Didache*. I have myself suggested that *5 Ezra* (the two Christian chapters which come at the beginning of 4 Ezra) provides a further interesting parallel. *5 Ezra*, which may have been written shortly after A.D. 135, also stems from a community which sees itself as "the little ones" and in which Christian prophecy continues.[11]

Schweizer suggests that Matthew was written in Syria, possibly in Antioch. This is the traditional view, but, surprisingly, Schweizer does not mention one of the strongest arguments in its favour. The first clear evidence of use of Matthew comes from Ignatius, Bishop of Antioch. The opening verse of his *Epistle to the Smyrneans* ("in order to fulfil all righteousness") seems to reflect knowledge of Matt. 3:15, a redactional verse which stems from the evangelist's hand.

There have been several other attempts to locate Matthew's community. G. D. Kilpatrick (1946) proposed a southern Phoenician city, perhaps Tyre or Sidon, but our knowledge of these cities in the final quarter of the first century is so limited that it is not easy to make out a case either for or against them. S. van Tilborg (1972, 172) proposes Alexandria and B. T. Viviano (1979) suggests Caesarea Maritima. But perhaps the most interesting fresh suggestion is made by H. D. Slingerland (1979) who believes that Matt. 4:15 and 19:1 both reveal the redactional hand of the evangelist and confirm that he is writing somewhere *east* of the Jordan. Hence both Antioch and the Phoenician sea coast are unlikely.[12]

As on so many of the issues touched on in the essays in this volume, discussion will undoubtedly continue. But unless scholars follow the lead of Schweizer and Luz (and a small number of other Matthean specialists) and attempt to set Matthew in the wider context of early Christianity there is a real danger that the debate will become sterile.

The essays included here discuss a wide range of topics and examine in detail a number of most important passages in the Gospel. Three related topics are conspicuous by their virtual absence: the relationship of Matthew's community to contemporary Judaism, his use of the OT and his attitude to the law.

On the traditional view Matthew was the first Gospel to be written. Its author was a disciple of Jesus who wrote in Hebrew or Aramaic for a Palestinian Jewish-Christian community. This view became untenable once it was generally accepted that since Matthew had used Mark in *Greek*, he was unlikely to have been a disciple of Jesus.

A number of scholars have argued that Matthew's community had not yet broken its links with Judaism after AD 70.[13] G. Bornkamm (1956, 19f) for example, suggests that the pericope about the temple tax (17:24–7) shows that "the congregation which Matthew represents is still attached to Judaism and that it in no way claims for itself exemption from the taxation of the diaspora congregations ... the disciples of Jesus pay the Temple tax as free sons, merely in order not to give offence" (19f). "The struggle with Israel is still a struggle within its own walls" (39). W. D. Davies uses Bornkamm's phrase "a struggle within its own walls" to describe Matthew's relationship to Judaism. He provides a very detailed study of the reconstruction of Judaism which took place at Jamnia following the fall of Jerusalem in A.D. 70, and suggests that a number of passages in the Gospel, and chapters 5–7 in particular, may be seen as the Christian answer to Jamnia.

Davies' stimulating contribution has been widely acclaimed, but many scholars are not persuaded that Matthew's community still retained very close links with Judaism of the Jamnian period. G. Bornkamm modified his position between the 1956 essay quoted above and the 1970 essay included in this volume. In the latter he notes, with reference to Matt. 18:19f that Matthew's community, although still very small, knows itself to be *cut off* from the Jewish community ..." (p. 88).

Although Bornkamm's earlier position is still defended, in future it will need to be set out much more thoroughly if it is to remain plausible. It may prove possible to make some progress by exploring the "limits of tolerance" within first-century Judaism. There must have been "boundaries" beyond which innovation was unacceptable. But even if our knowledge of the development and structures of Judaism in the period immediately after A.D. 70 increases, this view will probably still founder on two crucial passages. At 21:43, in a redactional verse, Jesus says to the chief priests and elders, "the kingdom of God will be taken away from you and given to a nation producing the fruits of it";[14] and at 28:15, in the only such passage in Matthew, "the Jews" is used in a thoroughly Johannine way and seems to indicate that the Matthean community saw itself as a separate and quite distinct entity over against Judaism.

If Matthew's community has cut all its ties with Judaism, is the evangelist a *Gentile* Christian whose community is neither attacking nor defending itself against any strand of Judaism in the Jamnian period, A.D. 70–100? Were most members of Matthew's community Gentiles for whom discussion with Judaism had become either impossible or irrelevant?

This general approach has been defended by a number of scholars. They claim that the evangelist betrays his ignorance of contemporary Judaism—a point we discussed briefly above. Some have suggested that Matthew's permanent rejection of Israel is so clear and strong that it must have been written by a Gentile, since no Jewish Christian would have been capable of such a view of Israel.[15]

But the evidence can be explained very differently. The intensity of Matthew's anti-Pharisaism in redactional passages suggests to some scholars that the evangelist must have been *a Jew*. "Whereas the Gentile Luke speaks of the synagogue with the detachment natural to one for whom it is a foreign institution, Matthew speaks as one from whom it has only recently become an alien institution."[16] Once again *5 Ezra* provides an instructive parallel: anti-Jewish and pro-Gentile views are even more pronounced than they are in Matthew, but from its form and contents there can be no doubt that its author was a Jewish Christian.[17]

On any view Matthew's polemic against Israel is such a distinctive feature of his Gospel that some account must be given of it. Some acknowledge, with great regret, that Matthew's attacks on Israel were intended to be taken at face value. L. Gaston, for example, claims that since Matthew taught the Church to hate Israel, the redactor Matthew, as distinguished from the tradition he transmits, can no longer be part of the personal canon of many Christians. Gaston appeals to Luther's hermeneutical criterion: "We commend Christ against Scripture" (1975, 40).

But not all scholars have reached such a drastic conclusion. In a sensitive discussion of Matthew's "anti-Judaism" S. Légasse (1972, 426) emphasizes that the evangelist is primarily concerned to instruct his Christian community; he is as harsh on unfaithful Christians as he is on unbelieving Jews: Christians can also be called "hypocrites" (7:5) and condemned as such (24:51). Judgement on Christians can be severe – as 21:11–12 confirms.

For many Christians today Matt. 23 is embarrassing. The unremitting attack on scribes and Pharisees seems to contrast sharply with passages such as 22:38 and 5:43–8 which speak of love of one's neighbour. A monograph has been devoted to this difficult chapter by D. Garland (1979). He emphasizes that in Matt. 23:1 Jesus is portrayed by the evangelist as addressing both crowds and disciples. The inclusion of disciples indicates that the discourse is intended by Matthew to be a warning to the leaders in his own church. Matt. 23 has a pedagogical function: the same judgement which befell the leaders of Israel awaits the unfaithful leaders of Christ's community (215).[18]

In ten passages in Matthew (some scholars add up to four further passages) the OT is cited in a quite distinctive way. These "fulfilment" citations have intrigued scholars for a long time and their origin is still under keen discussion. There is general agreement that the passive of the verb *plēroō* which is found in all the introductions to the citations is particularly important. All these passages function as "asides" of the evangelist and not as part of his narrative; they all have a mixed form of the OT text which is less close to the Septuagint (LXX) than other passages in Matthew where the OT is cited.

K. Stendahl claimed that these passages contained a special type of biblical interpretation, a *pesher* translation which presupposes an advanced study of the Scriptures (in the "school" of Matthew); the OT text is treated in somewhat the same manner as in the Habakkuk scroll discovered at Qumran. These views have not gone unchallenged; Stendahl himself has offered important modifications in a new preface to his influential monograph (2nd edn 1968).

G. Strecker concluded that although the formula which introduces the fulfilment citations contains Matthean wording, the citations themselves cannot be the work of the evangelist himself as they differ considerably from the LXX which the evangelist normally follows: they come from a source which is used in a rather pedantic way to set the history of Jesus back in the past as a chronologically and geographically distant event.

Several other important contributions to this rather technical debate have been made.[19] Almost the only point on which there is general agreement is that there are important differences between the fulfilment formula quotations and the other citations of the OT found in Matthew. I am not at all sure myself that such a sharp division does justice to the evidence. If an individual OT passage has been translated (at whatever stage) in a fairly free way (as was customary), or if the form of the citation has been adapted to the context in which it is set, it then becomes difficult to prove that individual quotations are drawing on a particular text form. And, in addition, it is now becoming clear that both the Hebrew and Greek textual traditions of the OT were very much more fluid in the first century than most scholars who have studied Matthew's use of the OT have assumed.

Even after a good deal of very detailed work it is clear that the origin of many of the evangelist's OT citations is an unresolved issue. There seems to be reasonable certainty at only one point: the introductory fulfilment formulae which *precede* many of the OT citations are a distinctive and important Matthean refrain.

Matthew's presentation of the attitude of Jesus to the law is an equally difficult theme. It is not surprising that J. P. Meier can comment rather shrewdly that the carefully constructed views of many recent scholars on "Matthew and the Law" rudely collide with certain redactional texts in Matthew and – worse still – with statements made by the scholars themselves elsewhere in their own monographs (1977, 43)!

In an influential essay G. Bornkamm (1956) emphasized that for Matthew the law is binding down to the last jot and tittle. Matt. 5:17–19 may be directed against a tendency to abandon the law. For Matthew the right interpretation and the essence of the law is summed up in Jesus' command of love to God and to one's neighbour (22:40), and in the evangelist's formulation of the golden rule (7:12).

G. Barth (1960) argues that Matthew is opposing two views: against antinomians who wished to abolish the law, he stresses its continuing validity; against rabbinic Judaism he emphasizes the right interpretation of the law. The evangelist's Christology leads him to raise the love-commandment to be the criterion for the interpretation of the law.

In a careful study of the most crucial passage of all, Matt. 5:17–20, J. P. Meier (1977) argues that these verses do not contain, as so many scholars have conceded (often almost in desperation), disparate material loosely strung together.[20] The core of 5:18 is a traditional "conservative" statement which has been redacted by the addition of the final clause "until all is accomplished":

the most insignificant part of the law will not lose its binding force until all things come to pass in the eschatological event, the death–resurrection of Jesus. 5:17 (which has been heavily redacted by the evangelist) and 5:20 (probably a Matthean creation) are interpreted along these lines. Meier is forced to concede that 5:19 seems like an "undigested morsel", a "literary fossil" (165f) which probably originated as a corrective of "moderate" Jewish Christians over against the very stringent position taken in the original version of 5:18.

From this sketch it is again clear that an individual scholar's understanding of the whole structure of Matthean theology will determine to a considerable extent his exegesis of particularly difficult and important passages. There is general agreement that in his emphasis on "fulfilment" Matthew implies that Jesus *modifies* in some ways contemporary understandings of the law. But it is far from easy to spell out precisely what "fulfilment" and "modification" mean. At this point scholars tend to appeal, not always very convincingly, to the evangelist's Christology or to his eschatology in order to expound his attitude to the law.

But even if we appeal to the structure of Matthew's theological thought it is far from easy to determine exactly how Matthew's community practised the law from day to day. We may simply have to accept that the evangelist was less creative as a theologian and less consistent than some of his modern students have supposed. There may well have been diverse attitudes to the law among the members of Matthew's community: perhaps the evangelist has made use of disparate traditions at his disposal and has not always striven hard to be fully consistent.

The preceding paragraphs have given examples of some of the unresolved issues in Matthean scholarship and have shown that scholarly interest in this Gospel is keener now than it has ever been. Matthew's Gospel was more widely used and more influential in the early Church than any of the other Gospels. Today it is very much a storm centre.

But what of the future? How will Matthean scholarship develop over the next decade or two? It is rash to "play the prophet", but several possible lines of advance may be mentioned.

There is an urgent need for full-scale commentaries, for Matthew has not been as well served as have the other three Gospels.[21] The task is daunting, for we need commentaries which will not only assess critically recent Matthean scholarship but which will also attempt to develop individual lines of interpretation of the whole Gospel.

Scholarly interest in many aspects of first-century Judaism is considerable and significant advances are being made, especially by J. Neusner and his pupils. Few Matthean specialists have yet taken these advances sufficiently seriously.

Although there has been plenty of interest in the relationship of Matthew's community to Judaism, few scholars have followed the example of L. Goppelt and M. Simon and set this question in the wider context of Christian-Jewish relationships in the first and second centuries.[22]

There are also some grounds for hoping that the new interest of students of early Christianity in the social sciences will bear fruit in the future. But perhaps we should not be too optimistic: this Gospel may well lend itself to study along these lines rather less readily than some other early Christian writings.

In recent years Matthean scholarship has been dominated by redaction criticism. Undoubtedly this method has been very fruitful, as we have seen, but unless its assumptions and procedures are reconsidered carefully it may become increasingly barren. And if our understanding of the origin and purpose of the Gospel is to be clarified further, redaction criticism will certainly need to be complemented by a variety of other approaches

NOTES

1   "Luke-Acts, A Storm Center in Contemporary Scholarship", *Studies in Luke-Acts* ed. L. E. Keck and J. L. Martyn (Nashville, 1966; London, 1968) 15–32.

2   See, for example, G. D. Kilpatrick (1946) and G. Bornkamm, G. Barth and H. J. Held (1963).

3   For a detailed discussion of recent Matthean scholarship see G. N. Stanton, "Origin and Purpose" (1983).

4   W. R. Farmer (1964) has attempted to revive the Griesbach hypothesis. On this view Matthew's Gospel was the first to be written, Luke used Matthew, and Mark used both Matthew and Luke. J. M. Rist (1978) rejects firmly the Griesbach hypothesis and Marcan priority; he argues that Matthew and Mark are independent of one another.

5   G. Bornkamm (1963) 228.

6   See R. Brown (1979) 71–74 for a useful survey.

7   "Die des Uria: Zur Bedeutung der Frauennamen in der Genealogie von Matthäus, 1:1–17", *Tradition und Glaube*, Festgabe K. G. Kuhn ed., G. Jeremias et al. (Göttingen, 1972) 246–76. Brown's criticisms (see note 6) of this view are not convincing.

8 See J. P. Meier (1976) 25f for a discussion of this point.

9 G. Strecker's monograph (1962) is entitled "The Way of Righteousness. Studies in the Theology of Matthew".

10 Przybylski provides a valuable study of righteousness in Matthew, the Dead Sea Scrolls and the Tannaitic writings.

11 See G. N. Stanton (1977) 80ff.

12 Slingerland suggests Pella, but his reasons are not convincing.

13 See, for example, R. Hummel (1966[2]), W. D. Davies (1966) and M. D. Goulder (1974).

14 See W. Trilling (1964[3]) 58ff for a detailed defence of the view that 21:43 stems from the evangelist's own hand and for a discussion of its wider implications.

15 See especially K. W. Clark (1947).

16 D. R. A. Hare (1967) 165.

17 See G. N. Stanton (1977) 74f.

18 A similar view is defended by E. Schweizer (1974) 38 and 116ff, and by S. van Tilborg (1972) 168f.

19 For a useful survey see F. van Segbroeck (1972).

20 See also the excellent study by U. Luz (1978).

21 Two commentaries have been published recently. F. W. Beare (1981) has provided a solid commentary, but his comments on individual passages are often very brief and he takes little account of the most recent phases of Matthean scholarship. R. H. Gundry's commentary (1982) is stimulating but rather idiosyncratic: he adopts a thorough-going redaction critical stance, arguing that the evangelist has composed several key redactional sections himself and has not used earlier traditions; he also insists that the author is Matthew, the disciple of Jesus.

22 L. Goppelt, *Christentum und Judentum im ersten und zweiten Jahrhundert* (Gütersloh 1954); M. Simon, *Verus Israel* (Paris, 1964[2]).

1

*Matthew as Rabbi and Catechist**

ERNST von DOBSCHÜTZ

The Gospel according to Matthew is the first in the present order of NT writings and this sequence goes back to the second century. No wonder that this Gospel more than any has determined people's ideas and that it has been normative for both the outline of the life of Jesus and the individual form of the Lord's deeds and words. Until the eighteenth century that was undisputed. Only in 1786 did Storr venture the opinion that Matthew might have been dependent on Mark. When in 1838 this idea was taken up simultaneously by Wilke and Weisse it established itself victorious, despite the set-back it suffered in 1841 from Bruno Bauer's radical hypothesis about Mark. In the so-called two-source hypothesis, as this was worked out especially by H. J. Holtzmann in 1863, Weizsäcker in 1864, and Bernhard Weiss in 1872, it lies at the basis of all modern research. There are only a very few individual scholars who carry on with the older view: Zahn, Schlatter, G. Dalman, and others. As the last of the Tübingen school, Adolf Hilgenfeld fought right up to his death for the priority of Matthew with tenacious zeal, and the same arguments have recently been adduced by G. Schläger. But these individuals can no more make headway against the broad front represented by Jülicher, Wernle, Wellhausen, etc. than their wrongly interpreted individual observations can against the total impression. Nevertheless it is no wonder that even among other researchers who have grown up completely under the dominance of the two-source theory, the traditional influence of Matthew continues to be felt. It therefore seems to me desirable to establish certain points once again as firmly as possible.

---

* First published in *ZNW* 27 (1928) 338–48. Translated by Robert Morgan.

I

In a large number of recent monographs[1] we find the observation that Jesus began by taking over the preaching of the Baptist. The Baptist too is said to have proclaimed the nearness of God's kingdom and to have attached his demand for repentance to that. This goes back to the fact that Matt. 3:2 formulates the preaching of the Baptist in exactly the same terms as Matt. 4:17 does the first preaching of Jesus. But is this correct? Are we methodologically justified in using this source in this way in the face of the different evidence of the other Gospels? Our answer is: No, because one of the characteristic peculiarities of Matthew is that he likes echoes. Unlike the more literary educated Luke who aims at as many variations as possible, when Matthew has once found a formula he sticks to it as much as possible and uses it repeatedly. This harmonizing tendency can be observed as early as the introduction to the story of the Baptist and Jesus in Matthew. Both at 3:1 and at 3:13 he has *paraginetai* ("came") whereas his source had something different at Mark 1:4 and 1:9.[2] We may also compare 4:23, "to heal every disease and every infirmity", with 9:35 and 10:1.

Matthew very often has the same thing twice. He twice repeats the saying of Jesus that he was not sent except to the lost sheep of the house of Israel, in the mission discourse at 10:6 and in the story of the Canaanite woman at 15:24. In the first passage his special source which we cannot check may have contained this, but in the second he inserted it himself into the Marcan tradition.

He also twice has the saying from Hosea 6:6, "I desire mercy and not sacrifice", at 9:13 in the meal with publicans, and at 12:7 in the sabbath controversy over plucking corn. In both cases it seems to be an addition of our evangelist. We know that it was a favourite saying of Rabbi Jochanan ben Zakkai who used it to console himself and his disciples over the loss of the Temple and the possibility of sacrifice.[3] Of course this is not its significance in the Gospel; but one might suppose that the evangelist had earlier belonged to the school of Jochanan (see below). Matthew twice uses the saying about the first being last, at 19:30 (from Mark 10:31) and at 20:16 at the end of the parable of the Labourers in the Vineyard, which is probably his own addition.

Matthew twice inserts the address, "O wicked and adulterous generation", into the demand for a sign (which the two sources cause to be told twice): at 12:39 and at 16:4 which echoes Mark 8:38, "in this adulterous and sinful generation". This is lacking in the parallels at Matt. 16:26 and Luke 9:26, which is exceptional. At the demand for a sign in 8:12 Mark has only "this generation". But from Luke 11:29 Q seems to have had "evil generation". Together with the influence of Mark 8:28, this accounts for Matthew's expanded formula not only in the Q passage Matt. 12:39, but also in the passage taken from Mark at Matt. 16:4.

Matthew twice includes on his own account the clause *parektos logou porneias* (5:32) or *mē epi porneią* (19:9) ("except in a case of unchastity") in the prohibition of divorce. The Mark 10:11 and Luke 16:18 parallels to the latter passage do not have it. It seems to reflect the influence of rabbinic tradition (see below).

Twice he adds to the saying, "to him who has will more be given" his own phrase *kai perisseuthēsetai* ("and he will have abundance"), at 13:12 (= Mark 4:25; Luke 8:18) and at 25:29 (Q; Luke 19:26). This is perhaps an echo of the *kai prostethēsetai hymin* ("and still more will be given to you") at Mark 4:24.

The motif of compassion upon the leaderless people in the feeding story (Mark 6:34) is included by Matthew not only (in abbreviated form) at 14:14, but also as early as 9:36, in an expanded form. Matthew includes the warnings of the eschatological discourse 24:9–14 (= Mark 13:9–13) also in the mission discourse, as early as 10:17–22. He has sayings of Jesus about oaths at both 5:33–7 and 23:16–22. He includes the Baptist's phrase "brood of vipers" (3:7 = Luke 3:7, Q) on the lips of Jesus in his discourse against the Pharisees at 23:33 as well; that parallel particularly deserves our attention.

Add to this that our evangelist duplicates whole stories: the healing of two blind men (9:27–31 = 20:29–34 = Mark 10:46–52); and the healing of a dumb demoniac (9:32–4 = 12:22f, probably Q, = Luke 11:14). Matthew's delight in correspondences is quite clear.

His harmonization of the voices from heaven at the baptism and transfiguration is particularly characteristic. He takes the *houtos* ("this") from 17:5 (= Mark 9:7) and puts it in place of the address in the second person at 3:7 (= Mark 1:11). Conversely he supplements 17:5 with *en hǭ eudokēsa* ("with whom I am well pleased") taken from 3:17, so that 17:5 only goes beyond the voice at the baptism (3:17) with "listen to him" provided by Mark 9:7.

The harmonizing tendency is particularly clear in the doublets, i.e. the sayings which Matthew takes over both from Mark and from Q. The wording of the sayings is different in both sources but Matthew tries so far as possible to harmonize them. Compare Matt. 10:38,39 and 16:24,25 with Luke 14:27; 17:33 and Mark 8:34,35.

21

And compare Matt. 13:12 and 25:29 with Mark 4:25 and Luke 19:26: Matthew also includes in the second passage the *ap' autou* ("from him") which does not fit at all well in Q's participial construction, because he has taken it over in the first passage from Mark's relative clause.

The conclusion of all this is that when we find in Matthew two passages with the same wording we must recognize that this is his own work, not earlier tradition. When we apply this to the question about the Baptist, it means that the evangelist has taken the idea of preaching the Kingdom of heaven from the words of Jesus and introduced it into the preaching of the Baptist. It was not there originally. The Baptist preaches an imminent judgement and in connection with that the coming of a judge. Jesus preaches the coming near of the Kingdom of God of which he is himself the bearer, though he does not speak of that. That sums up the whole difference between these two, and it should not be blurred. The Baptist proclaims threats of damnation, repentance, flight from the world; with Jesus there comes a message of salvation, faith, affirmation of the world.

Matthew's harmonizing of their content is prepared at the formal level by Luke who at 3:18 applies the verb *euangelizesthai* ("to preach good news") to the preaching of the Baptist; Heb. 4:2 extends it to the OT promise.

II

It is well known that Matthew repeats five times the formula, "and it happened, when Jesus had finished these sayings" (7:28; 11:1; 13:53; 19:1; 26:1). Matthew thus clearly designates the conclusion of his five large groups of sayings. Some people have believed that these five passages can be assigned to his source, the sayings source, which on this view was divided into five parts, and they have then connected it with the fact that Papias' well-known work, *Interpretation of the Words of the Lord*, was divided into five books.[4] This theory again overlooks the fact that Matthew likes to repeat his formulae. In one passage, the first, it was in fact provided by his source, as can be seen by comparing 7:28 with Luke 7:1. In none of the other passages does Luke provide any such parallel to Matthew's formula. Thus it is clear that the four other applications of the formula do not come from the source but are due to the evangelist himself.

By way of analogy I refer to Matthew's frequent formula *en ekeinǭ tǭ kairǭ* ("at that time") which he uses without chronological precision simply as a transition, just as he inserts his *tote* ("then") without ado for Mark's connecting "and". He first has the formula at 11:25 where it is evidently taken from Q (cf. Luke 10:21). It then crops up at 12:1 and 14:1.[5] On this cf. *en ekeinais tais hēmerais* ("in those days") at 3:1, which comes from Mark 1:9.[6]

Or another example: the saying about weeping and gnashing of teeth in the material about drawing the Gentiles into the messianic meal (Matt. 8:12 = Luke 13:28, from Q). But Matthew has it five more times: in the parables of the Tares among the Wheat, and the Dragnet (13:42,50); and the king's Feast (22:13), the Servant in charge (24:51), and the Talents (25:30).

There is the frequently repeated introductory formula to Matthew's "formula quotations" – "in order that it might be fulfilled which was spoken by the Lord through the prophet" (or some such) – at 1:22; 2:15,23; 4:14; 8:17; 12:17; 13:35; 21:4; or "Then was fulfilled" – 2:17; 27:9. These all stem ultimately from Mark 14:49 = Matt. 26:54,56.

III

Matthew's delight in stereotypes is at once apparent in chap. 1 in the genealogy with its forty-fold repetition, "A begat B". The saying of the Lord at 5:22 contains *enochos estai* ("shall be guilty of") which occurs three times and *hos d'an eipē* ("whoever says") which occurs twice. 5:29ff has "throw it away; it is better that" twice; 5:34ff has *mēte en ... hoti* ("neither by ... because") four times. In these sayings of Jesus it is probably not the evangelist who creates the stereotype. He takes it from the tradition—but he likes doing so. He could have avoided it, as a comparison with the parallels in Luke shows.

There is also the pleasure Matthew takes in the schematic use of numbers. He counts three times fourteen generations in the genealogy and has clearly made the beatitudes up to eight by filling them out with individual traditions. Luke still shows what the original four were. Similarly he has increased the examples of Jesus "perfecting" the law from two to six. The source had as examples for 5:17 only the first two "you have heard that it was said to the men of old ... but I say to you" – namely, the sayings about murder and adultery (the fifth and sixth commandments). This follows from the fact that (a) the third example about the bill of divorce and the fourth about oaths do not fit at all well into the scheme of the command being broken by the sin of the thought;

and (b) the material of the fifth and sixth examples is found in Luke too, but in a quite different form, without the antithesis to the law. It can similarly be shown from formal observations in the three examples for 5:20 which follow in 6:1–18, that at least vv. 7f, 9–13, 14f are the evangelist's insertions from other traditions.[7]

<h1 style="text-align:center">IV</h1>

Now where does this inclination towards stereotype and formula in our evangelist come from? There are two possible explanations which do not exclude but supplement each other:

(a) It is rabbinic style. To anyone who knows the talmudic tradition, this uniformity, carried often to the point of boredom, will be sufficiently familiar. One need only read a little in the Strack-Billerbeck extracts from the talmudic literature to get a very strong impression of this. I recall once again Matt. 5:22 where Jesus imitates, clearly ironically, the style of the rabbis when he says, "But I say to you that everyone who is angry with his brother shall be liable to judgement; whoever insults his brother shall be liable to the council, and whoever says, 'You fool!' shall be liable to the hell of fire."

Our first evangelist is plainly a Jewish Christian who has undergone a rabbinic schooling. He is a converted Jewish rabbi. This inner relationship with rabbinism is the reason why Matthew is the Gospel modern students of rabbinism always most like working with. Strack-Billerbeck dedicate their whole first volume of 1,055 pages to it, in contrast to only 867 pages for the other three Gospels and Acts all together in volume 2. It is much the same in Adalbert Merx's commentary on the Gospels, and with Gustaf Dalman, G. Kittel, J. Jeremias, and others. Dalman still insists that Jesus himself used the expression "kingdom of heaven", whereas for anyone who looks at the Gospels in a source critical way it is clear that this expression, common among the rabbis, has only got into the gospel tradition through Matthew. He has it even where his sources can be shown to have "kingdom of God". His expansion of the simple form of address, "Father" (Luke 11:2) to "Our Father who art in heaven" at 6:9 and the replacing of Jerusalem by "the holy city" at 4:5, contrary to Luke 4:9 (Q) and at 27:53 is also rabbinic. Recognition that this evangelist is a former rabbi makes sense of the verses 18 and 19 inserted between Matt. 5:17 and 20. These verses are less concerned with the law observance that is important for all Christians than with the teaching about the law that concerns the rabbi. It also makes sense of the much disputed sayings in 16:17–19 where Peter is so to speak installed as Christian chief rabbi. ("Binding and loosing" here refer to doctrinal authority to decide which of the law's commands are obligatory and which are not). It also makes sense of the beginning of the discourse against the Pharisees, peculiar to Matthew, at 23:2–3, with its full recognition of the doctrinal authority of the scribes who sit on Moses' seat.

The addition "except for adultery" made to both the passages prohibiting divorce, at Matt. 5:32 and 19:9 (cf. above) is also rabbinic. It is above all reminiscent of the interpretation of Deut. 24:1 in the school of Shammai which instead of *côth dabar* ("something shameful") inserted *děbar 'irwāh* ("a case of impurity")[8] for which *logos porneias* would be an exact translation.

We have already seen above that the author of Matthew was perhaps a pupil of Rabbi Jochanan ben Zakkai. That would agree well with the material we have considered and would point us to the period around A.D. 90–100.

Certainly this Gospel with its universalist conclusion, 28:18ff, is not Jewish-Christian in the strict sense of the word, but the author is using a Jewish-Christian source from which he takes the sayings in 10:5f (which are clearly more narrow than Jesus' own attitude).

This view of the author as a converted Jewish rabbi provides the best explanation of the so-called formula quotations that are so frequent in this Gospel. They do not go back to the Greek Septuagint Bible but direct to the original text. A pupil of the rabbis and only a pupil of the rabbis would think of getting a literal fulfilment of Zech. 9:9 at Matt. 21:5f by introducing two animals. This supposition makes complete sense of the one basic tendency of the Gospel, which is to show that Jesus, in truth the Messiah of Israel, was deprived of his mission's success amongst his people by the Jewish people's and their leaders' own guilt. Consider the contrast in the infancy narrative between the king of the Jews, Herod, who hunts the child Jesus and the Gentile wise men from the East who look for him. Corresponding to this, at the end is the bribing of the Roman guard at the tomb by members of the Jewish authorities who thus deprive their people of faith in the resurrection of Jesus, and so of his blessing.

(b) The other explanation lies in the clearly catechetical interest of the author, who aims in this Gospel to provide the Christian community with a kind of church order and catechism of Christian behaviour. This catechetical aspect finds expression in the many catchword compilations of the evangelist, such as 6:5–15 on praying, 6:19–34 on cares, 7:1–5 on judging and so on. It is in fact an old rule in catechetical practice that there is nothing so effective in driving a point home as stereotyped repetition. This explains the forms of expression, the doublets and above all the assimilation which we have observed above.

It is plain that the explanations provided under (a) and (b) do not contradict each other but go hand in hand. The Jewish rabbi had become a Christian teacher and now used his catechetical skills in the service of the gospel.

V

A further brief word about the age of the Gospel. The traditional view that saw Matthew as the earliest Gospel, composed according to one tradition as early as the eighth year after Jesus' ascension,[9] continues to exercise some influence even today, and even amongst those who are convinced of the priority of Mark. That usually changes the sequence Matthew–Mark–Luke which we have in our New Testament, to Mark–Matthew–Luke. That is now by far the majority critical view, with some like B. Weiss stressing the total independence of the two later Gospels from one another, whereas others, following especially the work of E. Simons,[10] believe they can prove that Matthew was used by Luke. Apart from the names in the footnote, this is now the view of Jülicher, Feine, Appel and Dibelius.

Only a few up to now (including H. von Soden) have dared to reverse the temporal relation of Luke and Matthew and assert the use (if only in a secondary way) of Luke by the author of our first Gospel. I must include myself among these and would like to make a few observations in support of the position.

The idea of extending the presentation of Jesus' public activity (Mark) into a "life" by prefacing it with an account of his childhood accords perfectly with the manner of the educated Hellenist Luke. It is not really probable that the two evangelists who provide an infancy narrative should have hit on the idea quite independently. Matthew may well have got the idea from Luke even though he then developed it entirely in his own way.

Similarly, the idea of working the Q sayings material into the Marcan narrative seems to me to have started with Luke. It is here still carried out in a relatively primitive way by two insertions at

6:20—8:3, and 9:51—18:14. In Matthew by contrast we find a far more complicated combination of the two sources.

Luke evidently has a more original form of the Q tradition than M. One should not restrict oneself, as Harnack does in his study of *The Sayings of Jesus*,[11] to the particulars of the wording. At that point the literary artist Luke refines it. But the construction of the whole, the presentation of individual sayings in contrast to Matthew's composition of discourses, the shorter units in contrast to the way our first evangelist has filled them out, all tell in favour of the relative priority of Luke. Would Luke have omitted several of the beatitudes? Would he have scrubbed out the third and seventh petition of the Lord's Prayer? Would he have reduced the Sermon on the Mount to a third of its original size? The usual motive given for his doing this, namely that his Gentile Christian readers would not have been interested in the interpretation of the law, is in the first place actually false, and secondly only accounts for a small part of the extra material in Matthew, and thirdly is contradicted by what we have already seen above about the way in which Matthew composed precisely this part of the Sermon on the Mount.

Luke 4:1–13 provides a more correct account of the temptation story than Matt. 4:1–11, not only in the sequence of the three temptations, but also in that the middle one seems to have Jesus taken up into the air. The high mountain from which all the kingdoms of the world can be surveyed has been introduced into the story by a rationalizing Matthew. That Matthew represents a later stage than Luke is also apparent in the introduction to the Lord's Prayer. In Luke 11:1f it looks like a typical prayer given to the disciples at their wish, whereas in Matt. 6:9 it looks like a formula for prayer prescribed for the community by its founder. It is only a small step from here to the regulation of the *Didache* (8:3), "So you should pray three times a day."

In my opinion the decisive argument for Matthew knowing and using Luke at least in a secondary way alongside Mark and Q, is this: Mark 6:14–29 refers in the story of the execution of the Baptist quite innocently to "king" Herod. This was the title by which minor oriental princes were known among their subjects. Officially, according to imperial law, Herod did not have this status. Augustus had granted him and his brother the title tetrarch (meaning approximately "duke", in contrast to "ethnarch" as archduke). Luke, the educated historiographer uses the verb "to be tetrarch" not only in the synchronism of 3:1 but also at 9:7ff in the rudimentary parallel to the martyrdom of the Baptist from Mark 6:14ff. (When

Herod is mentioned elsewhere, at 13:31; 23:7,12; and also at Acts 4:27, his name is given alone, without any title.) But in the Matthew parallel at 14:1–12 it is remarkable that Herod is at the outset introduced in v. 1 as the tetrarch, but then subsequently in v. 9 he is called "the king". This is explicable in my view only on the supposition that Matthew, who takes no notice at all of the position in imperial law (at 2:22 he uses the expression "to be king" of Archelaus as well), is in the first passage influenced by Luke, but that later on, where the Luke parallel left him in the lurch, he simply fastened on to Mark. One might imagine that in reading Luke, Matthew made a few notes in the margin of his copy of Mark and then used them in his own writing up of this material.

This is how I would explain the numerous cases in which Matthew and Luke agree against Mark, which B. and J. Weiss explain by means of a more extensive Q source used also by Mark, others by the idea of a text of Mark which differs from ours, whereas E. Simons and those mentioned above suppose a secondary use of Matthew by Luke. But they all allow the reverse interpretation and this follows as soon as we are convinced on other grounds about the relative priority of Luke.

Luke belongs linguistically and theologically to the deutero-Pauline group of early Christian writings. His closest relation is the Epistle to the Hebrews. That puts him between A.D. 70 and 90, or around A.D. 80. Matthew shows us a catholicizing type. His emphasis upon righteousness, his sharp rejection of unlawfulness, and his quite statutory manner are not to be adjudged Jewish-Christian in the sense of the primitive community, but as catholicizing. The parallels to this are found in the Epistle of James, in the Pastoral Epistles, and in the *Shepherd of Hermas*. That points to the period about A.D. 90–110, or around about A.D. 100.

One proof of the great age of this Gospel has been that of all the Gospels it is the earliest known by other writers. *Barnabas* 4:14 is known to cite Matt. 22:14 with *gegraptai* ("it is written"). But it must remain a question whether this saying of the Lord really is drawn from the Matthean tradition. In the *Didache* and Justin too the sayings of the Lord agree most closely with Matthew's version, but even if this observation is correct it can still be interpreted in the reverse direction: Matthew was the Gospel most used in the second century because it was congenial to that period, and that, because it stems from this period or emerged shortly before. It seems to me it would be an interesting task to investigate how far Matthew as the latest of the synoptics agrees with the Fourth

Gospel which also belongs to this period. There are very interesting observations to be made about this.

NOTES

1 I name only W. Michaelis, *Taüfer, Jesus, Urgemeinde. Die Predigt vom Reiche Gottes vor und nach Pfingsten* (1928), and G. Gloege, *Das Reich Gottes im NT* (1928). The right interpretation is found as early as H. J. Holtzmann and Klostermann. On Matt. 3:2 Wellhausen interprets Kingdom of God on the lips of the Baptist as referring to the judgement – with what justification? But he does stress that it is not the gospel.

2 Besides this the time reference in Matt. 3:1 is borrowed from Mark 1:9 (see below).

3 W. Bacher, *Agada der Tannaiten*[2] I, 35.

4 The five concluding formulae come from Q, according to B. Weiss (Wendt is different). Q is divided into five parts according to A. Wright, *Some NT Problems* (1898) 266; and Papias: Eb. Nestle, *ZNW* 1 (1900) 252ff. The right line is taken by B. H. Streeter amongst others, in *Oxford Studies in the Synoptic Problem* (1921) 148.

5 Even more frequently in the lectionaries which like to use just this formula as introduction to a section (see Matthaei's apparatus, *passim*).

6 This was not considered by K. L. Schmidt, *Der Rahmen der Geschichte Jesu* (1919) 22.

7 The construction of the source and its revision can be clarified as follows: 5:17 (18,19) 20; with v. 17, vv. 21,22 (23,24,25,26,27), 28 (29,30,31,32,33–7,38–42, 43–8); with v. 20, 6:1,2–4,5–6 (7,8,9–13,14,15), 16–18.

8 Strack-Billerbeck I, 314ff.

9 Tischendorf on the subscriptions of Matt. (I. 212f) and von Soden, I, 1, 297f.

10 E. Simons, *Hat der 3 Evangelist den kanonischen Matthäus benutzt?* (1880), and all the literature listed in Holtzmann's *Einleitung*[3], 356.

11 *Beiträge zur Einleitung in das NT* II (1907).

2

The Conclusion of Matthew's Gospel*

A Contribution to the History of the Easter Message[1]

OTTO MICHEL

I

In the first place Matthew reshapes the story of the discovery of the empty tomb into an epiphany style and as a polemical apologetic against Judaism. He reports the discovery of the empty tomb in two clearly separate sections: vv. 1–8, and vv. 11–15. The material is unusually expansively related in the style of an ancient epiphany (appearance and description of a heavenly being, cosmic signs, the impression it makes on people)[2] and as a polemical apologetic (against the thesis that the disciples have stolen the body). The fourth evangelist also pays special and lengthy attention to the tomb tradition and it is clear that in both Gospels the evidential value of this is strengthened. Matthew then inserts the brief description of an appearance of Jesus to the women at the empty tomb (vv. 9–10), breaking the construction and composition of the whole chapter; but in the composition of Matthew as it now stands this does not represent a climax; it points rather beyond itself. This "interim appearance" has the same preparatory function that Jesus' appearance to Mary Magdalene has in the Fourth Gospel (John 20:11–18). Both Gospels recognize the women as witnesses of Easter, but both admit that the disciples were given a special commission and a new authority through the Easter event. *The Galilean pericope Matt. 28:16–20 corresponds to the Jerusalem one in John 20:19–23.* In its present form Matthew twice reports the instruction to the

*First published in German in *EvT* 10 (1950) 16–26. Translated by Robert Morgan.

disciples to go to Galilee and twice too the promise that Jesus will appear there to the disciples (vv. 7, 10). The two instructions come from different sources. The first form, which takes up the Marcan thread and which incidentally constitutes an unsolved riddle ("behold he goes before you to Galilee"), is preferable.[3] In the existing composition of the evangelist both hints underline the significance of the concluding scene (Matt. 28:16–20 cf. expressly v. 17, "and seeing him . . ."). The angel at the tomb and Jesus himself (= two witnesses, according to Deut. 19:15) become announcers and guarantors of the Galilean concluding scene, Matt. 28:16–20. *The very composition of the whole chapter points to the climax in Matt. 28:16–20.*

Amongst the various possibilities for interpreting Mark 14:28, 16:7, the attempt of E. Lohmeyer, *Galiläa und Jerusalem*, (1936) 10ff to relate *opsesthe* ("you shall see") eschatologically to the parousia still seems to me the most probable. Jesus' journey is the transition from the resurrection to the parousia. It will happen in Galilee. The parallel in Mark 10:32 is important, with Jesus "going ahead" (*proagein*) towards Jerusalem. There too (unfortunately often overlooked) the challenge to follow corresponds to the picture of Jesus going ahead. As Mark 14:28 shows, the addition "There will you see him" (Mark 16:7) is not original.

In Matt. 28 there is a remarkable discrepancy. Despite the double promise that they will see the Christ in Galilee (vv. 7, 10), the actual "seeing" in Matt. 28:17 has no decisive theological evidential value. It is simply an accompaniment for the word of the Risen One which follows. The "coming" of Jesus is very briefly related, unlike the "descent" of the angel from heaven (cf. Matt. 28:17 with 28:2). The actual Easter narratives avoid presenting the appearance of Jesus in the hellenistic sense of an epiphany.[4] If the original Easter shout was, "The Lord has risen indeed and has appeared to Simon" (Luke 24:33), or "he appeared to Cephas, then to the twelve" (1 Cor. 15.5), or "we have seen the Lord" (John 20:25) then what is striking about our text is the peculiar reserve as regards the vision: "and when they saw him they worshipped him, but some doubted" (Matt. 28:17). The commentaries show that this admission in the text is not easy to understand. One might think of a historical reminiscence (e.g. E. Klostermann), or perhaps the Thomas pericope could be recalled too (John 20:24ff) since this also struggles to overcome doubt and give the community certainty. For this reason it seems to me that Matt. 28:17 has to be fitted into the whole process of the Easter tradition. The later development of this tradition which goes beyond the Easter vision *and seeks a new certainty about the*

Risen One is clearly apparent in the two Gospels Matthew and John. Behind both Gospels stands the theological question: in what form does the community confess the Risen One, once the vision has become tradition and an event in the past?

It is again worth comparing Matthew with the Fourth Gospel: The blessing in John 20:29 takes it a step beyond the earlier stage of certainty about Easter ("because you have seen me, do you believe?"). In fact even the Fourth Gospel is aware that Easter faith came from seeing. But through this blessing the Risen One creates the possibility of coming to Easter faith without seeing. If one believes without seeing, the main weight falls on the authority of the proclaimer and his proclamation. The problem of *"seeing and believing"* is posed both in the gospel traditions (Mark 15:32; John 4:48; 6:30; 20:8) and in the Rabbinate with great seriousness, and the problem is always set in the context of the *"signs and wonders"* problem. The Gospels presuppose the Jewish desire for signs which support belief (Mark 15:32; 1 Cor. 1:22) and the message's explicit repudiation of that kind of demand. The Fourth Gospel in particular polemicizes in an explicit saying of Jesus against faith being tied to signs (John 4:48). The Gospel, including the Johannine Easter narrative, does of course recognize the confirmatory role of signs: even a sign can create faith (John 20:8 "he saw and believed"). But the demand for a sign is expressly resisted, surpassed, superseded. In this sense John 20:8 should be seen in the context of the gospel tradition and its understanding of signs. *But in John 20:29 the problem of "seeing and believing" becomes a new form of the certainty about Easter.* The appearances of the Risen One are assumed to be over and taken up into the kerygma. The kerygma confronts one anew with the decision of faith without vouchsafing the gift of seeing.

It should not, however, be overlooked that the Rabbinate also solved this problem of the relation between seeing and believing, and in a way that is related to that of John 20:29. According to a well-attested tradition, Rabbi Jochanan (d. 279) blamed and condemned a pupil who had not accepted an apocalyptic statement. The pupil sees the truth of this statement in a vision and confirms it to his teacher. Rabbi Jochanan replies, "You fool, if you had not seen it you would not have believed it; so you are one who laughs about the sayings of scholars" (*B. Bat.* 75a; *Sanh.* 100a; *Midr. Ps.* 87 § 2 = Strack-Billerbeck II, 586). Similarly Rabbi Schimeon b. Lakisch (about A.D. 250) can say: "A proselyte is more dear to God than those hosts which stood on Mt Sinai" (*Tanch.* 8a). Those hosts which stood on Mt Sinai were only brought to receive the kingdom of God by the signs (thunder, flames, lightning, earthquake, trumpet blasts) whereas the proselyte sees no sign and yet comes and yields himself to God and takes upon himself the yoke of the kingdom of God. Behind these different third-century traditions there lies the same basic idea: The words of the scholars (or the Torah) have an authority which does not need to be proved by a vision (or signs). A. Schlatter, in *Der Glaube im Neuen Testament* (1905³) 598 draws attention to the view that the appearance on Sinai took place so that they would not say: If only he had shown us his glory and his greatness, we would have believed in him; but now, because he did not show us his glory and his greatness, we do not believe in him.

It seems to me that Matthew and John are confronted by quite similar problems in the question of certainty about Easter. Neither underestimates the old Easter stories but both point beyond these into the future. Neither Matthew nor the fourth evangelist wants to deprive the *horama* ("vision") of its significance within the tradition; it remains an important aspect of the Easter story. But the vision is now taken up into the kerygma (preaching) and guaranteed by the kerygma. The problem of "doubt" is touched on in both Gospels. In Matthew the message of the Risen One and obedience to this word is the way doubt is overcome. In John the hearer is referred to the understanding inherent in faith itself; it can and may dispense with seeing. For Matthew the word of the Risen One contains the way to master doubt about the truth of the message and the reality of the Risen One. Despite the double *opsesthe* ("you will see") in v. 7 and v. 10 the kerygma becomes dominant. One might even say that *opsesthe* has lost some of its force. The historical framework recedes in Matt. 28:16–20 and gives free play to the kerygma itself. It was easy to introduce the report in Matt. 28:16ff. There is no mention at all of the effects of what happened or of Jesus taking leave of his disciples.

II

Let us analyse the three-part word of Jesus in Matt. 28:18–20. It consists of very different materials but these are here brought together in a definite theological arrangement. First comes the revelation or authority saying in v. 18b: *edothē moi pasa exousia* ("all authority is given to me"), and this forms the basis of the whole composition. There follows, as a "consequence" of this, the actual missionary charge in v. 19 (an imperative, *mathēteusate* ("make disciples") with two attached participles, *baptizontes* ('baptizing") and *didaskontes* ("teaching"), v. 20a).[5] The actual "missionary charge", the central section of the composition, brings the commis-

33

sion of the Risen One; in obedience to him, the event of Easter, and indeed the whole Gospel, reaches its fulfilment. Admittedly this missionary charge of Matthew is open to critical suspicions of having been liturgically enlarged or worked over. The conclusion of the composition consists of the promise in v. 20b:

> It was customary in Judaism also to end a book with a blessing and word of consolation. Thus *Sifre Num* ends with a reference to Num. 35:34 (omitting chap. 36) and the interpretation of the words "in the midst of which I dwell" (taking *šākan*, dwell, to refer to *Shekīnah*, presence). This interpretation repeats an earlier section assigned to Rabbi Nathan: "The Israelites are dear (to God). For wherever they went in exile the Shekinah was with them. They went into exile in Egypt: the Shekinah was with them. Because Scripture says, Was I not exiled in the house of your fathers when they were in Egypt in the house of Pharaoh? (1 Sam. 2:27)... and when they come back home the Shekinah returns with them". *The certainty that the Shekinah goes with Israel into exile accompanies Judaism into the Dispersion.* The next section produces a rabbinic scriptural interpretation through a parable: "What can this be compared with? It is like a king who says to his servant, When you are looking for me I am with my son. Whenever you look for me, I am with my son!" God remains present with his people, always and everywhere, even when they are impure. *Even in the Dispersion God's presence is with his people.*[6] This poses the question of the relation between Matt. 28:20b and this rabbinic conclusion.

We can take it that the three parts of this composition were originally independent, especially since there are parallels to each separate part: cf. Matt. 11:27 and John 3:35 with v. 18; Mark 16:15 with v.19; Matt. 18:20 with v. 20b.[7] So this combination of sayings of Jesus is secondary, as are other compositions in the Gospels (cf. for example, Matt. 11:25–30 or Mark 16:15–18).

> Most important here is the three part composition in Mark 16:15–18. It clearly contains earlier material. This begins with a shorter missionary charge in v. 15 which is more simply constructed than that of Matthew, but is shaped in the style of Mark 14:9. Could Mark 14:9 perhaps even be influenced by it? Then comes a formulated liturgical baptismal sentence in v. 16, carrying on the missionary charge (cf. Matt. 28:19). In this baptismal sentence what is noteworthy is the close connection between faith and baptism, with the emphasis on faith, as is clear from the way the second part continues (*apistein*, "to disbelieve", refers here to refusing to believe; *sōthēsetai*, "will be saved", and *katakrithēsetai*, "will be condemned", refer to the eschatological judgement of God). This baptism

sentence is stated apodictically as a community rule; it is wrong to see it as simply a "reflection on the necessity of baptism" (E. Klostermann). Finally there is in v. 17b and v. 18 an authority saying which appeals to the solemn *onoma* ("name") of Christ (*en tǭ onomati mou*, "in my name"). So unlike Matt 28:19, the *onoma* is understood here not liturgically but charismatically, and this is extremely important for the character of the two compositions. This authority saying is probably a further expansion of Luke 10:19 (= Ps. 91:13). Originally, in Ps. 91, it is about the special protection which the pious person enjoys under the shelter and in the shadow of the Most High (cf. Matt. 4:6 and parallel), not the sign of a hellenistic miracle-worker. If Luke 10:19 and Mark 16:17b–18 are accepted as connecting charismatic authority in the hellenistic sense with OT certainty about faith, then some family resemblance with the concluding promise of Matt. 28:20 is probable. But for all its resemblance to Matthew, Mark 16:15–18 should by no means be seen simply as an echo of that passage (against F. Hauck). The pieces of the Marcan composition also have a pre-history.[8]

All these compositions of sayings have come from individual pieces, and these have their own history. But the "compositions" themselves also have their particular significance within the history of the synoptic tradition. If Matt. 11:25–30 draws out the dignity and the authority of the "Son", for example, and Mark 16:15–18 the commission and authority of the apostle and missionary, then Matt. 28:18–20 seems to pose a problem: Must this composition really be understood in terms of its middle piece, the mission charge, – as usually happens – or is it not *right from the start christological*? This thesis, that Matt. 28:18–20 is to be understood christologically, would indeed be strengthened by R. Bultmann's supposition that originally the missionary charge did not contain a triadic *onoma*, but a christological "into my name".[9] There is no need to dwell at length on the importance of this closing composition of Matthew for the Gospel as a whole. It is sufficient to say that the whole Gospel was written under this theological premise of Matt. 28:18–20 (cf. 28:19 with 10:5ff, 15:24; v. 20 with 1:23; also the return to baptism, cf. 3:1). In a way the conclusion goes back to the start and teaches us to understand the whole Gospel, the story of Jesus, "from behind". *Matt. 28:18–20 is the key to the understanding of the whole book*. How the Christ eschatologically "builds" the community (admittedly Matt. 16:18 was originally understood in a different way)[10] will have been understood by the evangelist in the christological terms of 28:18–20.

The conclusion of the chapter must still be fitted into the whole. *Our evangelist is not so much concerned with "seeing" as with understanding and obeying.* We have here (in a similar way to Matt. 11:25–30) a definite Christology being unfolded. It discloses the mystery of the *kyrios* ("Lord") in the form of a "revelatory discourse". This result corresponds to both the language and the outlook of the composition. The Easter message, "He is raised" (Matt. 28:6) and the Easter vision, "You will see him" (Matt. 28:7, 10) are surpassed by the *Easter knowledge* presented in Matt. 28:18–20. This is why the historical framework can recede and why too doubt about the vision can be admitted – it fits well into the overall construction.[11]

Our Matthean tradition sees Dan. 7:13–14 fulfilled in Easter; it is plainly a christological reshaping of the Daniel saying.

> LXX: And there was given (*edothē*) to him authority (*exousia*), and all the nations (*panta ta ethnē*) of the earth (*tēs gēs*) by race, and all glory were serving him. And his authority is an everlasting (*aiōnios*) authority which shall not be taken away, and his kingdom one which shall not be destroyed.

> Theodotion: And to him was given rule and honour and the kingdom, and all the peoples, tribes, tongues, shall serve him. His authority is an everlasting authority which shall not pass away, and his kingdom shall not be ruined.

The important thing here is the close connection of authority, rule, and the recognition by all nations that these are given. This motif is echoed at Phil. 2:11 as well as Matt. 28:18f. The Easter event is here thought of in terms similar to the *king's enthronement* in the ancient Near East: exaltation, presentation (announcement of exaltation), and enthronization (handing over of sovereignty) are now given to Jesus Christ as the Son of Man exalted to God. So Matt. 28:16–20, like Phil. 2:5–11, proceeds from the *exaltation* (not so much from the "being raised"). One recalls that in Phil. 2:5–11 too there is an already existing fixed liturgical tradition present. It depicts Easter as Christ's installation with the dignity of the *kyrios*: the confession *Lord Jesus Christ* derives from this event.[12] This christological tradition is clearly pointing from the start to this confession of Jesus as Lord. Matt. 28:18–20 corresponds to this in describing Jesus' installation as Son of Man, but is strictly speaking without the community's solemn confession of the title of the Christ which derives from this installation. The frequent occurrence in early Christian compositions and hymns, of reference to the "name" (*onoma*, Phil. 2:9; Mark 16:17) is evidently closely connected with the Easter event itself.[13] The "name" stands for the person himself, recalls the appeal, proclamation, instruction, confession of someone.[14] It is therefore not at all remarkable that Matthew's composition also includes a reference to a "name" in connection with baptism. The only remarkable thing here is that instead of a christological "name" we have a triadic one. Is this triadic "name" simply a paraphrase of the "name" of Christ, so that the proclamation of Jesus Christ can ultimately be expressed triadically, or has a christological reference ("into my name") been subsequently replaced by a triadic formula?[15] In any case it seems to me necessary to retain this "baptismal statement" whatever our reservations.

It must above all be stressed that the Lucan and Johannine Christology, unlike Phil. 2:5–11 and Matt. 28:18–20, inserts the ascension idea and so differs from the strict proclamation of Easter. Mark and Matthew know of no ascension idea as something distinct from Easter. In fact they even exclude this. Luke fixes the period of the appearances at forty days and then provides an ascension narrative (Acts 1:3, 9ff). John's Easter story also gives an explicit ascension saying of the Risen Jesus (John 20:17). Whereas in Matt. 28:10 the Risen One points to the Galilee appearance as the next event in the history of salvation, in John 20:17 it is the imminent ascension. We have to distinguish different forms of the Easter proclamation: resurrection, exaltation, enthronization, ascension, were originally different and independent ideas, and were only gradually harmonized and combined with each other. The history of each motif also indicates its particular significance. Analysis probably shows too that the Christology of the Johannine Easter story is older and different in kind from that of the farewell discourses. The combination of tradition and interpretation perhaps played a part here too in this christological process. It remains an open question when and where the resurrection of Jesus Christ was given soteriological significance. In the synoptic Gospels the Easter event is related first of all to Christ, not to mankind. It speaks of God's action which confirms the Crucified One who had been rejected by mankind.

The possibility that an earlier document from which the baptismal statement was perhaps absent has been worked over in Matt. 28:19, can probably be excluded (cf. *Did.* 7:1ff). The short form found in Eusebius' ante-Nicene writings can hardly be regarded as original.[16] Nevertheless, the sequence of the two participles, "baptizing ... teaching" is very difficult, since the *Didache* 7:1 order, "having said all this beforehand, baptize them", seems the natural one. It would admittedly make things slightly easier if the present participle "baptizing" could be replaced by the aorist "having baptized", as in the manuscripts B and D. The imperative, "make disciples", could then be strengthened by prefacing it with "having baptized". But this kind of solution fails to carry conviction. Baptism is an act of transfer. It establishes a belonging, and there is no avoiding seeing this "name" that is transmitted in triadic form as a normal confessional formula at the time of Matthew and the *Didache*.[17] This sign of baptism that is laid on people must be understood in terms similar to those suggested by the baptismal sentence in Mark 16:17. But it remains remarkable that after the resurrection of Jesus Christ early Christianity became again a movement of conversion and baptism (Acts 2:38). In Matthew "teaching" gains its own emphatic significance. The words which Jesus transmitted to the disciples are now his real legacy, and it becomes the task of the disciples to preserve and hand on the tradition in the form of the "commands" (*entolai*). Matthew thus underlines the special significance of the sayings tradition and reminds us of the related material of the Johannine farewell discourses which can likewise set the words of Jesus under the rubric "commands" (John 13:14; 14:15, 21; 15:10, 20). The concept of command does not have a legal flavour. What is meant is the "obligatory, authoritative word" of the gospel itself. Perhaps here too an old independent Easter tradition is glimmering through; the person saying farewell leaves behind his tradition and his "words" or "commands".[18] This transmission is wholly unecstatic. It does not make a gift of the Spirit central, though the triadic "name" includes a liturgical echo of the gift of the Spirit.[19] This traditional motif in the Easter event occurs elsewhere, as for example at Acts 1:21f. Whereas Matthew gives pride of place to the transmission of the teaching, John emphasizes the Church's ministry and its authority (John 20: 19–23). He too has a clear reminder of the giving of the Spirit, but in his case this is connected especially with the priestly office and its authority.

The first thing to grasp is that the concluding verse, John 20:23 has special significance and is clearly the climax of the scene. As with the end of Matthew, there is no account of the Risen One disappearing, because it is the words of Jesus that are decisive. The style of John 20:23 is not Johannine but an Old Testament–Jewish one (Strack-Billerbeck II. 585) that is alien to John. *One might even think of an Aramaic basis to this verse*. The antithesis, "forgive sins – retain sins" (i.e. count them), is well attested in the OT and in Judaism in the interpretation of Ps. 130:3 and elsewhere. It concerns God's own office in which only Jesus Christ, and since this point (John 20:23) the disciples also, have a share. Retaining sins means here: ascertaining that the conditions necessary for forgiveness have not yet been met. So here too the Christ transmits his authority, and the gift of the Spirit and the presupposition for this. Note especially that the antithesis, "forgive sins – retain sins", does not quite correspond to the rabbinic phrases about "binding" and "loosing" found at Matt. 16:19. We may perhaps assume that this disciples' authority is oriented towards a future Pentecost event and a pouring out of the Spirit as in Acts 2. There is something new here: the transmission to the disciples of authority to forgive sins at the founding of the community ("life-setting").

To understand the concluding promise at Matt. 28:20 it is necessary to compare it with the conclusion of the related composition, Mark 16.15–18. The promise of signs to accompany them, depicted in detail at Mark 16.17–18, is replaced in Matthew by the Risen Christ who supports the proclamation and testimony by his presence. "I am with you" is often a paraphrase for divine protection in Scripture and occurs particularly in revelatory passages (Gen. 28:15; Judg. 6:12; Acts 18:10). Matt. 18:20 is related, though here the connection between Christ and the Shekinah emerges more clearly.[20] Here too one can see an old theological idea being reshaped. The imminent eschatological turn of the ages is replaced by a period of waiting, even unto the consummation. We have here a new understanding of time and of the situation, and this is characteristic of this whole composition.

III

One final point, usually overlooked in the commentaries, should be noted. The present composition expressly emphasizes the motif of conclusion, completion, totality, as is clear from the use of "all" people (*pantes*) and "everything" (*panta*): "all authority" (v. 18), "all nations" or Gentiles (v. 19), "everything I commanded you" (v. 20), "always" (all days, v. 20). The mission charge in Mark 16:15 is very similar: "into all the world" and "to every creature". So it is a *cosmic* event which is rather similar to the hellenistic missionary preaching, as found for example in the *Odes of Solomon* 33. Here "grace" comes down from heaven, climbs a high mountain and lets her voice ring from one end of the earth to the other.[21] Since the exaltation of Jesus Christ the dividing wall of the law has fallen away and the gospel has become a message for "all nations", i.e. for all people, without reference to the law.[22] When the mission

39

charge was fixed in this last form, the road to the Gentile world had already been taken and the "Church" which handed on the words of Jesus had already spread. Matthew has preserved the word of Jesus and sharpened afresh his readers' obedience to it. But in the triadic "name" and in the promise "I am with you", the knowledge of Christ which stretches from the past into the present and interprets the old message is summarized. The holy name of God and the presence of God that is promised with it provide the basis, and are handed on to Jesus' community in christological form. In the exalted Lord, God himself appears.

NOTES

1 A lecture given at the Marburg Theological conference (NT section) on 28.3.1950. See also O. Michel, "Menschensohn und Völkerwelt", *Evangelische Missionszeitschrift* (1941) 257ff.

2 On the related concept of "epiphany", cf. M. Dibelius, Hermeneia Commentary, *The Pastoral Epistles* (Fortress 1972) 104: "Strictly speaking, the religious term 'epiphany' means the appearance of a divinity that is otherwise hidden, manifested as a *deus praesens* either in a vision, by a healing or some other helping action, or by any manifestation of power." Cf. also 2 Macc. 3:24ff as the best example of what is meant. In Mark 16: 1–8 we have only the interpreting angel; the emphasis is upon the proclamation. Cf. also H. Windisch, "Die Christusepiphanie vor Damascus", *ZNW* 31(1932) 1ff. Matthew's "epiphany" aims to express the conviction that it is now God himself who is beginning to speak through his messengers.

3 The word "to go before" is clearly metaphorical speech deriving from shepherds going ahead and leading their sheep (cf. John 10:4; "he goes before them") (*emprosthen autōn poreuetai*). On this problem cf. E. Lohmeyer, *Galiläa und Jerusalem* (1936) 12ff.

4 Cf. the investigations of the resurrection narratives by Lyder Brun, Jack Finegan, E. Lohmeyer, E. Hirsch, P. Althaus, W. Michaelis.

5 On the linguistic usage of *mathēteuein* ("to disciple") in Matthew I refer to my 1941 essay (n.1 above), 263 ff. It is striking that this expression is more hellenistic than "to make disciples and baptize" in John 4:1 – but notice the same combination of these two things in both Gospels.

6 I am obliged to my colleague K. G. Kuhn in Göttingen for the reference to *Sifre Num.* 35:34.

7 It has long been recognized that Matt. 18:20 is Jewish Christian and equates the Risen One with the Shekinah (cf. material in Strack-Billerbeck I, 794; R. Bultmann (1963) 147f, 149, 150f). It is no coincidence that the "name" of Christ is stressed in this Easter saying.

8 Cf. R. Otto, *The Kingdom of God and The Son of Man* (ET 1938).

9 R. Bultmann (1963) 151 also sees the special significance of the "name" in the

synoptic proclamation (Mark 9:37, 41; Matt. 7:22; 18:20; 28:19; Luke 24:27). This "name" of Christ is clearly the guarantee for the presence of Jesus Christ. It is efficacious not on account of the divine properties but because the Risen One combines and guarantees his historical word and action through his "name". Cf. W. Heitmüller, *Im Namen Jesu* (1903) 335: "As against the calling upon the Epitheta in paganism and Judaism the Christian combines with the name of Jesus a reference to the events of his history."

10 Cf. O. Michel, *TDNT* 5, 139.

11 That this form of the baptismal command belongs not to the beginning but the end of the apostolic age has been rightly emphasized by critical theology (e.g. A. Loisy and others). But the present form has emerged from a tradition which has been handed on and changed, and which in Matthew refers to the Exalted One who attests himself in his word.

12 Cf. E. Lohmeyer, *Kyrios Jesus* (1928).

13 The material is in part, though only in part, worked through in W. Heitmüller (n.9) 223ff. There must have been some connection between the "authority" which is given to Christ and the "name" which he leaves behind for his disciples.

14 This obviously includes the power of the "name" in exorcism and katharsis (purification, healing) to which W. Heitmüller attaches such great weight.

15 Cf. on this, *Did.* 7:1 as the nearest parallel. As early tradition *Did.* 7:1ff has special weight. The *Didache* knows of different forms of baptismal act and evaluates them: baptism "in running water" is the original form and constitutes the rule. More recent forms which have established themselves in the Church are not so highly respected.

16 It is perhaps unlikely that the short form of the mission charge found in Eusebius is connected with the "secrecy discipline" of the community. Cf. F.C. Conybeare *ZNW* 2 (1901) 275ff. E. Rigenbach, *Der trinitarische Taufbefehl* (BFCT, 1903).

17 W. Heitmüller (n.9) 121–2 is right about this.

18 Cf. also Luke 22:28ff. On the analysis of these verses cf. Bultmann (1963) 158f.

19 It is an important fact that Matt. 28:19 and *Did.* 7:1, 3 place the triadic formula under a single "name" ("into the name . . ."). Triadic formulae are popular in hellenistic antiquity, but require a thorough theological interpretation. This threefold "name" in Matthew clearly aims to summarize the peculiarity of early Christian proclamation as against other baptismal formulae and cannot be taken in the sense of later trinitarian doctrine. Cf. E. Norden, *Agnostos Theos* (1913) 348ff.

20 The "I am with you" is in a way related to the Paraclete motif which has been much investigated recently. Unfortunately N. Johansson's book *Parakletoi* (1940) has not gone into this connection. "I am with you" is probably even richer than the "Paraclete" concept. The *Christus praesens* is God himself, who supports his disciples through the word.

21 Cf. E. Käsemann, *Das wandernde Gottesvolk* (1938) 27–32. The new proclamation "from the mountain" would thus assemble the new people of God. In discussion after my lecture I am indebted especially to my colleague E. Käsemann for his stimulus and assistance.

22 "All nations" is a formula found especially in eschatological or apocalyptic contexts in the Gospels. Cf. in Matthew: 24:9, 14; 25:32. That probably means also in this case of the baptismal command: the prophecy is now being fulfilled.

3

The Passion Narrative in Matthew*

NILS ALSTRUP DAHL

The passion narrative in Matthew is a suitable point of departure for a discussion of synoptic questions and problems in gospel criticism, chiefly because of the unusual simplicity of the data for source criticism at this point. The Matthean passion is very close to the Marcan. Every episode in the Marcan account is also found in Matthew, with the exception of two informative notes (Mark 14:51f; 15:21b) and some descriptive details (Mark 14:3–4, 7, 12–25, 40, 56–9, 67; 15:7, 44–5; 16:1–5). Still, it is even more noteworthy that the outline and order within the Matthean and Marcan passion narratives are without exception identical. To a great extent a verbatim or almost verbatim correspondence can be found. To compare Matthew and Mark with Luke and John makes the similarity between the first two especially striking. They contain two variations of one and the same account.

The great majority of the critics have assumed that Matthew is dependent on Mark. Attempts to prove dependence the opposite way have been uniformly unconvincing.[1] Alternately, one could propose the use of a common source, an Ur-Markus. But within the passion story such a hypothesis would mean only a superfluous complication of the picture; such an Ur-Markus would be only a pallid double for our Mark. It is extremely unlikely that Matthew used written sources other than Mark for the passion narrative. We can be confident at *this* point, as at perhaps no other, that we possess the author's sole written source.

Precisely because the source critical situation is so simple at this point, it is all the more important to recognize that this result of critical analysis cannot resolve every problem in the Matthean

* First published 1955. Reprinted from *Jesus in the Memory of the Early Church* by N. A. Dahl (1976) 37–51.

passion narrative. The existence of scholars who defend the priority of Matthew confirms this.[2] Moreover, whoever rejects Matthean priority must concede that some weighty evidence supports it. Almost all of the observations may be reduced to a common denominator: within the passion narrative, as elsewhere, Matthew has a more "Jewish" character and stands closer to the original Palestinian milieu of the gospel message than does Mark. This fact cannot counterbalance the weight of the evidence that speaks for the priority of Mark, but it does require an explanation. Source critical assumptions alone cannot provide a satisfactory explanation.[3] In addition to the literary dependence on Mark and the editorial work of the first evangelist, we must pay serious attention to the significance of Matthew's church environment: his geographical and historical situation, existing traditions, liturgy, preaching, and school concerns.

We may almost take for granted that the "church of Matthew" had some knowledge of Jesus' passion prior to its acquaintance with the written Gospel of Mark. Still, the fragments of the *Gospel of Peter* illustrate how the tradition continued to grow and change even after all four Gospels were known. We must thus reckon with an intermingling of written and oral tradition and understand Matthew's literary revision of Mark within the framework of early Christian history.[4] In what follows I shall attempt to elaborate and establish these theses.

The special traditions of Matthew are only secondarily inserted into the Marcan order. This is obviously the case in the account of Judas' death (27:3–10). Not only does it break the connection between 27:2 and 27:11, but it also stands at the wrong place chronologically; in 27:3–10 the chief priests and elders are in the Temple, while immediately before (27:2) they are with Pilate. If this verifies the priority of the Marcan version, there can still be no doubt that Matthew used traditional material with a long prehistory.[5] The core must go back to the tradition localized in Jerusalem, as evidenced by the aetiology in 27:8. Even if none of the details is historical, the account of the horrible end of Judas reflects the impression the betrayal made upon the early Palestinian church.

The account of the miracles at the death of Jesus is also a later insertion. This is shown by the premature mention of the appearance in Jerusalem of the resurrected saints after the resurrection of Jesus (27:51b–54). A secondary tradition is presented in the apologetic legend of the guards at the tomb (27:62–6; 28:2–4; 11–15). It obviously arose in connection with discussions that were carried on with the Jews. Because the legend is incompatible with the intended anointing of the body of Jesus (Mark 15:1), it is at least conceivable that the legend presupposes a version of the story of the empty tomb in which the anointing did not occur (cf. John 20).[6]

Thus the special traditions prove, on the one hand, that Matthew is secondary to Mark and, on the other, that Matthew also knew oral traditions in addition to the written Marcan account. Moreover, the special traditions influenced the redaction of the material taken over from Mark. This is clearest in the story of Judas in which 26:15 (Zech. 11:12) anticipates the report of the betrayer's death (cf. 26:23–5). The motif of the guard at the tomb (no theft of the corpse!) is anticipated in Matthew's peculiar emphasis on the soldiers' keeping watch at the cross (27:36 replacing the chronological reference in Mark 15:25).

In the largest portion, about four-fifths of the Matthean passion, Matthew recasts Mark. Many of the differences are hardly based on deliberate corrections but simply on the adaptation of the language and narrative style within the passion story to Matthew's characteristic mode.[7] Especially remarkable is the frequent reappearance of narrative sentences from Mark in the form of statements in direct speech in Matthew; I consider this a decisive proof of Matthean dependence.

The eucharistic pericope presents the most formal example; Matt. 26:27 has *piete ex autou pantes* ("Drink of it, all of you") in contrast to the *epion ex autou pantes* ("they all drank of it") of Mark 14:23. In a similar fashion the chronological reference of Mark 14:1 reappears in Jesus' words in Matt. 26:2: "after two days the Passover is coming". Even elsewhere Matthew has shaped or expanded statements in direct speech from Marcan material.[8] In part this may be no more than the hand of the evangelist. But the preference for direct discourse may well reflect the style of subsequent retelling of the story in the written text. Within the eucharistic pericope, for example, the adaptation to direct speech had already occurred in liturgical recitation.

Even where Matthew does not employ direct speech one finds alongside verbal correspondences free reminiscences from Mark. For example, the phrase "leaving them again he went away and prayed, saying the same words", is found in the second petition in Gethsemane in Mark, but in the third in Matthew (26:44). The phrase "they sought false testimony" in Matt. 26:59 is an anticipation of the characterization of the witnesses in Mark 14:56f.[9] Perhaps Matthew even takes for granted that his readers are familiar with the Marcan account when he speaks simply of going to a certain man in the account of the preparation for the passover meal (26:18). In any case, 26:67–8 presuppose the blindfolding of Jesus reported by Mark; only in that way does the question *tis estin ho paisas se* ("who is it that struck you?") make sense. This confirms that the Marcan Gospel is known not only to the author of Matthew but also to the community within which and for which he writes.

It often remains uncertain to what extent the reshaping of the Marcan narrative rests on the redactional work of the evangelist and to what extent it occurred in the community even before the story was once again fixed in writing.[10] The question is not vital, for the first evangelist is an independent author to a much less degree than is Luke; rather, he is the preserver of tradition, a scribe, and he stands within a living tradition.

Agreements of Matthew and Luke against Mark are not numerous and almost exclusively concern the choice of words.[11] That Luke should have known the Gospel of Matthew is extremely improbable. All agreement ceases with the end of Mark. No agreement with the special material in the Matthean passion is found in Luke. Both evangelists make Pilate a witness to the innocence of Jesus, but they do it in entirely different ways. However, small agreements occur in spite of mutual independence. Luke frequently omits Marcan statements that are also missing in Matthew; this fact enhances the importance of the agreements. A second common source, such as a passion narrative in Q, is not a real possibility.[12]

In some cases, the evidence supports Streeter's hypothesis that the agreements arose through a secondary harmonization within the textual tradition;[13] in others it remains completely conjectural.[14] But in order to be able to explain all data in this way the whole textual history must be reconstructed using a presupposition from literary analysis: agreements of Matthew-Luke against Mark are secondary; agreements of Matthew-Mark against Luke and Luke-Mark against Matthew are primary. This is not advisable. The harmonizing of the copyists was scarcely conscious or methodical. Rather, they adapted the text being copied to the wording familiar to them. Matthew and Luke would have done the same thing in their reproduction of the Marcan text. However, the other wording to which they had access was not fixed in writing but was an oral tradition continuing along-side Mark or arising from Mark. The accumulation of minor agreements in a few pericopes is noteworthy: the trial before the council with mocking, the denial of Peter and, above all, the burial. The common omissions – for example, the second cock-crow or the scheme of the days of the passion week – could possibly be explained as peculiarities of the written Marcan version that were not able to hold their own over against the wider stream of tradition.[15]

Within the passion story, agreements between Matthew and John against the others are more significant and interesting than those between Matthew and Luke: the mention of the name of Caiaphas, the account of a plot to kill Jesus, Judas' greed, the identification of the betrayer, emphasis on Jesus' sovereign power at the arrest, the inscription placed on the cross, the name "Jesus" in the inscription, Joseph of Arimathea as a disciple of Jesus, the newness of the tomb, and the appearance of the resurrected Jesus to the women at the tomb. The wording of parallel pericopes, and some cases of the stereotyped phraseology furnish additional points of contact.[16]

No single hypothesis is sufficient to explain all John's contacts with the Matthean version of Marcan material and with his special traditions. Some may be accidental; others may be ascribed to a "tendency" common to both evangelists. But such explanations are not sufficient. Besides the burial episode and the christophany at the tomb, the logion in the account of the arrest is of primary importance: *apostrepson tēn machairan sou eis ton topon autēs* Matt. 26:52; *bale tēn machairan eis tēn thēkēn* ("put your sword into its sheath") John 18:11. Such similarities do not demand John's literary dependence on Matthew. That there were points of contact between the pre-Johannine and pre-Matthean traditions is more probable. It is difficult to say this with certainty because the possibility also exists that elements of Matthew's text have been orally transmitted to John. If this is true, and there are some indications that it is at least part of the truth, it would prove that details from Matthew have passed into an oral tradition to be fixed again in writing by John. In any case, the agreements between Matthew and John are evidence of the interplay of written and oral tradition.

We should also mention Matthew's Semitisms at this point. Matthew generally improves Mark's Greek. However, there are a few cases where the language of Matthew has the more semitic character. We find names such as *Mariam* ("Mary") instead of Maria and *nazōraios* ("Nazarene"), foreign words such as *rabbi* and *corban*, biblical idioms such as *ekteinas tēn cheira* ("he stretched out his hand") 26:51, and the paratactic construction, "come down now from the cross and we will believe" (27:42) where Mark's subordinate clause is better Greek. Several other typically Matthean idioms and phrases are considered Semitisms by experts in the field.[17] Influence from the Hebrew OT is present not only in the formula quotations in 27:9–10 but also in the designation of Joseph of Arimathea as a wealthy man (27:57; cf. Isa. 53:9). Matthew presupposes an audience familiar with the peculiarity of the Galilean dialect (26:73). Such observations do not prove the priority of Matthew over Mark or the existence of an Aramaic proto-Matthew. Rather, the assimilation and influence of Greek gospel literature within a semitic-speaking area appears to be a recurring phenomenon in the early Church. Such assimilation does not exclude the possibility that a chain of indigenous tradition continued parallel to it. Examples of this include the Aramaic *Gospel of the Nazarenes* and possibly the old Syriac versions and the Semitisms of Codex D.[18]

Consequently, we may assume that the Matthean Gospel took shape in a bilingual or trilingual community. Certainly the liturgical language of that community was Greek. But, that community combined its use of the Greek Mark with a "school" activity which still worked with texts and traditions in Hebrew and Aramaic.[19]

Matthew relates the passion more closely to the OT than does Mark. This is not surprising. Even before a written passion story was available, texts from the OT (e.g. Ps. 22) were read as descriptions of the passion of Jesus, and this practice continued even later, as best exemplified by the *Epistle of Barnabas*. The allusions to the OT peculiar to Matthew, or made more explicit by him, show how the references were occasioned by previously existing traditions. The OT texts, for their part, helped to shape the accounts.[20]

As an aid to the reconstruction of the course of events, the chief value of the Matthean passion lies in the light it throws upon the Marcan passion narrative. There are, however, a few passages where historical considerations favour the priority of Matthew. That Matthew knows the name of the high priest Caiaphas has little if any significance. But the form of the name "Jesus Barabbas" (27:16–17 codex θ, etc.) is so striking that it must be not only an original Matthean text but also an authentic historical tradition.[21] In the episode of the mocking of Jesus by the soldiers, historical probability argues for the scarlet robe of Matthew (27:28) in contrast to the purple of Mark.[22] The reference to Elijah (27:47ff) seems to presuppose the Hebrew *Eli, Eli* in the cry from the cross; this text is better supported in Matthew than in Mark. In the trial scene Matthew seems to offer the older tradition when he omits from the words of Jesus the addition "a temple made with hands – another not made with hands" (26:61); the same is true when he leaves out the assertion that statements of the witnesses who quoted these words did not agree (Mark 14:59).[23]

In such cases, the greater historical probability is no certain proof that old, authentic tradition has been preserved. The impression of historical accuracy could be the result of improvement by the redactor. Indeed, in the passion narrative of the "historian" Luke this may well be the case. But Matthew is hardly interested in the historically probable. One must therefore allow for acquaintance with traditions independent of Mark.

My concern here is not to decide individual cases. It is rather to show the complexity of the problem, and to indicate how many factors must be taken into account even in an area of the synoptic problem where the source critical question can be answered clearly and simply. We will not succeed if we follow a purely literary approach. To be sure, the Matthean passion is a revision of the Marcan account, but the reshaping is not simply the result of the literary activity of a redactor. It has its *Sitz im Leben* within a specific church which esteemed Mark's Gospel and which possibly read it in worship. But in this milieu, oral tradition was still living and the study of the OT was pursued.[24] Here and there the possibility exists that the secondary Matthean version contains an authentic tradition, but what is more important is that it shows how a specific church community understood and interpreted the passion of Jesus.

With this I come to the second part of my exposition: the theology of the passion narrative in Matthew. There is the danger at this point of over-interpretation; not all deviations from Mark are determined by a theological tendency. However, in the composition as a whole and in many details, a specific understanding of the passion story characteristic for Matthew emerges. What is at stake in this interpretation is the significance of the passion of Jesus for the Church in its relationship to the synagogue.

As in the other Gospels, so in Matthew: the passion story is dominated by the conviction that Jesus suffered as the Messiah. Jesus' passion is his road to enthronement. Matthew depicts the appearance of the Resurrected One on the mountain as a revelation of the already enthroned Christ to whom all power has been given, who gives to his disciples the great commission. Corresponding to Mark's description, Jesus' suffering is portrayed as the road of the humiliated Christ: rejected by the leaders of Israel, betrayed by Judas, forsaken by his disciples, condemned by the council, denied by Peter, mocked by many – up to the cry of forsakenness on the cross, "My God, My God". As in Mark, the passion of Jesus is portrayed in conjunction with OT psalms of suffering; Jesus walks the road prescribed for him so that Scripture may be fulfilled (26:54, 56). Matthew emphasizes more strongly than does Mark how Jesus' own word is also fulfilled (26:2; cf. 27:63; 28:6). A motive for the insertion of the Judas story (27:3–10) was a concern to show that the word of woe concerning the betrayer has been fulfilled (26:24). Matthew emphasizes the voluntary character of Jesus' suffering. An example of this is the modification of the Gethsemane pericope (cf. esp. 26:42). A saying of Jesus is the signal that first sets the whole event in motion (26:1–2; cf. 26:18, 25 and also 26:50). These are all familiar observations; Dibelius, for example, has shown how in Matthew Jesus in the midst of the passion remains the Son of God endowed with power.[25]

The hearer of Matthew's story hardly doubts for a moment that twelve legions of angels would have been at the disposal of Jesus the Christ if he had prayed for them. But that was a moral impossibility (26:53; cf. 26:61, *dynamai,* "I am able"). The crucifixion is not a profound mystery in the same way as in Mark; the account is constantly illuminated by the faith of the Church. The resurrection follows as self-evident. In Mark the anticipation of Jesus' resurrection in 27:53 would be impossible, or at least stylistically inappropriate. In contrast, the hearers of the Matthean account know all the time that he who was crucified is resurrected. The messiahship of the Crucified One is thus understood from the perspective of the Christian faith.[26] Luke (23:2) and John (19:12) refer each in his own way to the political aspect of the messianic question. In Matthew such historical reflections are remote. He makes the Jews condemn and mock Jesus as the Christ of the Christian confession, "the Christ the Son of God" (26:63–6). Jesus' self-confession, identical with the Christian confession, is a blasphemy in Jewish ears as is the assertion that the Crucified One is God's Son (27:40, 43). In the trial before Pilate it is not so much a question of the King of the Jews (27:11; cf. Mark) but rather of Jesus who is called Christ (27:17, 22).[27] The identity of the crucified Jesus as the Christ of Christian confession is presented in constant opposition to his rejection by the Jews.[28]

Of primary importance is the Barabbas episode. The care with which it is reworked demonstrates its significance for the Matthean passion. From the beginning the pericope is dominated by a question that poses the alternative: who do you want me to release for you, Jesus Barabbas or Jesus who is called Christ? With its acclamation, the mob concurs with the judgement of its leaders; this is indeed already the thought of Mark, but in Matthew it is set forth even more clearly.[29] From a special tradition Matthew added the reference to Pilate's wife (27:19) in which the Gentile woman declares

Jesus to be innocent. More important, however, is the elaboration of the pericope by Pilate's self-exoneration and the assuming of guilt by the Jews (27:24–5). Here the existence of any special tradition is open to doubt. An interpretation of the event is set in direct discourse: the Jews declare themselves responsible for the death of Christ. Pilate's declaration of innocence and the Jew's acceptance of responsibility are stylized in accordance with an ancient phraseology whose origin lies perhaps in the institution of blood vengeance. It played a role primarily within the sphere of sacred law; God is the avenger of innocent blood. Similar formulae are used in rabbinic legal procedure, where they serve primarily to exonerate the tribunal and to incriminate possible false witnesses.[30] In Matthew not only the term *haima athōon* ("innocent blood") in 27:4 (23:35) but also the maxim of 26:52, alluding to Gen. 9:6, belongs to the same complex of ideas.

Within the Matthean passion narrative an aetiological interest appears at several points (27:8, 28:15). This interest also stands in the background in the Barabbas pericope. Judas perishes because he is guilty of the innocent blood of Jesus; but for Matthew even the Jews of his time stand under the blood guilt that they have incurred. He probably understood the fall of Jerusalem as a corroboration of that guilt (cf. 22:7). That the assignation of guilt to the Jews is not a negligible aspect of the passion story for Matthew is confirmed by the preceding chapters of the Gospel. The parables in 21:28—22:14 and the speech in 23 are especially important in this connection. At its conclusion (23:35f) we hear of the "righteous blood" that shall come upon this generation. What one might call the theme of the passion narrative is stated in Matthew's conclusion to the parable of the vineyard: "The kingdom of God shall be taken away from you and given to a nation producing the fruits of it" (21:43).[31]

On the positive side, the blood of Jesus – of which the Jews have made themselves guilty – is seen as the blood of the (new) covenant, which is shed for many for the forgiveness of sins. The eucharistic pericope has a central place within the passion story. An indication of this is the reshaping of the account of the preparations for the Passover meal (26:17–19). According to Matthew, what is to be prepared for is not the eating of the Jewish Passover lamb but the first paschal feast of the new covenant; Jesus' *kairos* is near and he will celebrate Passover with his disciples in order to institute the Eucharist. The eucharistic pericope itself (26:26–9) is brought into relation to the contemporary celebration of the Church even more clearly than in the parallel traditions.

The entire passion (and resurrection) story has an aetiological significance; it explains the origin and the continuing basis of the Church's existence as the people of the new covenant, as the evangelizing, baptizing, and teaching community (28:19). Matthew emphasizes the failure of the disciples, though not quite as sharply as Mark.[32] The foundation of the Church's existence is not the faithfulness of the disciples but the faithfulness of Jesus and the forgiveness of sins through his blood. However, a paraenetic motif also appears in Matthew's portrayal of the disciples and their failure; he warns against false certainty and calls for faithfulness to the confession of Christ.[33]

For Matthew, disciples from all nations constitute the new community, as emphasized clearly at the conclusion of the Gospel. Within the passion story the events at the death of Jesus prepare for this (27:51-4). The earthquake and the resurrection of the deceased saints, related to Jewish interpretations of Ezek. 37, testify to the eschatological significance of the death of Jesus.[34] This special Matthean tradition is inserted between Mark 15:38 and 39 so that the event is illuminated in three ways: (1) The rending of the temple veil signifies the end of the earthly temple service and judgement upon Judaism. (Also, the providing of access to God? cf. Heb. 10:19f). (2) The resurrection of the saints points to the fulfilment of the promises made to the pious of the old covenant. (3) The confession of the centurion and his men that the crucified Jesus is Son of God foreshadows the conversion of Gentiles to Christ.

Matthew did not write his Gospel exclusively for Jewish Christians, but for the universal Church.[35] The evangelist and many members of his community were obviously of Jewish descent. But the separation of Jesus' disciples from the Jews is complete. Matt. 28:15 speaks of "the Jews" in an almost Johannine way. However, it is no accident that Matthew speaks of the Jews in this way only after the crucifixion, because the breach is first consummated by it. The people of the new covenant is the Church from all nations. Thus, the Church as represented by Matthew understands itself in terms of the passion and resurrection of Jesus; and conversely, the passion story of Jesus is related to the peculiar existence of the Church separated from the Jewish nation.[36] To this Church also belongs the OT as it is fulfilled in the history of Jesus. Consequently, one could say that in Matthew the passion of Jesus stands at the mid-point of a triangle whose angles are Old Testament, Church, and synagogue.[37]

We conclude with a brief word about the place of the passion narrative in the Gospel as a whole. On the one hand, Kähler's expression "passion narratives with an extended introduction"[38] proves to be true for Matthew much less than for Mark; the preceding chapters, above all the speech compositions, carry much too great a weight for that. On the other hand, it would also be one-sided to view chaps. 26–28 with B. W. Bacon as an epilogue to the five-fold work and to understand Matthew as a catechetical handbook.[39]

The passion narrative is linked to the teaching of Jesus by means of 26:1: "And it happened when Jesus had finished all these sayings". In the same way, Jesus' teaching is bound to the resurrection by 28:20, the word of the Resurrected One: "Teaching them to observe all that I have commanded you". It is certainly not accidental that both passages remind one of formulations at the end of Deuteronomy.[40] The evangelist understood his work as a sort of counterpart to the Pentateuch.

The passion of Jesus can only begin when Jesus has ended his teaching ministry. Those disciples added after Easter must learn to keep what Jesus commanded during his teaching in Israel. The whole post-Easter Church stands under the word that was addressed only to Israel before the passion. But like the Kingdom, this word is taken from the Jews and given to a nation which must learn to keep the commandments. On this basis must be explained the coexistence of apparent particularism and universalism in Matthew. The problem can be illustrated by means of chap. 10. The logia gathered there are obviously put together as instructions for the contemporary Church; however, the command to go only to the lost sheep of the house of Israel stands at the beginning of the chapter. For Matthew this specific command is applicable only to the pre-Easter situation. But Jesus' disciples in all nations must learn to keep all that he commanded on the occasion of the sending out of his apostles to Israel. Both belong together for Matthew: Jesus is *Christos* and *Didaskalos*, crucified Son of God and New Moses. This is in accord with the double character of the book as "gospel" and "handbook".

NOTES

1   A. Schlatter defended the priority of Matthew without success in *Der Evangelist Matthäus* (1929) and above all *Markus, der Evangelist für die Griechen* (Stuttgart: Calwer, 1935).

2   B. C. Butler (1951) argues almost exclusively from the sayings of Jesus. But cf. more recently W. Farmer (1964) and D. L. Dungan, "Mark – The Abridgement

of Matthew and Luke", *Jesus and Man's Hope*, ed. D. G. Buttrick (Pittsburgh: Pittsburgh Theological Seminary, 1970) 51–98.

3 In this respect J. Finegan, *Die Überlieferung der Leidens – und Auferstehungsgeschichte Jesu* (1934) is also unsatisfactory. The early form critics began to see the interrelationships among the synoptics within the history of traditions framework. Cf. G. Bertram, *Die Leidensgeschichte Jesu und der Christuskult* (1922) as well as M. Dibelius, *From Tradition to Gospel* (ET B. Woolf; New York: Scribners, 1935) and R. Bultmann (1963).

4 Cf. the correct and fruitful statement of the problem by G. D. Kilpatrick (1946) as well as by K. Stendahl (1954). The high probability of an interplay between written and oral sources has been established by the OT discussion initiated by H. S. Nyberg and carried forward chiefly by Scandinavian scholars.

5 Cf. Kilpatrick (1946) 44–6; Stendahl (1954) 120–6 and 196–8.

6 The story probably reached its present form in a community well acquainted with Mark. For in the words of Jesus in Matt. 27:63, *meta treis hēmeras* ("after three days") agrees with Mark 8:31; 9:31 and 10:34. Matthew himself uses *tē tritē hēmerā* ("on the third day") which is more exact chronologically, but he did not find it necessary to make the correction in his rendering of a statement of Jesus' enemies.

7 E.g. *tote* ("then") or *de* ("and") for *kai* ("and"), *eipen* or *ephē* for *legei* (all three words mean "he said"), a preference for *idou* ("behold") *ho legomenos* ("the one called") *symboulion lambanein* ("to take counsel"), conjunctive participles, frequent mention of the name Jesus. Cf. Finegan, 37f.

8 Cf. Matt. 26:36, 38–40, 42; and 26:15, 65f; 27:21. A complete list is given as Appendix I in *NTS* 2 (1955).

9 Further examples: 27:15 (for the crowd, cf. Mark 15:8); 27:32 (*exerchomenoi*, "as they were coming out", cf. Mark 15:20 *exagousin*, "they led him out," and 21 *erchomenon*, "coming"); 27:50 (*aphēken*, "yielded up", cf. Mark 15:37 *apheis*, "utter" or "yield up"); 27:55 (*pollai*, "many women", cf. Mark 15:41); 27:60 (*megan*, "large," cf. Mark 16:4). In such cases it is not necessary to assume an intentional redaction; the similarities of phraseology may simply be unconscious reminiscences.

10 A. Debrunner, *Coniectanea Neotestamentica XI in honorem Antonii Fridrichsen* (1947) 45–9 concludes from the use of *ap'arti* ("from now on") in Matt. 26:29, 64 that an intermediate stage lies between Mark and Matthew.

11 The "minor agreements" are chiefly found in these pericopes, Matt. 26:39–42, 50–2, 58, 63–4, 68, 75 (?); 27:54–5, 57–60. Cf. Appendix II in *NTS* 2 (1955).

12 E. Hirsch, *Die Frühgeschichte des Evangeliums* (1941) vol. II, 236–49 has argued for this.

13 Cf. above all B. H. Streeter, *The Four Gospels* (1927) 293–331.

14 Cf. Streeter, 325ff; Bultmann (1963) 272f.

15 Cf. Mark 14:40b, 51f, 72 (cf. v. 30); 15:21, 44f; 16:3. This explanation of the omissions within the passion story becomes more probable when viewed in the light of Matthew's and Luke's common omissions in earlier chapters.

16 Matt. 26:3–5, 7, 9, 15, 23, 25; 27: 29, 37, 57, 59, 60, 62, cf. Appendix III in *NTS*

2 (1955). P. Borgen, "John and the Synoptics in the Passion Narrative", *NTS* 5 (1958–9), 246–59.

17 On the Semitisms in Matthew, cf. primarily M. J. Lagrange (1927); further Butler (1951) 147–56. Cf. also M. Black, *An Aramaic Approach to the Gospels and Acts* (1946) 99f on Matt. 28:1; E. Lohmeyer (1956) on 26:10, 13, 23, 28, 69 and other passages.

18 Cf. Black, esp. 178–205, 212–21, where the persistence of oral tradition is noted. Concerning other contributions to the complex of problems, cf. A. F. J. Klijn, *A Survey of the Researches into the Western Test of the Gospels and Acts* (1949) 27ff, 146–50.

19 The conclusion of Kilpatrick (1846): "Our community was Greek-speaking" (103) has been modified somewhat by Stendahl's investigations in *The School of St Matthew*.

20 Cf. 26:15; 27:3–10 (on this Stendahl, 196f); 27:43 and further 26:67 (Isa. 50:67); 27:12 (Isa. 53:7?); 27:34 (Ps. 69:22); 27:57 (Isa. 53:9 MT). Ps. 31:14 seems to have had an influence on the form of Matt. 26:3–4; the psalm (cf. esp. vv. 12–19) could be read with Pss. 22 and 69 as a description of the passion. Finally, Luke 23:46 alludes to Ps. 31:6. Cf. K. H. Schelkle, *Die Passion Jesu in der Verkündigung des Neuen Testaments* (1949) 86ff. The minor variants in the citations 26:31, 54; 27:35, 46 support the relative independence of Matthew from Mark.

21 T. W. Manson has called my attention to the possibility that the full name "Jesus Barabbas" may have stood in the primitive text of Mark 15:7 as well.

22 Cf. R. Delbrück, "Antiquarisches zu den Verspottungen Jesu," *ZNW* 41 (1942) 132f.

23 Cf. J. Wellhausen, *Das Evangelium Matthaei* (1904), 141f, who surmises that Matthew has preserved the original even in 26:67.

24 Here we may conjecture that Matthew was already revered as an apostle and guarantor of tradition before the first Gospel was accredited to him. This would explain the identification of the tax collector with Matthew (9:9 and 10:3).

25 *From Tradition to Gospel*, 196–9.

26 G. Bornkamm, "Matthaus als Interpret der Herrenworte" *TLZ* 79 (1954) 341–6 comes to a similar conclusion from other material. Cf. his article, "End Expectation and Church in Matthew", in *Tradition* (1963) 15–51.

27 Cf. also the reminiscences of the Christian kerygma in 27:63, 64; 28:7.

28 As a rule Matthew designates Jesus' opponents as the chief priests and the elders (of the people) (26:3, 43; 27:1, 3, 12, 20; 28:11f, ef. 21:43), no doubt in order to emphasize that they acted as official leaders of the Jews. The legal aspect of the passion is also emphasized by the oath at the trial (26:67) as well as by Matthew's designation of Pilate as the governor (27:2, 11, etc.). The scribes appear only in 26:57 and 27:41, whereas in Mark they appear also in 14:1, 53 and 15:1. Could it be that the scribes were the contemporary opponents of the evangelist, while the chief priests and elders were considered the principal adversaries of Jesus?

29 P. Seidelin, "Den synoptiske Jesu", *Bidrag til Kristologien,* ed. L. Berner *et. al.* (1951), gives a few hints concerning the results of his unpublished studies on the passion story and writes among other things, "The real point of the Barabbas

episode is to eliminate Pilate from the question of guilt, because he was not a Jew, did not belong to the people, and was therefore irrelevant to this confrontation" (63).

30 Cf. 2 Sam. 1:16; 3:28f; 14:9; 1 Kgs. 2:31–3, 44–45; Lev. 20:9; Deut. 21:5ff; Sus. 46 Theod; *As Mos.* 9:7; *m. Sanh* 4–5; *T. Levi* 16:3; Acts 5:28; 18:6; 20:26. Cf. K. Koch (ed.), *Um das Prinzip der Vergeltung in Religion und Recht des Alten Testaments* (1971), esp. the essays by Koch and H. Reventlow.

31 Cf. Seidelin, 64f: on Mark, M. Kiddle, "The Death of Jesus and the Admission of the Gentiles in St Mark", *JTS* 35 (1934), 45–50.

32 As examples of modification, cf. the omission of Mark 14:40b and the insertion of "to see the end" in Matt. 26:58 and *pikros* ("bitter") in 26:75.

33 Cf. 26:22–5, 29 ("with you"), 31–5 ("because of me" – "of the shepherd" – "because of you"), 38, 40 ("with me"), 58, 69–75; 27:57 ("a disciple"); 28:8, 17.

34 Cf. H. Riesenfeld, "The Resurrection in Ezekiel xxxvii and in the Dura-Europos Paintings", *Uppsala Universitets Årsskrift* (1948) 11, where the correspondence between Matt. 27:51–3 and the representation of Ezek. 37 in the synagogue at Dura is demonstrated.

35 K. W. Clark (1947) 165–72 even accepts a Gentile Christian background for the author.

36 W. Hillmann, *Aufbau und Deutung der synoptischen Leidensberichte* (1941) comes to a similar conclusion though he approaches the problem quite differently: The first evangelist "takes up the question of his readers, which has to do above all with the internal and external vindication of the Christian church, and he justifies this new community by appeal to the events and the teachings of Jesus, based on faith in his true Messiahship" (264).

37 On this cf. A. Oepke, *Das neue Gottesvolk* (1950) who speaks, for example, of a "peculiar . . . dialectical, triangular relationship" (42f). Cf. now W. Trilling (1959), also R. Hummel (1966).

38 *The So-called Historical Jesus and the Historic, Biblical Christ* (1964), 80, note 11.

39 One major point of departure for this theory is the five-fold occurrence of the concluding formula: 7:28; 11:1; 13:53; 19:1; 26:1. Cf. B. W. Bacon (1930) 80–2; repeated by Stendahl, 25. Regarding Matthew as a "handbook", cf. Stendahl, 20–9.

40 On Matt. 26:1, cf. Deut. 31:1 (LXX), 24; 32:44f. On Matt. 28:20, cf. Deut. 29:8; 30:8, 10, 16; 31:12; 32:46.

4

Quis et Unde?*

An Analysis of Matthew 1–2

KRISTER STENDAHL

The tendency to harmonize the material in the different Gospels is deeply rooted in the Christian tradition and manifests itself especially in the treatment of what we are used to call the infancy or nativity narrative in Matt. 1–2 and Luke 1–2. In spite of comments and observations to the contrary, the study of Matt. 1–2 labours under the conscious or unconscious presupposition that Matthew here is doing – in his own manner, to be sure – what Luke is doing in his two first chapters, i.e. giving an account of the birth of Jesus.[1] This presupposition is constantly reinforced by the *quaestio facti*. Only within this presupposed framework of "birth narratives", the differences between Matthew and Luke – or, as it mostly happens, between Luke and Matthew[2] – are properly discussed. These differences are well known and need only be pointed out in their main features:

1 Matthew. The genealogy comes first, runs from Abraham to Jesus called Christ; it is revised – leaving out e.g. three of the kings mentioned in the OT (Ahaziah, Joash and Amaziah), and with obviously too few generations in its third part – according to a pattern (3 × 14), and follows the ruling Davidic line. Its most distinctive feature is the mentioning of the four women: Tamar, Rahab, Ruth and Bath-Sheba ("the wife of Uriah").

Luke. The genealogy has no relation to the birth narrative; it is connected with the "Son of God" of the *Bath Qol* at the baptism of Jesus (3:22). The genealogy runs in the opposite direction, from "Jesus ... being the son (as was supposed) of Joseph" by a chain of simple genitives all the way back to "... the son of Adam, the son of God". Thereby it forms a corroboration of the message of the *Bath Qol*. The circle closes itself. The line to David goes via Nathan, i.e.

* First published in *Judentum, Urchristentum: Kirche*, ed. W. Elester (1960) 94–105.

a non-ruling line of the Davidic family. The Davidic element is not stressed; the point seems to be: Son of God.

2   In Matthew Joseph is the main person. It is he who receives the revelations and through him the action progresses. Dreams are the vehicles of revelation, a phenomenon peculiar to Matthew.[3]

In Luke Mary is the recipient of revelation and Joseph is described as he who stands by.

3   None of the events mentioned in Matt. 2 are mentioned or alluded to in Luke 1–2: The visit of the Magi, the flight into Egypt, the massacre in Bethlehem, the return to Judea and the continued flight to Galilee and Nazareth. Furthermore, according to Matthew Joseph and Mary live in Bethlehem[4] and their settling in Nazareth is due to special guidance at a later time; according to Luke Joseph and Mary live in Nazareth, they go to Bethlehem for the specific purpose of the census, and they return to their home town Nazareth, 2:39. There is no evil Herod in the background, only shepherds and pious Jews, Simeon and Anna. And there is the elaborate parallelism between the Baptist and Jesus.[5]

4   In Matthew the text seems to rest on formula quotations, one for each point in Matthew's account.[6] There are no such in Luke, where the relation to the OT expresses itself in allusions, and these are materially and formally concentrated in the canticles.[7]

Such differences are more drastic than anywhere in the canonical Gospels – the synoptics *versus* the Fourth Gospel included. They should warn against treating Matt. 1–2 and Luke 1–2 as alternative birth narratives. The carefully organized structure of Matthew makes it unnatural to approach these divergencies by a direct discussion of the "source" or "sources" behind Matt. 1–2.[8] Whatever the sources, Matthew works here with a clarity of purpose, which should allow us to find out what *he* thinks that he is doing with his material. Such a first step is the most reasonable, since the organizing principles, and especially the formula quotations, are not confined to these two chapters, but are applied also to material of a synoptic nature.[9] But in chaps. 1–2 this method has totally formed the material, a sign of the fact that at the time of the Gospel this material had not yet frozen into a given form.

Matt. 2 is dominated by geographical names. This is the more striking in contrast to chap. 1, which has not a single one,[10] not even where we would expect them, i.e. in 1:18f. The chapter begins with the mentioning of Bethlehem of Judea, it takes us to Egypt, describes the massacre at Bethlehem, takes us out of Egypt back to the Land of Israel, bypasses Judea, takes us into Galilee and settles down in Nazareth. For Matthew this itinerary is not a frame secondary to his intention. On the contrary, these geographical names constitute what is really important to him, as can be seen from his use of the formula quotations: the common denominator for the four formula quotations in chap. 2 is that they all contain geographical names, names which substantiate the point reached in the "itinerary". At two points it becomes obvious that the four Matthean quotations have the location rather than the "event" as their foci.[11]

1   The prophecy, "Out of Egypt did I call my son", is placed by Matthew not where the call out of Egypt takes place (v. 19), but where Egypt occurs for the first time (vv. 13–15). Hence it is obvious that Matthew wants to nail down "Egypt" in the itinerary.

2   LXX^{A}א*, Vulgate, Aquila and the Targum[12] all suppress the geographical name Ramah,[13] in Jer. 31 (38):15, in a manner typical of the LXX,[14] by translating "on high". This may well be the prevailing interpretation in Judaism and hence Matthew's use of the geographical name is not self-evident, but stressed in order to serve a geographical quotation.

If the geographical information is what gives the structure to Matt. 2, then this chapter gives the answer to a question, similar to the two raised in John 7:41f "Is the Christ to come from Galilee? Has not the scripture said that the Christ is descended from David, and comes from Bethlehem, the village where David was?". In the Fourth Gospel these questions are left open – a literary device or an actual witness to John's lack of knowledge or lack of interest in any Bethlehem tradition.[15] But the question must have been a real one: How was it that Jesus the Messiah came from a Galilean village?[16] Hence the *whole* second chapter of Matthew has its climax in its last verse ... "that he should be called *Nazōraios*" ("Nazarene").[17] The chapter shows how God himself, according to prophecies and through divine and angelic intervention, leads Joseph, and thereby Jesus, from Bethlehem to Nazareth. The cry in Ramah then forms a prophetic alibi: it is obvious that they had to get the boy out of Bethlehem. The title to be written over the chapter would be: How it came to pass that the Messiah came from Nazareth. It gives in a sense the opposite answer to that given in Luke, where Nazareth is the self-evident point of departure and "Bethlehem" comes into the picture through the census. In a similar fashion, in Luke Nazareth is the point of departure for the whole ministry of Jesus; it is the way in which his neighbours renounce him that sends him out on his mission, Luke 4:16–30. Also in Matthew the christological geography[18] is not confined to chaps. 1–2. The thought expressed in 2:22f is reinforced as the point of departure for the whole ministry of Jesus also in Matt. 4:12–17; but now it is not Nazareth[19] that counts, but Galilee, and in accordance with Mark 1:21 Matthew sees Capernaum as the centre of Jesus' Galilean ministry. The transfer to Capernaum is substantiated in the phrase "toward the sea" (4:15). Yet, in Matt. 2 the issue was of a more specific nature: Bethlehem-Nazareth.[20]

Granted that we have found the correct key to the composition of Matt. 2, there remain the far more complicated questions concerning the origin, form and nature of the material which Matthew has made use of. It looks as if the story about the Magi, which has many striking features of its own, has already, prior to Matthew's use of the material, been an integral part of an account where "the struggle of the King against the Messiah"[21] is described in a language which draws on the similar motif in Exodus.[22] This assumption is strengthened by the mentioning of Herod's name nine times, and at all points of progress in the account, even after his death (v. 22). Nevertheless, in its Matthean form the chapter answers the question "Bethlehem-Nazareth", and it does so for apologetic purposes.

Such an understanding at Matt. 2 would also serve to elucidate two famous problems regarding Matt. 2:1–12: (a) It has remained a puzzling fact that this pericope has no explicit reference to the Star-prophecy in Num. 24:17. This prophecy, of messianic significance both in Judaism and the early Christian testimonies,[23] seems to lie just under the surface in the Matthean account.[24] Now we can explain why it remains there, since the formula quotations here are organized only to serve the geographical account. (b) The unique way in which the Bethlehem-quotation lacks the usual Matthean introductory formula is easier to understand if we see the apologetic tension between "Bethlehem as expected" and "Nazareth as revealed". This coincides with the situation of John 7, to which we just have referred.

Once it has been recognized how chap. 2 is totally focused in its geographical names, it appears that chap. 1 has not only a similarly apologetic purpose,[25] but also a similar structure, now centred around personal names. Already the way in which the two chapters end on a similar note and in a similar form points in this direction: "He shall be called a Nazarene"/"and he called his name Jesus". We have mentioned the striking absence of any geographical names in the first chapter.[26] Of greater significance is the observation that from the point of view of literary form, 1:18–25 could be called a legend of divine name-giving.[27] The revelation of the angel and Joseph's obedient answer is the nucleus of the pericope. Vv. 18–19 give the background; note the "behold" in v. 20, preceded by the summarizing "as he considered this". The formula quotation from Isa. 7:14 should be understood as not belonging to the message of the angel. It is Matthew's interpretative comment, this in agreement with all the other formula quotations in Matthew[28]. As a divine giving of the name, 1:18–25 has its genuine Matthean point and climax in its last words, as had chap. 2.

Most commentators give the disposition of Matt. 1–2 by drawing a decisive line of demarcation between the genealogy (1:1–17) and the "Matthean birth narrative" (1:18—2:25).[29] This is a striking example of Lucan influence upon Matthean exegesis. But it should be recognized that the whole of chap. 1 has its own integrity and that the line of demarcation really lies between the two chapters. The genealogy in its Matthean form points to what follows in 1:18–25 by its accentuation of the Davidic line. This is clear from the way in which David is epitomized in vv. 1 and 17, possibly also by the formula "three times fourteen", since in Hebrew the letters of the name David have a value of $4 + 6 + 4 = 14$;[30] and in 1:6 the royal status of David, and only of David, is stressed.

The link between the genealogy and vv. 18–25 is more specific in the mentioning of the four women Tamar, Rahab, Ruth and Bath-Sheba. The common denominator for these four women is found in that they all represent an "irregularity" in the Davidic line, an irregularity which is not only overcome by God's recognition of them as mothers of Davidic descendants: exactly by the irregularity the action of God and his Spirit is made manifest.[31] But as was the case in olden times, such divine interventions lead to slander from contemporaries who do not understand the ways of the Lord. In this light Matthew presents his apologetic argument about how Jesus was engrafted into the Davidic pedigree.

This argument is introduced by the phrase: *tou de Iēsou Christou hē genesis houtōs ēn* ("now the origin of Jesus Christ was thus") 1:18. The unusual word order[32] indicates that Matthew consciously refers back to the constellation of the name Jesus and the title Christ in v. 16 (*Iēsous ho legomenos Christos*, "Jesus, who is called Christ").

Matthew is now to explain the details of this last point of the genealogy, a point where the nature of the case has caused a rather complicated formulation.[33] He says: But as for this last link in the genealogy, "Jesus[34] Christ", his origin[35] was this wise. Thus already the syntactical form of v. 18a indicates that vv. 18–25 are the enlarged footnote to the crucial point in the genealogy. The usual translations, "Now the birth of Jesus Christ was on this wise"[36] are under Lucan influence, as is definitely the title e.g. in Huck's *Synopsis*, "The Birth of Jesus". As a matter of fact, the birth of Jesus is not described in Matthew, where the points are rather the angelic revelation to Joseph, and the naming of the child (eight days after its birth?; Luke 2:21). Schlatter has been more sensitive to the Matthean material in 1:18–25 when he calls the pericope, "The implanting of Jesus into David's line".[37] This engrafting is described with considerable precision, in a way aimed at overcoming slanderous remarks by placing Joseph in that same attitude of suspicion, and by showing how Joseph's hesitation was overcome by the angelic revelation. Hence the suspicion is not that Joseph should have been the actual father to the child, but that Mary should have deceived him.[38] But even this rebuttal is secondary to Matthew's intention. The genuine point is that the angel encourages Joseph, the son of David, to make this child a Davidic child. Thereby Jesus' place in the genealogy is explained. God has ordered this engrafting. Furthermore, the name Jesus is shown to be according to God's order. On both these points Joseph is explicitly reported to have obeyed: he takes Mary to his wife and he gives her child the name Jesus. The fact that the name Jesus is interpreted directly, without translation, has been used in favour of a semitic source.[39] This is by no means necessary. That Jesus meant "Saviour", could have been presupposed knowledge; Gospels are not missionary material. The reason could also be of a more formal nature: an angelic message should not be loaded with interpretative comments of the sort which, on the other hand, could well be attached to Immanuel, since this verse is in itself a commentary added by the evangelist. The Spirit or an angel neither quotes nor interprets.[40]

If we were to take our key from chap. 2 strictly, we could surmise that the salient point in the quotation from Isa. 7:14 was Immanuel, i.e. the personal name; such an understanding would also make the explicit translation "God with us" more natural. Then "the virgin shall conceive and bear a son" would be the *basis* for the application of the title Immanuel, not the point itself.[41] That Immanuel is meant by Matthew as a title is clear from the plural *kalesousin*, "one will call him ...", this against all known OT texts.[42] It should be noted that, while Isa. 7:14 was not – as far as we know – used as a messianic prophecy in Judaism, it stands within the Davidic line. And the title Immanuel underscores the messianic function of Jesus, who is to set his (!) people free from their sins. In short: the Immanuel prophecy substantiates the significance of the name Jesus as expressed in v. 21, an interesting and typically Matthean contrast to the easy conflation in Luke 1:31![43]

The two messianic/christological designations Jesus and Immanuel, lead us to consider finally the relation of Matt. 1:18–25 to the biblical witness to the Virgin Birth. It is obvious that the supernatural birth of Jesus was known to Matthew, and the tradition was apparently known well enough to have given rise to slanderous remarks. But it is equally clear that Matthew is not announcing the birth story. Furthermore in Matthew the Virgin Birth story is theologically mute, no christological argument or insight is deduced from this great divine intervention. There is little reason to read the Immanuel prophecy in the direction of "incarnation". The context suggests rather a Jewish, messianic understanding, In Jesus' messianic deeds God visits his people and sets them free from the hardships which their sins have justly caused.

NOTES

1 If this be what Luke actually is aiming at. In any case, he differs substantially from Matthew in the epic breadth; this is in accordance with his introductory remarks (1:1–4) and manifests itself already in chaps. 1–2. The descriptive element goes together with the explicit stress on the place of the event in Jewish history (1:5) and World history (2:1, cf. 3:1–2). See further M. Dibelius, *Jungfrauensohn und Krippenkind* (1932) (= M. Dibelius, *Botschaft und Geschichte* I, 1953, 1–78). The tendency to *describe* what originally was *believed* is one of the creative forces in the development of Nativity Gospels; see O. Cullmann, "Infancy Gospels" in E. Hennecke, *NT Apocrypha I* (ET 1963) 363–6. It is significant that Luke – not Matthew – shows the first signs of "filling in the gaps" in the historical continuum (Luke 2:40, the visit to Jerusalem at the age of twelve; and 2:52). It is also only in Luke that the Virgin Birth serves as an explicit reason for Jesus being Son of God: "therefore ..." (1:35). See H. Conzelmann, *The Theology of Saint Luke* (ET 1960) 172. Cf. Dibelius' summary of the aim of the Lucan account; 80 (78). For a more recent analysis of Luke 2:1–20 as a totality, see K. H. Rengstorf, "Die Weihnachtserzählung des Evangelisten Lukas", in *Stat crux dum volvitur orbis*, (Festschr. H. Lilje, 1959) 5–30; cf. also R. McL. Wilson, "Some Recent Studies in the Lucan Infancy Narratives". in TU 73 (1959) 235–53, especially its reference to R. Laurentin, "Traces d'allusions etymologiques en Luc 1–2", Biblica 37 (1956) 435–56; 38 (1957) 1–23; also *Structure et Théologie de Luc 1–2* (Paris 1957).

2 The two major studies of the Virgin Birth both agree in taking their point of departure in Luke, treating Matthew as corroborating or supplementary material: V. Taylor, *The historical evidence for the Virgin Birth* (1920); J. G. Machen, *The Virgin Birth of Christ* (1930), cf. F. Kattenbusch's extensive review in *Theologische Studien und Kritiken* 102 (1930) 454–74. More sensitive attention is given to the Matthean material by K. Bornhäuser, *Die Geburts- und Kindheitsgeschichte Jesu* (1930) and, to some extent, G. Erdmann, *Die Vorgeschichten des Lukas- und Matthäusevangeliums und Vergils vierte Ekloge* (1932), but even so they seem to labour under Lucan "pre-understanding".

3 *Kat' onar* ("in a dream"): 1:20, 2:12, 13, 19, 22, see also about Pilate's wife, 27:19. In Acts the term used is "a vision in the night" or similar, 16:9; 18:9.

4 This does not follow with absolute necessity from Matt. 2:1 where a harmonizing exegesis could make a case for Nazareth *e silentio*; the line of demarcation to be drawn between chaps. 1 and 2 (see below, 59f) further minimizes the possibility of such an argument. But 2:22–3 remains the decisive stumbling-block for such harmonization: To Matthew Galilee and Nazareth are new data, divinely revealed and prophetically announced.

5 See P. Benoit, "L'enfance de Jean-Baptiste selon Luc 1", *NTS* 3 (1956/7) 191–4. It may be of some significance for further study of the Lucan material that it thus deals with *two* messianic figures, one priestly and one royal. For the assessment of John-Jesus, see J. A. T. Robinson, "Elijah, John and Jesus: An Essay in Detection", *NTS* 4 (1957/8) 263–81.

6 The genealogy is, in its own way, of a similar nature, v. 17 forming virtually a statement of fulfilment.

7 Apart from the strong allusion to Isa. 7:14 in Luke 1:31, cf. Matt. 1:21, 23, there is no clear coincidence in quotations between Matthew and Luke. For an ingenious but hardly convincing relation between Matt. 2:23 and Luke, see B. Gärtner, *Die rätselhaften Termini Nazaräer und Iskariot* (Horae Soederblomianae 4, 1957) 8–18.

8 See B. W. Bacon (1930) 154–64. A detailed argument for different sources and a minimum of Matthean activity has been given by W. L. Knox, *The Sources of the Synoptic Gospels* II (1957) 121–8. His argument forces him to split the formula quotations in Matthew between different sources and subsequent stages in the development of the Gospel.

9 Bacon, 155, following Streeter, stresses this "parasite-nature" of the Matthean material. There are also more internal reasons for ruling out the possibility that the quotations gave impetus to creating facts, events or legends, see K. Stendahl, (1954) 194–202.

10 Except in the phrase "the deportation to Babylon" in 1:11, 12, 17, where it serves as a temporal designation.

11 In the fourth quotation (2:23) there is no alternative; for the purely geographical meaning of Nazarene in Matthew, see below, n. 17.

12 I.e. in the actual saying, but "Ramah" is retained in the fuller exposition of the verse.

13 On the identification Ramah-Ephrath(a)-Bethlehem, see Jeremias, *Heiligengräber in Jesu Umwelt* (1958) 75.

14 On the treatment of geographical names in the LXX, see I. L. Seeligmann, *The Septuagint Version of Isaiah* (Mededelingen en Verhandelingen van het Vooraziatisch-Egyptisch Genootschap "Ex Oriente Lux" 9, 1948) 76ff.

15 Cf. also 7:52. In his commentary Bultmann goes as far as to say, "The Evangelist knows nothing, or wants to know nothing of the birth in Bethlehem;" (ET 1971) 306 n.6. Against this see C. K. Barrett *ad loc.* It seems reasonable to see the Johannine attitude as one where "Bethlehem" is an adiaphoron; the Johannine answer is rather to be found in John 1:46 where the question "Can anything good come out of Nazareth?" is met by "Come and see."

16 G. K. Kilpatrick (1946) 54, phrases the question: "If Jesus, commonly associated with Nazareth, really belonged to Bethlehem, how came he to spend by far the greatest part of his life at Nazareth?" But the length of residence is of no interest to Matthew (cf. above, n. 1), only "Nazareth" and the Galilean point of departure, which is implied.

17 For our argument at this point the discussion about *Nazōraios* ('Nazorean")/ *Nazarēnos* ("Nazarene") as sectarian name or geographical designation is of no consequence. To Matthew the issue is purely geographical. For the latest discussion of this problem and of the source for the quotation, see B. Gärtner, op. cit., and A. Medebielle, "Quoniam Nazaraenus vocabitur", *Studia Anselmiana.* 27–8 (1956/7) 136–9. *Nazarēnos* could be considered a (Marcan) Latinism, so Bacon (1930) 164; cf. the way in which the different writers refer to the Essenes *essēnoi/ esseni* (Josephus, mostly, and Pliny) and *essaioi* (Philo), see W. Bauer, in Pauly-Wissowa, *RE*, Suppl. 4 (1924) 419.

18 W. Schmauch, *Orte der Offenbarung und der Offenbarungsort im Neuen Testament* (1956), is of little help at this point. He recognizes other elements in Matthew (15), but takes his refuge in the Johannine material to substantiate his thesis (16f).

19 The reading *Nazara* (B *pc* k) in Matt. 4:13, accepted by Tischendorf and Westcott-Hort is doubtful, see A. Schlatter, (1963⁶), ad loc. Influence from Luke 4:16?

20 Thus the structure of Matt. 2 lies even closer to the core of the discussion "Galilee and Jerusalem" than its two independent protagonists suggested. E. Lohmeyer, *Galiläa und Jerusalem* (1936) and R. H. Lightfoot, *Locality and Doctrine* (1938) e.g. 115. The more recent contribution to this discussion, L. E. Elliott-Binns, *Galilean Christianity* (1956) has hardly fostered the discussion since it moves from the specific into ever more uncontrolled generalities.

21 So Schlatter, (1963⁶) 25.

22 The Exodus imprint is seen especially in the unexpected – hardly generalizing: Blass-Debrunner *Grammar* ET 1961, § 141 – plural "those who sought" (v. 20; Exod. 4:19), and the more general suggestiveness of Moses/Jesus, and Egypt-Land of Israel, see Jeremias, *TDNT* IV, 870f. The Jewish background to the whole chapter is however of a broader nature since similar patterns of events have clustered around Abraham, see Strack-Billerbeck I, 77f, cf. *Jewish Encyclopedia* I, 86; and Laban-Jacob, see D. Daube, *The New Testament and Rabbinic Judaism* (1956) 189ff; cf. L. Finkelstein, in *HTR* 31 (1938) 299f.

23 See E. Burrows, *The Oracles of Jacob and Balaam* (1939) 71–100; and for Qumran and the Damascus Document A. S. van der Woude, *Die messianischen Vorstellungen der Gemeinde von Qumran* (Studia Semitica Nederlandica 3, 1957) e.g.

212ff, et index sub Num. 24:17; cf. F. M. Cross Jr, *The Ancient Library of Qumran* (1958) 169 on the Star as the priestly Messiah at Qumran.

24 See Stendahl (1954) 136.

25 This is generally recognized for 1:18–25; for 1:1–17 see below, concerning the reference to the four women.

26 See above, p. 57; cf. Klostermann, commentary, on 1:18, "the place and the time ... remain in the dark."

27 Cf. Gen. 16:11, 15; 17:19; 21:3 and also Judg. 13:3; Strack-Billerbeck I, 63. This aspect is stressed by R. Bultmann (1963) 292.

28 The sole example to the contrary would be in 2:6, a quotation placed on the lips of the scribes; see, however, the end of the preceding paragraph. Note also the tenses in 1:22f (*gegonen*, "took place", and *hexei*, "shall conceive").

29 So e.g. the commentaries by W. C. Allen, A. H. McNeile, and especially Lohmeyer. I have earlier followed this common and, at first glance, obvious approach; see *Peake's Commentary on the Bible* (ed. H. H. Rowley and M. Black 1962). Schlatter comes closer to the truth, but does not capitalize on the distinction between Matt. 1 and Matt. 2, this partly due to his overall theme for these chapters: "God's actions at the birth of Jesus", which gives a misleading emphasis to the "events".

30 On this and other aspects of the Matthean genealogy, see J. Jeremias, *Jerusalem at the Time of Jesus* (ET 1969) 292. A fresh approach to the genealogies as means of historical writings has been made by O. Linton in a penetrating and pioneering study, *Synopsis historiae universalis* (Copenhagen: 1957).

31 That this is the only possible interpretation has been demonstrated beyond doubt, with special attention to Tamar, by Renée Bloch, "Juda engendra Pharès et Zara, de Thamar", *Mélanges A. Robert* (1957) 381–9. This against G. Kittel in *TDNT* III, 1f.

32 See Blass-Debrunner, *Grammar* (ET 1961) §271, 142. Cf. Matt. 10:2 *tōn de dōdeka apostolōn ta onomata estin tauta* ("the names of the twelve apostles are these"). Yet, in 1:18 the relation to the preceding is even stronger, since not only "Jesus Christ" but also "the birth" is taken from the preceding context, see n. 35.

33 So F. C. Burkitt, *Evangelion Da-Mepharreshe* II (1904) 262.

34 Omitted by e.g. Klostermann and Lohmeyer, mainly on the basis of syr[sin cur] (also 71 latt). The textual problems are here of a sort which cannot be solved apart from the exegesis. Hence we would argue for the reading *Iēsou Christou* on the basis of our interpretation, and we do so in fundamental agreement with Burkitt's penetrating textual analysis, op. cit., 260–5.

35 I read *genesis* ("origin"), and take it to retain its genealogical sense (cf. Matt 1:1) Luke 1:14 notwithstanding; this is the natural sense in Matthew if we were not under the sway of Lucan and traditional "Christmas-pressure". On *Biblos geneseōs* (Matt. 1:1), see also the extensive study by M. Lambertz in Festschrift F. Dornseiff (1953) 201–25 and J. Lindblom, "Matteusevangeliets överskrift", *Teologiska studier tillägnade E. Stave* (1922) 102–9. O. Eissfeldt, "Biblos geneseōs, in *Gott und die Götter* (Festgabe E. Fascher; 1958), observes that the toledot-formula signifies "clearly the points at which a narrowing of the horizon takes place (34)",

and on the basis of Matt. 1:18 he understands *Biblos geneseōs* as "record of the origin" (36).

36 So King James' Version, which is representative of most translations; cf. Klostermann and Lohmeyer.

37 Op. cit., 7.

38 X. Léon-Dufour, "L'annonce à Joseph", *Melanges A. Robert* (1957) 390–7, follows the same line as Schlatter, 15, in interpreting Joseph's attitude as one where awe and piety make him hesitate in taking Mary to his wife. But within this interpretation he makes significant observations about Joseph's role as the "namegiver" and the Davidic link.

39 On the complicated problem of Aramaic/Hebrew at this point, and for the general discussion see P. Nepper-Christensen (1958) 84ff. Furthermore Matt. 1:21, Luke 1:77 cannot be considered as a conscious allusion to Ps. 130 (129):8, as claimed by Kilpatrick (1946) 54; see rather W. L. Knox, op. cit., 126 n. 1.

40 Stendahl (1954) 159; cf. Luke 1:31.

41 This "basis" is of course not insignificant in the total context. Note the additional *holon* ("all") in the introductory formula (cf. 26:56) which shows that the quotation sums up a whole chain of data. Nevertheless, it remains legitimate to ask where Matthew saw the point in this formula quotation.

42 Stendahl, 97f. Luke 1:31: *kaleseis* ("you will call").

43 The observations made by W. C. van Unnik concerning "Jesus" and "Immanuel" would, on the whole, strengthen such an interpretation, see his article "Dominus vobiscum" in A. J. B. Higgins (ed.), *New Testament Essays, in memoriam T. W. Manson* (1959) 287f and nn. 58 and 59.

5

*The Concept of History in Matthew**

GEORG STRECKER

A history of modern synoptic criticism would show that in the nine-teenth and early twentieth centuries the method of analysis was almost entirely source criticism.[1] The source critics tried to ascertain what literary and historical relationships existed between the synoptic Gospels. They reached a conclusion which is today still widely accepted, that this relationship is best explained within the framework of the so-called "two source theory". This is that Mark is the oldest Gospel and was used as a source by Matthew and Luke, and that in addition Matthew and Luke had access to a second source, the so-called Q source, which contained mainly sayings material. The real theological motive during this period of source criticism in gospel study was without doubt the quest of the historical Jesus. Since the individual Gospels could not be harmonized to produce a "life of Jesus" out of them, the quest led to the reconstruction of sources which were then made the basis for answering the historical question.

It was the New Testament scholar William Wrede who in his book published in 1901, *The Messianic Secret in the Gospels*, put in question these consequences for the life of Jesus drawn from the two-source hypothesis.[2] Wrede saw that Mark's Gospel did not contain a psychologically based unity that could provide the basis for a reconstruction of a life of Jesus. He pointed out the discrepancies in the construction of the Gospel. These cannot be understood as reflecting an authentic life of Jesus tradition, but must mean that different streams of tradition have influenced the shape of the Gospel. Accordingly, Wrede understood the familiar messianic secrecy theory in Mark in terms of the history of the tradition. The

* First published in *EvT* 26 (1966) 57–74. Partly reprinted in translation in *JAAR* 35 (1967) 219–30. First section translated by Robert Morgan.

idea that during his earthly ministry Jesus revealed himself as the Christ only in secret, presupposes two different kinds of traditions: on the one hand there is the tradition of the community's faith in Jesus as the one who was enthroned as Christ at the resurrection; and on the other a life of Jesus tradition in which Jesus did not publicly confess himself as the Messiah. These two traditions were fused together prior to Mark into the idea of the messianic secret. This kind of history of traditions explanation represented a decisive advance in gospel criticism. Whatever one's judgement about the details of Wrede's interpretation[3] it brought into view the stream of tradition that lies between the Gospels and the historical Jesus, and thus pointed NT scholarship in new directions. The authors of the Gospels were subsequently no longer to be seen primarily as more or less reliable witnesses to an authentic life of Jesus tradition, but as the exponents of the on-going historical life of the Christian community. The actual development of this Christian community is presupposed by and reflected in the Gospels themselves.

The literary critical method called form criticism, developed by M. Dibelius and R. Bultmann at the start of the 1920s[4] followed the route indicated by Wrede. It concentrated on the history of the pre-synoptic tradition, i.e., the period after the life of Jesus but before the composition of the Gospels. It tried to classify the data in the tradition by formal criteria, and combined historical statements with this analysis by trying to establish its *Sitz im Leben* (life-setting).

It was natural that in drawing the consequences of Wrede's history of traditions initiative, and making methodical use of it, form criticism dealt only peripherally with the gospel writings themselves, and saw these as merely the provisional final stages in the development of the material in the tradition. In contrast to this we can therefore call the latest period of research a new phase of gospel criticism. Interest has been concentrated here on the "redaction" of the Gospels. This expression covers the process of editing and compiling the different units of tradition. We shall call this recent trend in the use of literary critical methods "redaction criticism",[5] even though it is not really a new "method" but simply the application of already existing methods to a limited area. It considers the redaction of the Gospels and their theological conceptions insofar as these can be delineated historically. It is closely connected with form criticism in that both these approaches and the older history of traditions work presuppose a far-reaching stream of community traditions, and see both the redactor and the traditions available to him as standing under the influence of the community's tradition, i.e., as exponents of the community's faith. But whereas form criticism stressed the kerygmatic accentuation of the units of tradition and in some cases the "sermon" as the basis of the tradition's emergence, redaction critical research seems to imply a tendency to admit that the authors of the Gospels have a historical, not a directly kerygmatic purpose. This takes up again, although in a greatly modified way that no longer focuses on the authentic life of Jesus, the historically accentuated view of the Gospels held by the liberal life of Jesus research.

The aim of what follows is to present the results of a redaction critical analysis of Matthew oriented to its understanding of history. A preliminary methodological observation is thus necessary. In working out the historical situation and theological conception of the evangelist it is important to determine in principle the relationship of tradition and redaction. This relationship cannot be resolved by a simple alternative between the editor's "agreeing" with his tradition or a "difference" between them. It is rather a matter of "both-and". As spokesman for a community the evangelist stands on the ground of his community's tradition. He indicates his fundamental agreement with the tradition he represents by his selection of material too. On the other hand, the Gospels are not seamless unities. They contain breaks and tensions which cannot be subsumed under the single theme of the redactor's conception. This poses for the redaction critic the task of drawing distinctions within the pre-redactional tradition and asking about the genuinely redactional statements which may reflect the central thrust of a particular Gospel, as seen by the redactor himself.

Matthew's understanding of history presupposes the change in the theological situation which took place around the turn from the first to the second Christian generation. The primitive Christian community emerged from the Easter faith in the Kyrios Jesus who had risen from the dead. The content of its faith was the expectation that the return of its Lord would take place during that generation. Even before the first generation was past, therefore, the question arises how the problem of the delay of the parousia should be met and how the originally eschatological conception could be fitted to the fact of a continuing history.[6] The following period tried in different ways to master this problem. They constructed forms of church institutional life which could outlast that period. They established an ordained ministry; they discovered the significance of tradition as a factor which would guarantee the unity of the Church as time progressed. The redactors of the synoptic Gospels had a hand in the beginnings of this movement, which has also been given the label "early catholicism",[7] in the sense that they presuppose an awareness of the delay of the parousia as a fact, and have drawn consequences from the changed theological situation by their new orientation in history. If their theological situation is conditioned by a conviction that the Christian community has to reckon with an indefinitely extended history of mankind in the future, that means also that the course of history itself comes into focus. One has to give some account not only of the future, but also of the past.[8] This is the task posed for the redactors of the synoptic Gospels. They collect the Jesus material in the tradition and arrange it in a way that tries to respond to the changed theological situation. This situation is characterized firstly by the necessity of considering the problem of "time" or "world" as the historical locus of Christian existence. This implies, secondly, the task of asserting the original relation of Christian existence to the eschaton. That sums up the question to be asked in analysing Matthew here: In what way has the redactor of the first Gospel taken account in his modification and compilation of traditional material, of the theological situation of his generation; and that means by what specific understanding of history does he respond to the problem area that exists?[9]

I

The first inference from our recognition of the theological-historical background of the synoptic redactions is that there was a *"historicizing"* of the traditional material by the redactor Matthew. In the period between the life of Jesus and the time of the gospel writers, there were already individual units of tradition and collections of traditional material, which contained "historical" statements about the place of the tradition in the life of Jesus. Thus, the pre-synoptic collection of the passion narrative was connected with the end of Jesus' life. The Q source represented an early form of the Gospels insofar as it contained a primitive, chronological arrangement of the speech material, for it probably began with the tradition of the preaching of John the Baptist and ended with the apocalyptic speech of Jesus. Finally, with its outline – "from the appearance of John the Baptist to the passion and resurrection of Jesus" – the Gospel of Mark already anticipated the essential elements of a portrayal of the life of Jesus. Matthew, however, extensively amplified the outline of temporal references that he found in these sources. To the Marcan outline he prefixed a genealogy of Jesus, as well as the infancy narrative (in chaps. 1–2). Even if this implies a theological interpretation, since here Jesus is already presented as the Son of David and as the one who fulfills the promises given to the people of Israel, still a historical intention is at the same time involved. By enlarging Mark's outline with respect to the beginning of Jesus' life, Matthew indicates that he is reflecting on the past as such. It is no accident that Luke proceeds in exactly the same way; he also amplifies the Marcan source with an infancy narrative and a genealogy of Jesus. If Luke has rightly been called a "historian" – the existence of Luke-Acts confirms to a certain extent the validity of this designation – then this parallelism might lead us to suppose a historical tendency in Matthew also. But beyond that, Matthew elaborated his Marcan source in terms of chronology. Contrary to Mark, he inserted in his Gospel at characteristic points the chronological formula *apo tote* ("from that time on ..."). This formula characterizes the beginning of Jesus' preaching;[10] it marks the beginning of the first passion prediction as an introduction to the last stage of Jesus' way to passion, death, and resurrection (16:21); and it is inserted into the Marcan outline at the beginning of the betrayal of Jesus by Judas (26:16). This formula, like the numerous other indications of chronology in Matthew's Gospel, is not meant to express a development of the life of Jesus, but it nevertheless emphasizes a temporal, linear movement, in contrast to the traditional material.

Another example of Matthew's historicizing of tradition may be taken from the realm of geographical concepts. If one compares Matthew and Mark in respect of the idea of the "house" in which Jesus stays, it is evident that in Mark we find a topological meaning. The concept of "house" is a part of the theory of the messianic secret and refers to the place of revelation, which is separated from the public; here, the paradoxical unity of the revealed and hidden messiahship of Jesus becomes clear. Thus, according to this idea in Mark's Gospel, the "house" is not fixed geographically; it can be found anywhere that Jesus' revelatory activity requires.[11] In Matthew, however, the situation is different. By the way he chooses and frames the corresponding Marcan passages, Matthew shows that he understood the motif primarily in terms of geography rather than topology. The "house" is located at a certain place in the Palestinian region, at Capernaum.[12] This corresponds to the fact that only Matthew designates Capernaum as Jesus' "own city" (9:1), and he alone can speak of Jesus "dwelling" in Capernaum (4:13). This means

71

that the originally topological idea has become geographically limited.

Not only chronological and geographical statements are used in the first Gospel to point out the historical character of the traditional material. The use of a special source of collected quotations is much more important in this connection. Matthew made his own use of this collection in the so-called "formula-quotations" of his special material.[13] In the framework of redaction, the formula-quotations presuppose, in accord with their pre-Matthean meaning, that the promises of God to the people of Israel have found *fulfilment* in the life of Jesus. This means on the other hand that the promises have found fulfilment in the *life of Jesus*. Without doubt, Matthew emphasized the latter, since the quotations are connected with temporal and, above all, geographical statements about the life of Jesus. Accordingly, the different stages of the life of Jesus – Bethlehem, Egypt, Nazareth, Capernaum – are emphasized.[14] This is also shown by the fact that biographical details are made known (so, for example, Jesus' performance of miracles or his entry into Jerusalem). This means that Matthew uses the formula-quotations to interpret the history of Jesus as a unique event, temporally and geographically distant from his own situation. The inclusion of these quotations in the Gospel expresses the historical-biographical tendency of the redactor.

This historicizing adaptation of traditional material also implies a specific understanding of the content. Matthew is the only one of the evangelists who transmitted a logion about limiting Jesus' proclamation to the people of Israel: "I was sent only to the lost sheep of the house of Israel" (15:24). This saying appears also in 10:6, as a missionary command to the disciples. Especially on the basis of this latter passage it has been supposed that here lies a self-interpretation on the part of the evangelist. According to this opinion, the saying must be regarded as an expression of Jewish-Christian self-understanding, an expression of Matthew's community which wanted to restrict missionary effort to the Jewish people.[15] However, Matthew belongs to a gentile-Christian generation, which pursues as self-evident the universal mission to all nations, as the end of the Gospel makes clear.[16] The exclusiveness of the mission to Israel, apparent in this logion, finds no explanation in the situation of the redactor, but rather corresponds to his historical reflection: only for Jesus, and thus for the disciples in the lifetime of Jesus, is this restriction valid. Only during the life of Jesus is the proclamation directed exclusively to the people of Israel, to call them to repentance. Matthew shows that this call is constantly rejected, above all by the Pharisees and Sadducees, the representatives of theology. Whereas the Jewish people are characterized in the first part of the Gospel as a chorus that applauds the deeds of Jesus, by contrast in the passion the entire nation joins the cry demanding crucifixion (27:22). After the condemnation of Jesus, the priority of Israel is abolished and the mission is broadened and directed without exception to all nations of the world.

Hence, it becomes evident how Matthew understood history, and which historical aspect he followed when historicizing the traditional material. The course of history was conceived as a sequence of periods: the central epoch of history is the "time of Jesus", the time when Jesus is sent exclusively to the people of Israel. This is brought to expression by the frequent use of the christological title "Son of David" with reference to Jesus; the "Son of David" is the promised Saviour of Israel.[17] The disciples of Jesus are a part of the uniqueness of this epoch. Like the mission of Jesus, their preaching remains at first directed exclusively to the Jewish people.[18] And while Jesus is presented as the elevated *kyrios*, who shows no anthropomorphic emotions, feels neither "indignation" nor "pity",[19] and demonstrates that his power as a miracle worker is beyond all human imagination,[20] the disciples of Jesus are portrayed in the same idealizing way. As followers of Jesus they possess "understanding" and they do the will of God.[21] So, the time of Jesus is a unique, unrepeatable, holy, and ideal epoch in the course of history, to the unity and completeness of which the figure of John the Baptist also contributes. For John, as is said in 21:32, "came in the way of righteousness" before the public appearance of Jesus, and like Jesus and his disciples, he proclaims the call to repentance motivated by the nearness of the Kingdom. Thus, the time of Jesus, from birth to resurrection, became a unitary period of revelation through the one proclamation.[22]

The time of Jesus is preceded by a time of preparation, which, like the period of the fathers and the prophets, points forward to the life of Jesus.[23] It is also a time of preparation in that it is the period when the call of the prophets is rejected and the prophets are murdered.[24] It has ended with the life of Jesus, involving the rejection of Jesus' call to repentance and the loss of Israel's priority in *Heilsgeschichte*.[25] The time of Jesus is followed by the time of the Church, the time of world mission. This epoch is to last until the eschaton breaks in. For the period immediately before the end will be a time of extreme tribulation, of false prophecy, persecution, and temptation,[26] which are characteristics already specifically present in the time of Matthew's community.[27] Therefore, all these are signs not of a new period, but rather of the last phase of history moving straight to its goal. They are signs of a history unfolding in three epochs, the centre of which is the time of Jesus as the time of revelation.

II

Matthew's periodicizing represents, however, only the formal aspect of his concept of history. Unlike Luke, who is restricted primarily to showing "the fact" of the sequence of periods, Matthew was concerned to work out in detail which meaning and which task were implied within this history. This can be shown by the fact that he submitted the traditional material not only to a historicization, but, moreover, to an *"ethicization"*. As a comparison with the Q tradition attested in Luke shows, Matthew has combined the sayings material into five blocks of speeches and has underscored them in the framework of his Gospel with five similarly composed formulae.[28] According to Matthew's understanding, the time of Jesus is a time of proclamation, in which the ethical demand is raised, as the content of the speech tradition, especially of the Sermon on the Mount, makes clear. It is in this ethical demand that the period prior to Jesus had its aim, for the people of Israel had rejected the demanding will of God proclaimed by the OT prophets. And from here the period of the Church can be understood, which follows upon the time of Jesus and his ethical proclamation.[29]

This concept of history, focused as it is on the ethical demand, becomes evident in Matthew's presentation of the life of Jesus, when he modifies the traditional material in a practical-ethical sense. The pre-Matthean tradition took a stand on the question of divorce and without any exception characterized separation and subsequent marriage as adultery, as is shown in Mark's Gospel and in the Q source. Matthew, by contrast, has inserted an exception clause. The pre-Matthean rule holds good "except on the ground of *porneia* ('unchastity')" (5:32, 19:9). Thus, Matthew has mitigated the judgement, which was originally more rigorous, and by producing a practicable law has taken account of the needs of the community in his time. In a similar way, the commandment against oath-taking, expressed in the series of antitheses, has been changed. While in the pre-Matthean tradition this commandment ended with an exhortation to absolute trustfulness ("Let your yes be yes, and your no be no"), Matthew has completely reversed the original meaning: "Let what you say be simply 'yes, yes', or 'no, no'; anything more than this comes from evil" (5:37). For, thereby, the originally absolute commandment has been broken and a formula has been quoted, which was used in Judaism in place of a fully spoken oath, when there was oath-taking.[30] The formula may well have been customary in Matthew's community. Here is a further example of the redactional alteration of the tradition and of the adaptation of the traditional material to the situation of the community: the demand of Jesus, which is the central point in the course of history, is an ethical-practicable rule.

The ethicizing modification of the traditional material becomes apparent, above all, in the Matthean tendency to express the ethical demands with formulae that set forth principles. Thus, the commandment of love for God and neighbour appears as the summation of the OT (in 22:27–40) and as the summary of the Sermon on the Mount.[31] Even if the individual commandments of Jesus in Matthew's Gospel cannot be subsumed in every case under the love commandment,[32] still the intention is apparent to present the ethical proclamation of Jesus in the form of principles. This does not mean that a commandment to love, given in the form of a principle, stands in contrast to a concrete realization of the goal. On the contrary, it is understood in an ethically practical sense. This also becomes clear, when the proclamation of Jesus is contrasted with Pharisaism. In Matthew's Gospel Pharisaism does not primarily reflect the situation of contemporary Judaism,[33] but rather has the function of a topos, which represents the attitude of unbelief and thus also of iniquity, in contrast to the ethical demand. Like the Sadducees as the representatives of the official theology, the Pharisees accept the demand of the ceremonial law as obligatory for themselves. Thus, they exhibit concretely the attitude of "hypocrisy", which is contrary to the ethical demand of Jesus and which recognizes only the observance of external forms, without a corresponding inner disposition.[34] In contrast, the ethical demand of Jesus, according to Matthew, radically claims an identity between external and internal attitude. Unlike the hypocritical attitude of the Pharisees, this demand is to be fulfilled without regard to human reward.[35]

According to Matthew's understanding, the commandment of Jesus is more than just a call for the correspondence of external and internal attitude. As the commandment of love it is at the same time the demand for a righteousness that is different from that of the Pharisees and scribes. By demanding a radical and far-reaching ethical attitude it claims more than the Pharisaic tradition (cf. 5:20). It appeals to the OT, in the sense of claiming to be the fulfilment

75

and not the abolition of the OT commandments (5:17). But still it is not identical in detail with the OT law. In spite of its positive relation to the OT, it is not just the demand of a "new Moses",[36] but the law of the *kyrios*, whose authority is not of a derivable sort but can be recognized by the mighty eschatological works of Jesus.

This can be seen even more clearly if we ask about the motivation of Jesus' ethical demand. The attempt has often been made to explain the motivation of Jesus' command of righteousness in Matthew's Gospel by comparing it with the doctrine of justification in Pauline theology. According to this suggestion, the ethical demand would be preceded by an indicative "righteousness" as the gift of God, which is prior to all effort of men and thus limits it. This suggestion has often been supported by referring to the beatitude, where the expression "those who hunger and thirst for righteousness" (5:6) presupposes the idea that "righteousness" is a gift of God.[37] If so, there would be a parallel in the Pauline definition of the relation between indicative and imperative, according to which the imperative of the new life arises from the indicative of the new being. Nevertheless, the beatitude in 5:6 has the sense, not of a desire for a gift from God, but of great human effort directed towards realizing the demand of righteousness.[38] The Matthean understanding of "righteousness" does not imply the thought of a righteousness given by God, but a righteousness realized by men, which is the same thing as justice.

The motivation for Jesus' ethical demand, therefore, does not arise from the idea of a previous gift, but is to be derived from another connection in Matthew's theology. Like the preaching of John the Baptist, the teaching of Jesus is directed to the eschaton.[39] Jesus announces the Reign of God and God's judgement according to one's deeds. Correspondingly, the beatitudes of the Sermon on the Mount are nothing other than conditions for entry into the Kingdom of God.[40] That the ethical demand of Jesus is directed toward the eschatological future follows from Matthew's concept of reward and punishment. At the last judgement reward and punishment for each individual will be meted out according to his deeds. This motivates the ethical demand out of the future and intensifies the responsibility of individual Christians in the present.

Because of this motivation out of the eschatological future, the ethical demand of Jesus can also be called an eschatological demand, all the more so as it is eschatologically motivated, not only out of the future, but also in the present.[41] That is to say, it is an eschatological demand in so far as the eschatological Reign of God is thought to be present in the demand of Jesus. Like the proclamation of the ethical demand, the mighty works of Jesus are signs of the present Reign of God.[42] This means, however, that the "gift" of God's Reign cannot be separated from the demand; rather, the indicative of the Christ event is identical with the imperative of the demand for righteousness. Salvation is present in time by the demand of Jesus.

Thus, the real mission of Jesus within history according to Matthew's understanding is the proclamation of the ethical demand in which the still-awaited Reign of God has become present. This demand is also represented by the exemplary conduct of Jesus during his earthly life. Hence, the entire life of Jesus, through word and deed, is a presentation of the ethical demand, that is, the "way of righteousness".[43]

III

What function does the Church have within a course of history thus conceived? This question implies a methodological problem: the interest of the redactor is directed to the past, to the time of Jesus' life; therefore, the Gospel must be explained primarily in terms of Christology, not in terms of ecclesiology. Matthew's understanding of the Church is not expressed directly in his Gospel.[44] On the other hand, Matthew's historicizing of the traditional material has not led to an authentic presentation of the life of Jesus, but is – even by its implied consciousness of the distance between past and present – an expression of the redactor's theological self-understanding and as such also reflects Matthew's understanding of the Church. If we now look for expressions that give some information about Matthew's understanding of the Church, we can state that to Matthew's interpretation of history in terms of "historicization" and "ethicization" there corresponds an *"institutionalization,"* or "ecclesiasticalization", of the traditional material.

The Gospel of Matthew, even more strongly than the parallel synoptists, gives evidence of the existence of church officials. Even if there are no certain details about how these church officials were classified in Matthew's community, still it is probable – according to 23:34 – that Matthew presupposes "prophets, wise men, and scribes" as officials in the Christian community, and that he especially esteems the position of a Christian scribe, as can be seen from the logion 13:52. Moreover, we should recognize that even the pre-Matthean sayings material shows a specific character that must have been influenced by the way of thinking typical of the scribes. This is shown, for instance, by the frequent use of the principle of "round numbers" or by the quotation-source, which is influenced by the idea of fulfilment, and by the fact that these same elements play a not unimportant part in Matthew's redaction. If perhaps one should avoid speaking of a "school of Matthew" without a terminological limitation, nevertheless all of this indicates that the redactor, like the tradition that preceded him, has modified the traditional material in line with concepts characteristic of the scribes.[45]

In addition to these traces of the existence of church officials, we find clearer evidence of the beginning of institutionalization. In 18:15ff Matthew has pictured the basic features of a disciplinary practice established by the Church, according to which the assembly of the local community has the right to take disciplinary action against unrepentant members and to exercise the power of binding and loosing, that is, to exclude or to re-admit a member. This action of the community in the present time has the assent of the exalted Lord; it has an eschatological consequence. Exclusion from the Church's fellowship is identical with eschatological condemnation, just as readmittance is equivalent to the repeal of such a judgement. Matthew's community administers an eschatologically qualified system of discipline.[46]

The presentation of the sacraments also corresponds to an institutionalization of the community's life. According to Matthew's understanding, the baptism of Jesus represents "fulfilment of righteousness".[47] This means that the sacrament of baptism is generally seen from the viewpoint of obedience to the demand for righteousness. In the redactional context, Matthew has not attempted to establish baptism as a sacramental occurrence, nor does the baptismal formula quoted in triad form in 28:19 have any support in the redactional material. The decisive tendency of Matthew's redactional activity points in the direction of a legalization of baptism. Baptism is an expression of "conversion", which stands at the beginning of Christian life, and therefore it is an initiatory rite which introduces one into the corporate body of the community. Likewise, Matthew's presentation of the words of institution at the Lord's Supper expresses this twofold concept: on the one hand, the community fully possesses the power to forgive sins, as is evident when it administers its system of discipline; and on the other hand, the sacrament is understood essentially as a fulfilment of the eschatological demand of Jesus. This becomes clear in the imperative forms that Matthew gives to the words of institution.[48] The sacrament of the Lord's Supper is not above the institutional activity of the community, but is part of it, and thus is a further example of the institutionalization of tradition.

From here the function of the Church within Matthew's concept of history becomes evident: the Christian Church represents the ethical demand in time.[49] By proclaiming this demand the Church guarantees the continuity between the past time of Jesus and the present up to the final goal of history, which will be reached in a near or far future. The Church points the way that individual Christians have to go within the changes of the times.

Matthew's understanding of history, as expressed in his tendencies of historicizing, ethicizing, and institutionalizing, proves the fact that the Matthean redaction does not represent simply a collection of traditional material, but offers an independent theological view. This clearly verifies that Matthew's theology is not to be paralleled directly with other theological schemes in the New Testament. It corresponds neither to the older Jesus-tradition nor to Pauline or Johannine theology. Rather it gives evidence of the heterogeneity of the primitive Christian faith, which is represented by a complexity of different theological conceptions.[50] A responsible consideration of the bases of the proclamation and the Christian faith must observe such differences carefully and weigh their theological significance. It will not be able, despite all its legitimate criticism, to cast aside as irrelevant the message of Matthew,[51] namely the heightened responsibility of the individual towards the eschatological-ethical demand within the change of times.

NOTES

1   For classic synoptic source criticism, cf. H. J. Holtzmann, *Die Synoptischen Evangelien, ihr Ursprung und geschichtlicher Charakter* (1863); P. Wernle, *Die synoptische Frage* (1899); B. H. Streeter, *The Four Gospels. A Study of Origins* (1924). Some not very convincing criticisms of the two source theory, asserting the priority of Matthew, have come especially from B. C. Butler (1951); L. Vaganay, *Le problème synoptique* (1954); and W. R. Farmer (1964).

2   ET J. C. G. Greig (Cambridge; 1971).

3   In my essay on "The Messianic Secret in Mark" (ET C. Tuckett, *The Messianic Secret* volume in this series, 1983), I tried to show that the specifically Marcan secret is to be interpreted more in terms of redaction criticism than through the history of the traditions. It should therefore not be used to support the idea that the pre-Marcan Jesus tradition was unmessianic.

4   R. Bultman (1963); M. Dibelius, *From Tradition to Gospel* (1919, ET 1934).

5   Though they do not all cover the whole span of an evangelist's redaction the most important relevant monographs include on *Mark*; Marxsen (1959, ET 1969);

Burkill (1963); Trocmé (1963, ET 1975); on *Matthew*: Bornkamm, Barth and Held (1963); Trilling (1959); Strecker (1962); on *Luke*: Conzelmann (1953 ET 1960); W. C. Robinson (1964); Flender (1965, ET 1967).

6   Recent German work on the delay of the parousia includes articles by O. Cullman (*TZ* 1947; *TLZ* 1958); H. W. Bartsch (in his 1962 collection); Bornkamm (1951, rep. in his *Geschichte und Glaube* I); the monograph of E. Grässer (1960²). Conzelmann's 1953 monograph (ET 1960) drew the consequences of this for Luke in a particularly impressive and convincing way.

7   Cf. E. Käsemann, "Paul and Early Catholicism" in his *New Testament Questions of Today* (London, 1969) 236–51. W. Marxsen, "Der Frühkatholizismus' im Neuen Testament", *Biblische Studien* 21 (1958).

8   We must recognize with W. Trilling (1964³, 44f) that neither in Matthew (nor Mark, nor Luke) is there a contemporary problem about the delay. The real discussion of this problem belongs to the pre-synoptic stage of the tradition, and is to be located at the turn from the first to the second generation (cf. 1 Thess. 4:13ff). This does not of course exclude the possibility that the task of new orientation in an on-going history was not completed in the pre-synoptic stage of the tradition, and so was still a task for the authors of the Gospels.

9   Cf. Strecker, 1962. The remainder of the present article follows the translation in *JAAR* 35 (1967) 219–30, with footnotes renumbered (n.2 there = n.10 etc. here and in the reprint in *Wege der Forschung*, ed. J. Lange (1980).

10   4:17. Cf. the careful study of E. Krentz (1964). According to Krentz, the passage 1:1–4, 16 represents a composite literary unit referring to the David- and Abraham-sonship of Jesus. Starting from the *apo tote* ("from that time on") formula in 4:17 and 16:21 the structure of Matthew's Gospel is conceived as follows: (1) 4:16—16:20 ("kingdom"); (2) 16:21—28:20 (or 26:2) ("The Son of Man and his way to resurrection") (411). Concerning this division, however, we have to ask if the *basileia* ("kingdom") proclamation can really be understood as being the theme of the first main passage 4:17—16:20 – in contrast with 16:21ff (cf., on the other hand, also 18:23ff; 21:33ff; 22:1ff; 25:1ff etc.); on the other side, account has to be taken of the fact that the Son-of-Man subject is also presupposed in the passage 4:17ff (cf., e.g., 12:8, 32, etc.). Yet also the frequent attempts to reconstruct the composition of the Gospel on the strength of the five formulae of connection and transition (see below, note 28) cannot really convince; thus, the consequence at hand is that Matthew, instead of working out and arranging a detailed composed structure, was rather concerned to constitute the Gospel as a whole in terms of a continuous line, which can be fixed temporally and geographically, and the essence of which is to be characterized by "the proclamation and presentation of the eschatological demand".

11   Cf. Mark 2:1; 3:20, 7:17; 9:28, 33; 10:10.

12   Matt. 8:14; 9:10, 28; 12:46; 13:1, 36; 17:25.

13   Matt. 1:23; 2:6, 15, 18, 23; 4:15f; 8:17; 12:18–21; 13:35; 21:5; 27:9f. All of these verses (with the one exception of the redactional statement in 2:23) are quotations from the OT, the wording of which – despite a few traces of influence from the LXX – points to the Masoretic or to an unknown OT text. They have not been quoted originally by the evangelist Matthew, for he used the OT in the version

of the LXX, though he inserted them into his Gospel, as proved by the Matthean character of the introductory formulae. The widely held opinion, which recently has been repeated by A. Suhl (*Die Funktion der alttestamentlichen Zitate und Anspielungen im Markusevangelium* (1965) 35, n. 64), that the formula-quotations must be ascribed to Matthew, proves to be unavailing, as it is impossible to explain conclusively the textual and material discrepancies between the redactional LXX quotations and the specific type of the formula-quotations. Matt. 3:3 (= Isa. 40:3) is not to be connected with the formula-quotations of Matthew's peculiar material. This passage rather follows the text of Mark 1:3, and its introductory formula points back to Mark 1:2a, though it has been extended by Matthew; nor must the quotation Matt. 13:14f (= Isa. 6:9f) be listed here, which has rather to be understood as a post-Matthean interpolation, as has definitely been demonstrated by K. Stendahl's impressive study (1954) 131.

14 That the geographical line is extraordinarily prominent from the beginning of the Gospel up to 4:16, has rightly been pointed out by E. Krentz (1964) 413.

15 Thus, e.g., J. Munck, *Paul and the Salvation of Mankind* (1959) 263f; especially B. C. Butler (1951) 130f, who from the Jewish colouring of the pericope Matt. 15:21–8 deduces an argument to support the priority of Matthew against Mark and Luke.

16 Cf. Matt. 28:16–20; also 10:18; 21:33–46; 22:1–14; 24:9, 14; 25:32. In this respect I am in far-reaching agreement with W. Trilling, who in the third edition of his book emphatically points to the "universalistic gentile-Christian" character of the final redaction of the first Gospel (214ff). Cf. already K. W. Clark (1947).

17 Cf. Matt 1:1 (= Son of Abraham); 9:27; 12:23; 15:22; 21:9,15; 22:41–5.

18 Matt. 10:6.

19 Cf., e.g., Matt. 19:14 (against Mark 10:14); 8:3b (against Mark 1:43); 8:3a (against Mark 1:41).

20 See Matt. 8:13 (against Luke 7:10); 9:22 (against Mark 5:34); 15:28 (against Mark 7:24); 17:18 (against Mark 9:27); 21:19f (against Mark 11:14, 20f); 14:20f (against Mark 6:43f); 15:37f (against Mark 8:8f), and frequently.

21 Matt. 13:16, 51; 16:12; 17:13; cf. also the elimination of the Marcan concept that Jesus' disciples do "not understand": Mark 4:13; 6:52; 8:17f, 21; 9:6, 10, 32, etc. The idea that the disciples "perform God's will" is expressed especially in 12:49f (against Mark 3:34f).

22 The parallel between John the Baptist and Jesus (or Jesus' disciples) becomes evident by a comparison of 3:2 with 4:17. The chronologically difficult term "in those days" (3:1) can also be motivated by the presupposed material relationship.

23 Besides the genealogy of Jesus in 1:2–17 and the introductory formulae of the formula-quotations, cf. especially Matt. 11:13.

24 Cf. 23:29ff.

25 Cf. 21:39, 41, 43; 22:7ff; 23:38f; especially the cry for crucifixion and the Jews' declaration of their guilt in 27:22, 25 (the latter statement against Mark). It is characteristic of this concept that the naming of the Jewish people is changed; "Israel" is used in Matthew until after the crucifixion and resurrection, when the more distant expression "Jews" is applied (28:15).

26 Matt. 24:9–28.

27 Cf. 5:10ff; 7:15ff; 10:17ff; 18:6ff, and frequently.

28 Matt. 7:28; 11:1; 13:53; 19:1; 26:1 (the formula originates from Q; cf. Luke 7:1).

29 This is emphasized by 28:20 (the demand to observe all commandments of Jesus' teaching, and the promise that the exalted *kyrios* will be present in his community). Cf. A. Vögtle (1964) 266–94; G. Bornkamm (1971).

30 Cf. *Slav. Enoch* 49:1, and frequently; Strack-Billerbeck, I (1956²) 336f.

31 Matt. 7:12; cf. also 9:13; 12:7; 19:19.

32 Note especially the pre-Matthean legal formula in 23:23 (justice, mercy, and faith), but also the different concrete legal commandments, the content of which does not disclose any material relationship to the commandment of love.

33 Against G. D. Kilpatrick (1946) 113 ff. The fact that in Matthew's presentation of the "Sadducees" (who are frequently mentioned, though they had almost no political and religious function after the year 70) as well as in his presentation of the "high priests" there is an underlying "historicizing concern" has been rightly recognized by R. Hummel (1963) 20f; it was not realized by this author, however, that this insight should be applied also to the Pharisees and that the inferences drawn with regard to "the present situation (of Matthew's community)" must be secondary in comparison with the question of Matthew's theological and historicizing intention.

34 Cf., e.g., Matt. 6:1ff; 15:1ff; 23:1ff.

35 Cf. 6:1; 23:28, and frequently. The radical form of the ethical demand, in opposition to "hypocrisy" is also expressed in the pericope Matt. 19:16–26; here the list of the single commandments of the Decalogue and their subsumption under the commandment to love one's neighbour (19:18f) are followed by the demand for perfection as the demand to give up all possessions (19:21). This might be understood as an intended differentiation between a general Christian attitude limited to obedience of the commandments of the Decalogue on one hand, and the particular ethics of perfection on the other side. (Thus G. Kretschmar, "Ein Beitrag zur Frage nach dem Ursprung frühchristlicher Askese", *ZTK* 61 (1964) 27–67, in which starting from this point the line is carried forward to the early Christian proclamation and asceticism in Syria.) According to Matthew's understanding, however, 19:21 has rather to be interpreted as an expression of the idea that in keeping the commandments a radical human decision is implied. This may be confirmed by the fact that both the demand for righteousness and the demand for perfection are without distinction directed to the one aim: entering the Kingdom (5:20; 19:16f, 24, and frequently).

36 In his detailed study, W. D. Davies, (1964) 14ff, despite his readiness in principle to admit that there are elements of a Moses-Christ-typology in the first Gospel, arrives at a negative result: "Matthew presents Jesus as giving a Messianic Law on a Mount, but he avoids the express concept of a New Torah and a New Sinai: he has cast around his Lord the mantle of a teacher of righteousness, but he avoids the express ascription to him of the honorific 'a new Moses'" (108). This statement would probably have been made with no less decisiveness in the chapters dealing with the exegesis of single pericope, if the author had dealt with the questions of *Traditionsgeschichte* and *Redaktionsgeschichte* in a more intensive way.

37 Cf., e.g., E. Lohmeyer (1956) *ad loc.*

38 Even if we refer God's righteousness in 6:33 to "God's own doing of righteousness" and connect this with 5:48 (as P. Stuhlmacher does in his *Gerechtigkeit
Gottes bei Paulus*, 1965, 189; cf. in addition Matt. 5:45!), nevertheless in the
Gospel of Matthew this concept essentially has been interpreted in terms of
Christology and anthropology: man encounters "God's righteousness" in the
demand of Jesus; the "realization of the divine law" (E. Käsemann (1969), 105,
on Matt 5:6) is accomplished primarily in man's realization of the eschatological
demand proclaimed by Jesus. Undoubtedly this latter, not an apocalyptic-onto-
logical idea of God's righteousness, has been emphasized, since it forms the centre
of Matthew's theology; therefore, despite A. Schlatter's attempt to harmonize
"righteousness" and "grace" (1929, 234f), the difference between Matthew's
theological concept and the Pauline notion of *sola gratia* must not be overlooked.

39 Cf. Matt. 3:2 and 4:17.

40 Thus, rightly, H. Windisch, *The Meaning of the Sermon on the Mount* (ET
Philadelphia, 1951) 9 and frequently; cf. also M. Dibelius in *Botschaft und
Geschichte*, I (1953) 120.

41 Matt. 11:12. Cf. the corresponding connection with the proclamation of the
Church: 21:43 ("shall be given" as well as "shall be taken away" points to an
event, which does not occur only at the end of history, but also in time; it is of
historical significance: in the time of Matthew the Kingdom has been handed over
to the succeeding nation, in the time of the Church the Kingdom is present similar
to its presence in the *"heilsgeschichtliche Vergangenheit"* of the Jewish nation.)
Cf. also the aorist tense of the comparative phrases that introduce the so-called
parables of the Kingdom: 13:24; 18:23, and 22:2.

42 Cf. Matt. 8:29; 12:28.

43 Cf. Matt. 21:32.

44 This statement must be made especially in view of the third, and in many respects
modified, edition of W. Trilling's study. Trilling motivates his ecclesiologically
determined starting point by referring to "the present experience and reality of
the church and (to) the fulness of her faith", which is valid at any time (20). He
levels his criticism against a christologically accentuated interpretation of the first
Gospel, stating that this interpretation would imply "a shortening of perspectives
and an almost anxious narrowing of the concept of the Church", which he leads
back to "transient existential experiences and hermeneutical motifs" (19f).
Without question, however, Trilling's study in its very basis is determined by a
specific position, which comprises Trilling's extensive understanding of the
Church. This example is instructive enough to demonstrate the fact that the recent
discovery of historical criticism in modern Roman Catholic exegesis does not
automatically lead to an acceptance of the results of Protestant research. It is
rather to be expected that the interdenominational partnership within the application of the historical-critical method will bring about a clarification and classifica-
tion of exegetical problems, last but not least in such a way that the absence of
a common hermeneutical basis will become evident. In order to elucidate the
problem at hand it will be neccessary in the future to discuss the controversial
theological positions, which are underlying the exegetical work, in a more detailed
way.

45 By calling Matthew a "converted Jewish Rabbi" E. v. Dobschütz (1928) in this volume, p. 24 neglects the fact that the redactor of the first Gospel is dependent on a *Christian* scribal tradition. No one should deny the semitic tinge of this tradition nor its semitic-Jewish origin; however, this tradition becomes accessible to Matthew within a process of transmission. Its semitic character has increasingly been transformed according to the needs of a hellenistic environment; Matthew is the last active part within the course of such development of tradition.

46 Cf. the close parallel in John 20:23, according to which the disciples are entrusted with the authority to forgive sins by the risen *kyrios*. The difference between John 20:23 and the tradition of Matthew is significant. In the Gospel of John are lacking the eschatological-disciplinary interpretation of the power of binding and loosing as well as the juridical terminology that originates from the institution of excommunication of the synagogue.

47 Matt. 3:15.

48 Matt. 26:26–8.

49 This understanding of the Church relativizes the relationship between Church and world, since the nations of the world as well as the Christian community are judged according to the standard of the ethical demand (25:31ff). Trilling's assertion that such a relationship would contradict the parallel between the Church and the people of God according to 21:43 (154, n. 46) is not convincing at all; for, on the one hand, the parallel drawn between the Church and the OT-Jewish nation of God does not answer the question of the *tertium comparationis*, i.e., of the content which fills the notion of God's people as well as the concept of the Church. If we realize that the idea of God's people has been concentrated on the eschatological demand that is proclaimed and followed by the Church, the thesis mentioned above may be supported; on the other hand, the idea of the independence of the Church has not been given up – despite the relative character of the difference between Church and world – since the Church is aware of being bound to the *kyrios*, who not only endowed his community with the eschatological demand, but also entrusted it with the authority to forgive sins.

50 Cf. recently H. Köster, "ΓΝΩΜΑΙ ΔΙΑΦΟΡΟΙ: The Origin and Nature of Diversification in the History of Early Christianity," *HTR* 58 (1965) 279–318.

51 G. Kretschmar (see above n. 35) rightly calls the message of Matthew a "beneficial disturbance of the Church" (67). This characterization is especially justified, if it is acknowledged that Matthew's demand for righteousness includes radicalism *and* concreteness.

6

The Authority
to "Bind" and "Loose" in
the Church in
Matthew's Gospel:*

The Problem of Sources in Matthew's Gospel

GÜNTHER BORNKAMM

It is the purpose of the following study to set forth in a representative example, namely, the "Discourse Concerning the Congregation", the working method of the first evangelist and thereby to make a contribution to the problem of sources in the synoptic Gospels. Part I will answer the question: What sources has Matthew used in the separate units of his "discourse"? Parts II and III raise the further question: How has the evangelist worked with these sources and joined them into a unity? I hope that this methodical procedure will clearly demonstrate that the literary problems of the synoptic texts can be discussed fruitfully only in correlation with form-critical and redaction-critical research. The inferences and findings of this newest phase of synoptic research, as has been pointed out repeatedly (and justifiably) by its representatives, have not shattered the results of the two-source theory. Rather, they have extended it in a definite way, namely, into the field of preliterary tradition and its literary and theological shaping of the individual Gospels.

A method which isolates the literary questions and does not from the very outset build upon the insight of form criticism and redaction criticism must today be labelled as obsolete; it is an anachronism.

In this study of Matthew 18 the so-called two-source theory will not be presumed as a scientific "dogma", but will be tested from one paragraph to another, in detail and in general, as to its correct-

* First published in *Jesus and Man's Hope*, ed. D. G. Miller (1970) 1:37–50.

ness, or soundness. Only in this methodical way can we succeed in advancing towards true exegesis, and, what is more, in venturing to present well-founded theses about the Gospel's position in history, that is, in the history of theology and of the Church.

With rare unanimity recent exegetes speak of the discourse to the disciples in Matthew 18 as a "Rule for the Congregation" (*Gemeindeordnung*). The correctness of this description should not be contested; it will be fully confirmed in what follows. However, at first, it appears to be justified only by the style and content of the counsels for discipline of the congregation (18:15–17) and the logion of "binding" and "loosing" (18:18) related to it. The remaining context contains nothing of that which elsewhere in the early Christian literature pertains to church discipline, such as regulations for officials of the congregation (apostles, bishops, elders, and such like) in the Pastoral Epistles, or the rules for fasting and prayer, baptism and the Eucharist in the *Didache*. Indeed, as a matter of course one would not expect to find such regulations in a text compiled out of the words of our Lord. Still, it would be quite conceivable that in this "discourse" the evangelist might have worked in the prohibitions to the disciples who were being addressed with the honorary title of the Jewish scribes (Matt. 23:8–10), or even the sayings about the true piety – alms, prayer, and fasting (Matt. 6:1–18). Such, however, is not the case.

It would, however, be incorrect to describe only Matt. 18: 15–17 (18) as part of the "Rule for the Congregation" and to exempt the rest of the discourse from this form-critical description. Matthew 18 is so thoroughly composed as a unity that the entire discourse must be placed under one theme. The plan of the composition will come to light clearly after the small units of sayings which are worked into this passage have been defined.

I

As tradition history, the discourse is a rather variegated mosaic of source fragments of different kinds and origins:

1   The introductory group of sayings, Matt. 18:1–5, corresponds to what is found in Mark 9:33–7 (the disciples' dispute over rank). But here Matthew incorporates the "migrant saying",[1] which is encountered in Mark later, in the pericope of the blessing of the children (Mark 10:15).[2] Matthew renders in his own way this saying about "becoming as a little child" (Matt. 18:3f), which appears in various traditions.

86

2   The second group of sayings, Matt. 18:6–9, also follows Mark (9:42–8, warning against offences). Literary dependence is demonstrated by the fact that Matthew also takes over from his source the sayings about the hand and foot being an inducement to sinning, which Mark arranges under the key word, "scandal". It is noteworthy, however, that in Matt. 18:7 (= Luke 17:1) the tradition of the *"sayings source"* (Q) is already joined, which further on clearly emerges as basis for the group. (Matt. 18:15 = Luke 17:3; Matt. 18:21f = Luke 17:4).

3   Also, the parable of the lost sheep in Matt. 18:12f (= Luke 15:3–7) is derived from Q, which the evangelist adjusts to his total conception of the "discourse" by means of the "framework verses" Matt. 18:10 and 14.

4   The group of sayings, Matt. 18:15–20 (Matthew's special source), with which we shall be primarily concerned, is in itself a many-layered structure. The disciplinary instructions in vv. 15–17 clearly constitute a unity; the rest consists of independent single sayings. To what degree all this was already united with the "Rule for the Congregation" in a special tradition which Matthew took over, or to what degree this was done by Matthew himself, remains a question. However, we should not suppose that the evangelist gave any of the sayings their first editorial shape; they received their form beforehand. Note: (a) the three stages in the congregational rule itself (vv. 15–17), which embody the conditional style of law sayings. The rule is, in all probability, developed from the Q logion which is preserved in Luke 17:3.[3] This is suggested by the fact that in the first section of the rule, even as in the Lucan parallel, the possibility of resolving a conflict between brother and brother at an early stage is viewed positively. Matt. 18:15 could be understood as a mere variant on Luke 17:3; the Matthean version, though, being built more closely on the OT admonition in Lev. 19:17 to give no room to hatred and ill will against an offending brother.[4] However, the wording of Matt. 18:15 clearly shows that this first section is formulated with the further instances of a legal proceeding in mind, as specified in vv. 16 and 17: the *ean sou akousę* v. 15 ("if he listens") corresponds to the subsequent turns of expression *ean de mē akousę* v. 16 ("if he does not listen"; *ean de parakousę autōn* v. 17 ("if he refuses to listen to them"). Thus, the general drift of the sayings group undoubtedly moves towards the most extreme disciplinary possibility: the exclusion of the impenitent sinner by the assembled congregation. To the congregation is given authority to "bind" and to "loose"

87

which, according to the concluding saying (18:18), is also effective at the last judgement. (b) Verse 18, as is well known, is a variant of Matt. 16:19, and therefore an independent logion; but because the power to "bind" and "loose" is granted to the gathered local congregation, it is significantly distinguished from the word about Peter as the Rock of the whole Church. Also, it is certain that Matt. 18:18 refers to disciplinary authority and not, as Matt. 16:19, primarily to teaching authority. In our passage, the saying confirms the right, which is reserved solely to the assembled congregation, definitely to excommunicate the impenitent brother. The saying was apparently added as a conclusion to the rule of the congregation before Matthew.[5]

The terminology reveals that the rule itself (vv. 15–17) just as its conclusion (v. 18) came from Jewish-Christian tradition. In v. 17, "Gentile and tax collector" are named formula-like in the Jewish-exclusivist sense as those standing outside the religious and national community.[6] Similarly, the common rabbinic terms for teaching authority and disciplinary authority describe the office which is conferred on the scribes, that is, authority to declare something forbidden or allowed as well as authority to inflict or lift the ban. Though both the authority of teaching and of discipline is necessary for "binding" and "loosing",[7] this does not rule out the possibility that in Matt. 18:18 the emphasis is on discipline, and in Matt. 16:19 on teaching.[8] (c) Similarly, the double sentence 18:19f is obviously an independent, self-contained logion: the pledge of hearing prayer is grounded in the presence of the Lord among those who gather in his name. Here the Church, although still very small, knows itself to be cut off from the Jewish community; gathered no longer about the Torah, but in the name of Jesus, in faith in him and in confession of him,[9] and as such to be assured of his presence. But the relationship of 18:20 with the familiar Jewish saying in *Aboth* 3:2, "When two sit together and engage themselves with the words of the Torah, the Shekinah [a paraphrase for God's presence] is in their midst"[10] suggests that the Christian logion was formulated antithetically in relationship to the Jewish conception of the Shekinah. In the same way Matt. 18:19f must be regarded as belonging to a pre-Matthean special source which the evangelist, on grounds which still must be clarified, joins to the preceding sayings of 18:15–18.

5 We have already established that Matt. 18:21f again takes up the sequence of the Q sayings (cf. Luke 17:4), but is fashioned independently as a dialogue. Jesus' answer to Peter about the unlimited

readiness to forgive constitutes, as has already been said, the effective transition to the conclusion of the whole "discourse", the parable of the Unmerciful Servant; Matthew has contributed this out of his special source.

Source critical analysis has thereby confirmed that the "Discourse" in Matthew 18 is, from the standpoint of tradition history, a conglomerate of materials from very different traditions, and is a document typical of the working method of the evangelist who here, as also frequently elsewhere, alternates between his sources[11] and thematically unites materials out of Mark, out of the sayings source, and out of his special source, combining them through editorial accentuation and additions.

II

The leading motifs of the Matthean composition may be put forth still more explicitly. In the introductory sayings of the "discourse" (18:1–5), Matthew dispenses with particulars about location (Mark 9:33–5) which he had already indicated, instead, in 17:24. He does not mention the twelve and their dispute over rank (Mark 9:33–5), for in this passage the disciples definitely represent the congregation. Of primary importance is the placement of the pertinent question concerning true greatness in the Kingdom of heaven, which surely sets a standard for all that follows. It is formulated generally and, as a matter of principle, is put in a commanding position at the beginning (18:1), to be followed up explicitly in 18:4.

The movement of the "discourse" becomes more concentrated as the evangelist passes over the pericope of the strange exorcist (Mark 9:38–41) provided in his source, even as he also leaves out the chain of sayings in Mark 9:49f.

In the next part, Matthean composition becomes discernible in the leading theme "care for the 'little ones'" to which he co-ordinates the passages 18:6–9 and 10–14;[12] the "little ones", for which 18:1–5 prepared beforehand, refers now, quite obviously, to the disciples who "believe in me" (18:6). The term is more especially accented in 18:10ff as it is applied to those members of the congregation who are in danger of straying and perishing (18:10 and 14). Thus, in this context, the parable does not serve primarily for the proclamation of divine grace towards the lost; rather it serves to impress upon the congregation their duty to care for the straying.

The directions for church discipline (18:15–17, 18) are noticeably in tension with their contextual framework, that is, the immediately preceding parable of the Lost Sheep (18:12f), and the immediately following parable (18:23f). For the point of both these parables is untiring care for the erring brother and readiness to forgive without limit (18:21f) on the basis of the divine grace received. Even granted that the disciplinary rule takes into consideration someone being impenitent to the last instance, thus making forgiveness meaningless, yet the rule as such aims definitely at the final exclusion of the obdurate sinner from the congregation and thus from salvation; the possibility of a later repentance is not being considered. Does the evangelist consciously neutralize the rule by placing it in this context which was by no means forced upon him through the given tradition?[13] Surely, this is not his intention. But then the composition must have this meaning: to make apparent that the procedure of the congregation, though necessary for the sake of their purity, is an extreme possibility. Superior to it is the rule of life to which the whole congregation is subject, namely, the handing on of received mercy; this must not for a moment be forgotten. Apart from this context, and as a purely legal act, congregational discipline would become a pharisaic attempt to anticipate the last judgement and prematurely to separate the "just" from the "unjust" (cf. Matt. 13:24–30, 36–43, 47–50). Even though congregational discipline is an inescapable requirement, on no account should it be practiced, according to Matthew, with the intent of gathering a "holy remnant" in the Church. In this way the evangelist incorporates the Jewish-Christian tradition, but encases it in the fundamental motifs of Jesus' teachings, his concern for the humble and his call to humility, his love-commandment and the expectation of the coming rule of God and of the last judgement, in which the question about deeds of mercy will have to be answered. In agreement with Trilling[14] the "Rule for the Congregation" must be organized appropriately in four parts: (1) true greatness in the Kingdom of heaven (18:1–5); (2) care for the "little ones" (18:6–14); (3) correction of offenders (18:15–20); (4) forgiveness (18:21–35).

III

After considering the composition of Matthew 18 as a unit, we must now once more discuss the disciplinary rule in the setting of its immediate context (18:15–20). In doing so, we begin with the double saying 18:19f. What is its significance in relation to the preceding disciplinary rule? As far as I know, this question is not being raised by commentators, much less answered. At best there is a negative answer, such as by E. Klostermann, who remarks concerning the introductory phrase of v. 19, *palin amēn legō hymin* ("again I say to you") "... an artificial transition to another subject concerning the church". Thus it would be irrelevant to look for a special function of 18:19f in relation to 18:15–17. However, some weighty evidence requires further investigation: (1) We have seen that the evangelist constructed this "discourse" as a whole by very consciously and logically selecting and interweaving traditions of various origins, and through setting his own emphases. In no instance does he include a saying or group of sayings just because source and tradition provided it. We observe no thoughtless mechanism in his reproduction of traditional material.[15] (2) We have seen that with regard to Matthew 18, the evangelist was not bound by the limiting fact of a given source. The double saying is an independent logion and was originally not connected with 15–17 (18); therefore Matthew, in adding it, gives it its own introductory phrase. (3) The content of the double saying indicates an affinity of thought with 15–17 (18). As Trilling has correctly seen[16] it manifests a certain "ecclesiastical consciousness". The accent is not really on the (general) promise that prayers in the name of Jesus will be heard,[17] but on the fellowship of the congregation which is assembled in his name, and their becoming one in voicing the same request (*symphōnein*, "agree"/ *synagesthai*, "gather"). To this congregation is promised the presence of the exalted Lord in their midst. If this is correct, then the "anything" to which Matt. 18:19 refers, receives a very definite meaning, and the double saying receives a special function, namely, to undergird the "binding" and "loosing" authority which immediately before was awarded to the congregation.

Presumed obviously is the *Kyrios*-faith and the experience of hellenistic Christianity, which no longer lives only in expectation of the "Coming One", but by the presence and support of the exalted Lord until the close of the age. The promise, which at the end of the Gospel the Risen One gives to his disciples in a universal sense (Matt. 28:20), here applies also to the smallest local congregation.

It is both surprising and noteworthy that the belief and the experience of hellenistic Christianity, and the new self-understanding of the congregation (18:20), have found expression in a logion that obviously has been coined in correspondence with the Jewish Torah practice and conception of the Shekinah, though in a radically Christianized sense: "in the place of the Torah there is the *onoma* ("name") of Jesus, in the place of the Shekinah there is Jesus himself."[18]

How are we to interpret the fact that the logion was coined in view of that Jewish *theologoumenon* which refers to devotion to the Torah? Is Matt. 18:20 intended to point out an antithesis, that is, the superseding of the Torah by the name of Jesus and the presence of the exalted *Kyrios*? This would voice a conception which Matthew otherwise strictly rejects, namely, that Jesus had come to abrogate the law and the prophets (5:17–19). In the intent of the evangelist and of the congregation which he represents – the very congregation that makes the background for the saying 18:20 – the presence of the Exalted One in their midst can only mean and imply that the law which Jesus himself both fulfilled and interpreted, that is, his commandments and teachings, are to become obligatory for the congregation.

Thus Matt. 18:20 comes into close proximity to the last pericope of the whole Gospel: the commission of the Risen One to his disciples to make disciples of all nations, to baptize them in the "name" of the Father, the Son, and the Holy Spirit, and to teach them to observe all that he on earth has "commanded" them.[19] To this congregation is promised his presence and support to the end of the age (Matt. 28:19f).

Now it is clear that Matthew 18 has been constructed as the "Rule for the Congregation" under the strong influence of the basic principles of Jesus' teaching: his preaching about those standards which are valid before God – his call to repentance and humility (18:1–5), his love-commandment (18:6–14), and his demand for unlimited readiness to forgive (Matt. 18:21–35) – while being assured of the presence of the *Kyrios* in their midst and the expectation of the coming Kingdom. The marks of the Church (*notae ecclesiae*) of this congregation are thereby on principle distinguished from the Jewish congregation: no longer Temple and sacrifices, ritual laws and circumcision (the latter is not once mentioned in Matthew's Gospel), nor the rabbinical teaching of the synagogue, but neither a new cultic or hierarchical order; rather discipleship. Living as disciples and followers implies living by the mercy of God which in turn must be realized in the relation to the brother (18:21–35).

IV

What then is the significance of the "binding" and "loosing" authority of the congregation set in this context? To answer this question we shall have to elucidate the close relationship between the "Rule for the Congregation" (Matt. 18:15–18) and the authority given to Peter (16:17–19). As is known, it is only in these two passages, not alone in Matthew but in the synoptic tradition in general, that we find the term *ekklēsia* ("church") linked in both cases with the almost identical phrase about "binding" and "loosing". Yet at the same time, the differences are evident. In the earlier passage (Matt. 16:18) *ekklēsia* has obviously a general, "ideal", meaning, whereas 18:17 refers to the assembly of the (local) congregation. In this discourse on discipleship the same authority is conferred on the congregation which before is given to Peter alone. Also, apparently, Peter's "binding" and "loosing" authority refers primarily to teaching authority. From this we understand Peter's work to be fundamental for the existence of the Church and for her stability and continuance during the eschatological afflictions (16:20), which could hardly be asserted about church discipline.[20] To be sure, teaching authority and disciplinary authority are inseparably intertwined in this Jewish scholastic phrase about "binding" and "loosing", but this does not rule out, as was said before, that here one, there the other, meaning is more emphasized. At any rate, in Matt. 18:15–17 and 18 the authority for discipline comes to the fore. The authority of Peter thus refers to the teaching of Jesus entrusted to him as being valid and obligatory for the whole Church on earth, and according to which the sentences will be passed in heaven, that is, in the last judgement.

This corresponds to the role in relation to the disciples which Peter has in Matthew's Gospel. The evangelist did not change the function which he found traditionally ascribed to Peter, but in several passages he shapes it to a greater distinctiveness.[21] In Matthew's Gospel, too, Peter figures as the representative and speaker of the disciples; in this sense he has for them exemplary significance as the one who believes, but at the same time as the one who is troubled by faint-heartedness (14:28–31); as the confessor to whom "not flesh and blood" but the Father in heaven has granted the revelation in which faith is grounded (16:17), but at the same time as the one guilty of denying the Lord (26:69ff); as the one who loves Jesus and is concerned about him, but for that very reason who is endangered by a satanic temptation born of the prejudice of human thinking to divert him from his path of suffering and dying (16:22f). In his capabilities and incapabilities, in his ventures and failures, he is the exemplary disciple who in everything is dependent upon Jesus himself. He gives voice to the prayer for deliverance in affliction (14:30; cf. 8:25) as well as to the questions directed to Jesus when the disciples need his counsel regarding right conduct (17:24ff, 18:21f), and he receives Jesus' answer on their behalf. But at the same time a specific authority over against the congregation is thereby confirmed to him; he is made the rock and custodian of the Church.

What conclusion is to be drawn from this regarding the relation of the "binding" and "loosing" authority of the congregation (18:18) to that authority which has been conferred upon Peter alone (16:19)? This problem is frequently discussed under the aspect of tradition-history only. If the question is put in this way one must certainly affirm that Matt. 16:17ff is of an earlier date than 18:18.[22] However, we need not interpret this as finding in Matthew 16 an indication of Peter's historical position in the early Jerusalem church, and then in Matthew 18 a changed situation in the primitive Church when Peter had lost his position and a group of leaders in the congregation had taken his place.[23] In spite of the semitic language elements in the logion 16:17–19 which point to its relatively early date, there are weighty arguments for assuming that the version we find here does not come from the early Jerusalem church, but rather that it might have been shaped in another environment only after Peter's death.[24] There is no indication that historically Peter ever had the role which is ascribed to him in Matt. 16:17–19. Furthermore, this logion presupposes not only the resurrection of Jesus, but also the delay of the parousia and the continuation of the Church as an empirical entity characterized by an authoritative apostolic teaching tradition. Also, the designation "Ecclesia of Jesus" ("my church")[25] which was developed only in hellenistic Christianity in antithesis to the synagogue, has already been given its established place in Matthew. The authority bestowed on Peter, therefore, no longer refers simply to the Torah, but to the commandments and the teaching of Jesus, even though, as the one with "binding" and "loosing" authority, Peter is described as a kind of "supreme Rabbi".[26] From this we may conclude that the conferring on Peter of the authority to "bind" and to "loose" must be understood as an "ideal" scene containing traces of the beginning of a special Christian *halakah* in which we see the founding of the Church on Peter as the guarantor and authorized interpreter of Jesus' teachings.[27]

The disciplinary authority of the congregation in Matthew 18 ought, therefore, not to be understood as a rival tradition to Matthew 16, not even in the sense of a historical sequence, as though the congregation had replaced Peter. Rather, we must understand the meaning of these texts as being contemporaneous and see their essential correlation. That means: the congregation which acts in Matt. 18:15–18 knows itself as founded on the teaching of Jesus as guaranteed through Peter. The content and the lineaments of the "Rule for the Congregation" are, therefore, the outcome of that teaching.

The "discourse" of Matthew 18 thus turns out to be a significant document of the strained encounter between hellenistic and Jewish Christian traditions. Matthew and his congregation presuppose hellenistic Christianity which had already outgrown its Jewish origin, but they oppose the enthusiasm that wants to cut itself off completely from Judaism, and set forth the Church in terms of discipleship and obedience. The relationship between Jewish Christianity and hellenistic Christianity ought not, therefore, to be conceived according to the simple pattern of a replacement process. Truly to understand this process we must recognize the mutual penetration which is indeed evident in the whole Gospel of Matthew: the Jewish Christian hellenistic Christianity – it drew on its own heritage as a determining element and a corrective for enthusiasm at the same time. It would be wrong, therefore, to speak here only of a retrograde process of re-Judaizing.

Both in terms of church history and sociologically, the formation of Matthew's congregation is to be understood in a certain analogy to the formation of Jewish congregations in the Diaspora. This is indicated, too, by the fact that the evangelist locates his congregation in Galilee which is, as in the beginning of Jesus' own ministry, "Galilee of the Gentiles" (4:15). Jerusalem is no longer their home but the place of Jesus' last struggle with the representatives of Judaism, of his suffering, his death, and resurrection. But far away from Jerusalem, Peter's confession, the founding of the Church upon him as the rock, and the sending into the world of the disciples, take place. Also the evangelist localizes in Capernaum the conversation about the temple tax (17:24–7), which immediately precedes the discourse on discipleship in Matthew 18; there a standard problem among diaspora Jews is discussed, pointing out both the freedom of the Christian congregation from Judaism and their freely given adherence to Jewish rules ("not to give offence to them" 17:27). As to their self-understanding, however, the congregation can be compared to a special synagogue only on the grounds of their outward appearance. On the strength of her Lord's authority over heaven and earth, and in keeping with her origin, belief, and nature, the Church broke through former boundaries.

NOTES

1 Cf. W. Trilling (1964²) 108.

2 The opinion that Mark's version is basic for Matthew is confirmed by the following arguments: (1) The parallel sequence in Matthew/Mark continues till the second announcement of the suffering (Mark 9:30–2), it even includes the following dispute over rank (Mark 9:33–7); the discourse about the temple tax is a transitional passage taken from Matthew's special source. Mark 9:33ff offered to the evangelist thematically useful material from other traditions. In his composition, Matthew treated his basic source with some liberty: he transferred a later part to the beginning, Mark 10:15 = Matt. 18:3f (where he joined it to the saying about self-humiliation), and he omitted the apophthegm of the strange exorcist which he obviously regarded as not suitable for a discourse on the congregation. Furthermore, he made use of the logion Mark 9:40 for his mission speech where he included another version of it (Matt. 12:30). (2) Luke 9:46–50 corresponds to the Marcan version more closely and confirms it thus as the basic source.

3 R. Bultmann (1963) 141.

4 Cf. Lev. 19:17f: "You shall not hate your brother in your heart, but you shall reason with your neighbour, lest you bear sin because of him. You shall not take vengeance or bear any grudge against the sons of your own people, but you shall love your neighbour as yourself: I am the Lord." From this passage the Qumran community also developed a rule in different stages for its congregational discipline (1QS VI, 1 and Zadokite Document IX, 2–8). On these texts and their relation to Matthew 18 cf. W. Trilling (1964²) 117ff; H. Braun, *Qumran und das Neue Testament.* Both Qumran texts refer to an "admonition before witnesses"; however, the explicit call for witnesses' testimony is missing. In Matt. 18:16b it may be a secondary addition made by the evangelist himself. The meaning is obviously that those called in must witness not to the sin but to the impenitence of the offender. Cf. G. Barth (1963) 84 n. 2.

5 Cf. G. Barth, 91 n. 1.

6 Cf. W. Trilling (1964²) 115f; H. von Campenhausen, *Ecclesiastical Authority and Spiritual Power in the Church of the first three Centuries* (ET 1969) 126f. See similar usage of these terms also in Matt. 5:46f.

7 Cf. Strack-Billerbeck, I (1922) 738f; A. Vögtle, "Binden und Lösen", *Lexicon für Theologie und Kirche* II², 480–2; H. von Campenhausen, 126f.

8 Cf. H. von Campenhausen, 126f; R. Hummel, (1966²) 61f.

9 Cf. W. Trilling (1964²) 41f.

10 More in Strack-Billerbeck, *Kommentar* II, 314f.

11 Cf. R. Bultmann (1963) 328f and 353f.

12 Cf. W. Trilling (1964²) 110.

13 The sequential context of the Q tradition was, however, given to him (Luke 17:3f). But by interpolating other traditional material which in itself would not require to be inserted at this particular place, the evangelist adds to the passages 18:10–14 and 18:21–35 an important profile and distinctness. G. Barth (1963) 84 emphasizes strongly the contrast between 18:15–17 and the tendency of the context.

14 Trilling, (1964[2]) 106ff.

15 Also, the sayings group 18:8f was not just "dragged in".

16 Trilling, 120ff.

17 Matt. 18:19 thus points in another direction than Mark 11:24; John 14:–13; 15:17.

18 Cf. G. Barth (1963) 127.

19 Cf. on Matt. 28:16–20 G. Bornkamm (1963).

20 Cf. R. Hummel (1966[2]) 61; H. von Campenhausen 141, n. 4.

21 Cf. W. Trilling, 158f, R. Hummel, 59f.

22 So Bultmann (1963) 141f; W. Trilling, 157, etc.

23 So Bultmann, 141.

24 Cf. O. Cullmann, "Petros", *TDNT* VI, 104f; R. Hummel, 62.

25 Cf. W. Schrage, *ZTK* 60 (1963) 178ff.

26 Cf. Streeter, *The Four Gospels* (1924) 515.

27 Cf. R. Hummel, 59ff.

7

*The Disciples in the Gospel according to Matthew**

ULRICH LUZ

In recent years several monographs using redaction criticism have brought more clarity to the theology of Matthew's Gospel. Above all, Bornkamm, Barth and Held (1960, ET 1963), Trilling (1959), Strecker (1962) and Hummel (1963)[1] have helped to clarify several features of Matthew's theology even though in the interpretation of this Gospel we are still a long way short of a generally accepted overall view.[2] One of the points which still seems to be unclear is Matthew's understanding of the disciples. There are two tendencies evident in the interpretation of this. One can be characterized by the catchword "transparency". This is stressed by Hummel: the title "disciple" remains the exhaustive ecclesiological term.[3] G. Barth speaks of "an equating of the time of the Church with the time of the life of Jesus".[4] The other tendency is best described by the catchword "historicizing". That Matthew's understanding of the disciples has a historicizing thrust is stressed above all by G. Strecker: "The disciples, like Jesus himself, are set in an unrepeatable, holy past."[5] Other interpreters find both elements present in Matthew: "Matthew has consistently painted the situation of the post-Easter community back into the historical discipleship of Jesus without thereby dissolving the group of disciples in the salvation-history past into the eschatological self-understanding of his own day."[6] "On the one hand it is clear that we have before us here the preaching of the community in Matthew's time. On the other, these proclamations now have their etiology in the story of Jesus which substantiates them."[7] One notices a certain inconsistency in some authors. Neither historicizing nor transparency seems total. Strecker can say that the historical Peter is "transparent of the contradictions involved in being a Christian".[8] Conversely Hummel, who understands *mathētēs*

* First published in *ZNW* 62 (1971) 141–71. Translated by Robert Morgan.

("disciple") as an ecclesiological, not a salvation-history concept, sees Peter as "guarantor for the authority of legal and disciplinary regulations",[9] i.e. guarantor of the *halakah* in Matthew's tradition. This complex situation justifies a fresh treatment of the discipleship theme in Matthew. Special attention will be paid to historicizing and transparency in Matthew's picture of the disciples.

I

We begin by testing Strecker's theses. Can one really see a historicizing tendency in Matthew's understanding of the disciples, and if so, what is its meaning?

The first argument listed by Strecker goes as follows: Matthew identifies the disciples with the twelve.[10] It is true that the evangelist can on occasion fill out Mark's frequent *dōdeka* ("twelve") with *mathētai* ("disciples") (10:1; perhaps 20:17; 26:20). He can speak redactionally of the twelve disciples (11:1), and he can replace Mark's *dōdeka* with *mathētai* (13:10; cf. 18:1). But precisely this last possibility warns us to be careful: if Matthew can omit Mark's *dōdeka* in replacing it with *mathētai*, this shows not that the number of the disciples being twelve was important to him, but that he took it for granted. Above all, he never replaces *mathētai* in his tradition with *dōdeka mathētai* ("twelve disciples"). The result is that he speaks of the twelve more seldom than Mark.[11] A tendency to identify the circle of disciples with the twelve is already present in the pre-Matthean tradition, above all in Mark.[12] So we gain the impression, contrary to Strecker, not that Matthew consciously equates the twelve with the disciples, but rather that this had by his day already become established, and that Matthew is laying no particular stress on it. The analysis of the individual passages does not contradict this. Matthew does not speak of the twelve at all until 10:1. This tells against his consciously historicizing the disciples with the help of a consistent identification of disciples and twelve. It cannot be proved at any point before 10:1 that Matthew had any other disciples than the twelve in mind either.[13] But the fact that Matthew, unlike Mark, never establishes the group of twelve but presupposes it without comment at 10:1, shows how unimportant it is to him.[14] In short, a conscious historicizing by identifying the disciples with the twelve cannot be shown. Matthew is here simply following the tradition.

Another point at which Matthew might be thought to be historicizing the picture of the disciples is in their participation in Jesus' mission. Strecker[15] and Walker[16] especially have shown that in

Matthew's salvation-history conception the historical Jesus is sent only to Israel. This is particularly clear in the mission discourse in chap. 10, so we shall take this as an example to clarify the problem. The disciples are sent to Israel (10:5f) just as Jesus himself is sent only to the lost sheep of the house of Israel (15:24). The mission discourse is interesting for our concerns because Matthew has in his redaction consciously related the mission of the disciples to the mission of Jesus. As Jesus preaches only to Israel (cf. 9:35), so the disciples are sent only to Israel (10:5f, cf. 10: 17, 23). As Jesus has power to heal all diseases (4:25; 9:35), so have the disciples (10:1; cf. v. 8). One reason for Matthew's enriching the two miracle chapters 8 and 9 with miracle stories not found in the parallel chapters in Mark (1–3), is certainly that he wants to relate the authority to perform miracles, even their very details, to the authority of the master.[17] But it is clear that the historicizing in chap. 10 is not consistent. First an observation about its external shape: the disciples are indeed sent out in Matthew, but they do not come back – certainly in contrast to Mark and presumably also to the Q tradition. Instead, the mission discourse ends at 11:1 as follows: "And it came to pass, when Jesus had made an end of commanding his twelve disciples...". There is no mention of the disciples now going or later coming back. By contrast, both Mark and Luke (Q?) expressly mention the absence of the disciples. So we may say that in Matthew the disciples are evidently not sent out during the lifetime of Jesus: they have only got their instructions. So when are they sent out? This question does not seem to bother Matthew because he is concerned only with Jesus' instructions. Jesus' wishing to bring salvation to Israel naturally plays a large part in the redactor's construction of the discourse, as does the prophecy of persecutions which the disciples will experience from Israel itself (10:17, 23). But it is clear, especially in the second part of the chapter, that the period in which Jesus' instructions will be fulfilled is the post-Easter period. The post-Easter situation of Jewish Christians being persecuted by Israel shines through (10:17f). Gentile mission and Jewish mission seem to take place simultaneously (10:18).[18] In a whole series of sayings the redactor's wording itself makes it clear that it is intended to be understood as commands which are valid for the present (e.g. vv. 26, 30f). Elsewhere this is clear from the content.[19] Even the authority to perform miracles (vv. 1, 8) which is given to the disciples is probably an authority given to the Matthean community, as we shall see.[20] Finally, in this chapter the word *mathētēs* is clearly used in a sense which goes beyond the historical situation. Even though v. 24

can be understood as a general principle, this is no longer possible in v. 42. *Mathētēs* there must plainly be understood from the perspective of the Matthean community, i.e. it is transparent.[21] So we conclude that in the mission discourse there is no consistent historicizing of the understanding of the disciples.[22] That can at best be claimed more or less convincingly for 10:1–16. At the latest in vv. 17f the transparent character of the discourse is clear. But there is no formal break between 10:16 and v. 17. The commands of Jesus are in principle valid for all time.[23]

The expression *mathētēs* is fitted into the discourse's transparency for the present. It is of course true to say that Matthew intends to stress the mission of the historical Jesus to Israel. But this aim has not led to a consistent periodizing of salvation history.[24] The antithetical scheme "mission of the historical Jesus to Israel – mission of the apostles only to the Gentiles" seems one-sided, at least in its second part, as is shown by 22:3–6, and 23:34ff as well as by chap. 10. The rejection by Israel of its Messiah means God's judgement, but this does not exclude a mission of the Church to Israel. On the contrary, the fiasco of this mission demonstrates the rejection of Israel; its guilt and God's judgement are confirmed by this.[25]

A third argument which needs discussing is Matthew's idealizing his picture of the disciples.[26] For Strecker this is the result of the "distance of the redactor from his subject, ... a sign of the comprehensive historicizing of the gospel tradition: the disciples are ... set in an unrepeatable holy past."[27] Is this so? Matthew occasionally seems to improve the image of the disciples. That is clearest at 20:20ff (= Mark 10:5ff) where the mother makes the request instead of the sons of Zebedee.[28] In a few passages where Matthew seems to have a more favourable picture of the disciples the tendency to tighten up the composition is probably at least partly responsible. That is true of Matt. 19:23 (Mark 10:23f);[29] Matt. 20:17 (Mark 10:32);[30] Matt. 18:1 (Mark 9:33–5).[31] Abbreviation without change of content is found at Matt. 26:9 (Mark 14:5).[32] It is no use arguing in this connection that Matthew occasionally speaks emphatically about the disciples following Jesus, because he can speak equally emphatically about the crowd following him.[33] In a few passages Matthew changes the wording: in various places he reproaches the disciples for their little faith (8:26; 14:31; 16:8; 17:20); but he can also speak of the disciples' lack of faith (21:21) or their doubt (14:31; 28:17). Since these are not all passages in which a Marcan motif is reinterpreted but include some in which the motif first emerges, we cannot interpret them as a weakening of Mark's reproaching their unbelief. In a few places Matthew has erased the motif of the disciples' fear, especially where it was connected with Mark's motif of the disciples' lack of understanding (Mark 9:32;[34] 10:32; 16:8), but in a few places he has introduced or considerably strengthened it (Matt. 14:30; 17:6f; 28:4ff). The worship of Jesus by the disciples, which is mentioned from time to time, is not meant to describe the believing attitude characteristic of the disciples, but the appropriate attitude towards Jesus. That is plain from the fact that not only disciples but also other people fall on the ground before Jesus (8:2; 9:18; 15:25).[35] There is also the way Peter's image is considerably worsened in comparison with Mark.[36]

In short, the only point at which Matthew has quite consistently "improved" the picture of the disciples is in his elimination of the Marcan motif of their failure to understand. In Matthew the disciples do understand. And at this point Matthew is as consistent as he seems everywhere else to be inconsistent.[37] But if that is so, it is methodologically unsound to explain on the one hand his consistent and on the other his thoroughly inconsistent procedure by the same catch-phrase "comprehensive historicizing". Instead we must ask why Matthew treats the knowledge of the disciples differently from their other qualities.

The evidence for Matthew's removal of the Marcan motif of the disciples' lack of understanding has been exhaustively presented by G. Barth;[38] we can therefore refer to him. There is only one point at which we would differ from him. He thinks that understanding is given to the disciples whereas the people are hardened.[39] But the disciples would then have had no need to ask about the meaning of the parables, and at Matt. 13:10 they would not have had to do so. Mark 4:34 ("but privately to his own disciples he expounded all things") is also absent from Mathew. On this last point it can be said that the evangelist is heading consistently for his formula quotation at Matt. 13:35. Mark 4:34 is not absent but is brought up later at 13:36 where the disciples expressly ask for an explanation of the parable of the Tares among the wheat. But at Matt. 13:10 the evangelist simply adapts the disciples' question to the explanation which follows. Since Matthew has a longer passage between the disciples' question at 13:10 and the explanation of the parable of the Sower at 13:18ff, the formal incongruence of question and answer is considerably worse than in Mark. But above all, the disciples receive far more frequent special instructions in Matthew than in any other Gospel, and this contradicts the thesis of Barth.[40] It means that the disciples often fail to understand, but that they come to understand through Jesus' explanation (13:51). For Matthew it is important that the disciples do finally – after Jesus' instruction – understand. That fits 15:16 and 16:9 too where it is expressly said that the disciples do not *yet* understand. In each case this is followed by an instruction of the disciples the point of which is to remove their lack of understanding. It is then expressly stated at 16:12 and 17:13 that the disciples *now* understand, i.e. after this exhaustive instruction by Jesus. So Jesus is shown here as a good teacher who successfully gives the disciples full instructions about everything. They do not understand of their own accord. They come to understand through Jesus' instruction. The purpose of this common and consistently applied motif in Matthew is probably not to idealize the picture of the disciples. It is concerned with something else. When the eleven disciples are commissioned to teach all nations what Jesus has commanded them (28:20), the inescapable presupposition for this is that they should themselves have understood. A teacher who does not understand what he himself teaches is a blind man leading the blind.[41] Strecker himself has shown very well how the understanding spoken of by Matthew has a practical side too.[42] Corresponding to that, Jesus' teaching is also very practical; it is a teaching about the better righteousness.

So Jesus is the teacher who leads his disciples to understanding. Understanding is related to the teaching of Jesus. Faith and understanding are separated in Matthew. The disciples are men of little faith, but they do understand. Faith is directed to the person of Jesus; understanding is related to his teaching. In Mark the disciples' lack of understanding is conceived with reference to Christology. It applies to the person and later particularly to the suffering of the Son of God. In Matthew, by contrast, the disciples' understanding is directed to something different, namely to Jesus' teaching. It is no coincidence that understanding usually has an object here.[43] Where there could be no object Matthew deletes Mark's lack of understanding motif, but does not himself speak of the disciples' understanding (cf. 14:32f). So it is not only that in comparison with Mark the disciples have gained in understanding; the horizon of understanding has shifted too. Full understanding is for Matthew not the expression but the presupposition of Christian existence, and this consists in loyalty to the message of the historical Jesus. For Matthew understanding is the presupposition of both Christian life and Christian teaching. On the other side, Matthew's concept of faith has been detached from understanding and it has probably also been narrowed.[44] It is no coincidence that Matthew has taken up and reflected theologically, above all, on the usage of "faith" in the miracle stories, even though the more general use of the word was not unfamiliar to him. G. Barth put it like this: "The intellectual element ... is excluded from Matthew's concept of faith."[45] *Pistis* ("faith") becomes preponderantly trust. With the one exception of 16:8f, understanding is not the presupposition of faith[46] but is separated from it. Faith is directed at the miraculous power of the Lord which is still at work in the community; understanding relates to the teaching of Jesus. In terms of form criticism, "faith" is found largely in the miracle stories, "understanding" in the catechetical material. Theologically speaking, "faith" seems to be mainly linked to the exalted, and "understanding" to the earthly, Jesus. For Matthew faith is largely[47] the human attitude corresponding to the divine power of salvation, whereas understanding is the presupposition for loyalty to the earthly Jesus, i.e. for Christian ethics. Faith seems to be mainly correlated with the indicative of salvation, understanding more with ethics. And this lack of any close relation between faith and understanding which we seem to find in Matthew seems to present us with a fundamental problem about his theology.

A further observation corresponds to the disciples' understanding. In the first Gospel the disciples are basically designated as hearers of Jesus' message. That does not exclude the crowd hearing Jesus' message too. They too are hearers of Jesus' parables discourse. But the disciples' eyes and ears are called blessed because they not only hear and see but also understand it (13:16). Something similar is found in chap. 15. There too the crowd is present at the controversy dialogue with the Pharisees (15:10), but only to disappear again, at once, whilst Jesus explains the "parable" to the disciples (15:12, 15). Because the crowds to whom Jesus preaches in parables do not understand (13:13), they are a foil to the disciples who hear and understand all Jesus' instructions. In line with this, the disciples are always hearers of Jesus. They are never absent, not even after they have been sent out. It is not always self-evident that the disciples should be especially mentioned as hearers of Jesus. For example, it is not self-evident in the discourse of chap. 23, which apart from vv. 1–12 is directed at Israel. But there too the disciples are expressly named at 23:1 as among Jesus' hearers. In chap. 24 too it is not only a chosen few but all the disciples who are hearers of Jesus (24:3). Whether the Sermon on the Plain in Q was addressed to the disciples or to the people can no longer be ascertained since both the Matthean and the Lucan introductions and conclusions come from the evangelists themselves,[48] but it is notable that at 5:1 Matthew particularly mentions that it is disciples who hear the Sermon on the Mount because this does not naturally follow from his redactional composition of 4:25—5:2. In 16:24 too it is the disciples who are named as the hearers of Jesus' message. The crowds are here deleted. We have already mentioned that Matthew has a particularly large number of instructions to the disciples. In short, for Luke the apostles who are witnesses of all that Jesus did in the land of the Jews and in Jerusalem (Acts 10:39), and especially witnesses of the resurrection (Acts 1:22), are primarily *eye*-witnesses. But in Matthew the disciples are men who have heard and understood all that Jesus taught in his lifetime, i.e. they are *ear*-witnesses.

To summarize, we have not found a thorough-going historicizing in the understanding of the disciples in Matthew's Gospel. At only one point is Matthew consistent: discipleship is always related to the teaching of the historical Jesus. The disciples are hearers of that teaching and understand it. This is the presupposition for the definition of discipleship at Matt. 12:50 as doing the will of God.[49] The difference between Matthew and Luke seems to be that in Matthew the (limited) "historicizing" of the disciples is not connected with any idea of succession. That is clear, for example, in Matthew's picture of Peter, who is not to be interpreted as guarantor of the *halakah*, but as the model or "type" of discipleship, as Strecker has shown, in my opinion, convincingly.[50] This means that alongside the historicizing there is typification which frames it, and alone makes it truly meaningful. It is as pupils of the historical Jesus that the disciples become transparent and are models of what it means to be a Christian. That will be clarified in what follows, first by reference to the miracle stories.

II

The miracle stories in Matthew have been thoroughly investigated by H. J. Held, and we here latch on to the results of his work.[51] He has shown that in both Matthew's feeding miracles the echoes of the Eucharist already present in Mark become much clearer through Matthew's abbreviations of these narratives.[52] These echoes made it possible for the Christian hearer to understand his own experiences in the Eucharist in the light of the miracle reported in the story. Both the people who are filled and especially the disciples who share out the loaves and fishes, become transparent in the light of the eucharistic experiences of Christians.[53] However, neither story is simply made into a Eucharist story. The presence of the fishes, which are retained despite Matthew's abbreviation of Mark, and which do not fit the eucharistic practice of the Matthean community,[54] precludes that. The fishes and also the mention of the precise number of the baskets with the pieces of food left over, plus the giving of the numbers fed,[55] show that Matthew too sees the feedings as a matter of events which happened once in the historical past by the lake Gennesaret (where there are fish!). We must therefore say that it is precisely as past historical events that these two miracle-stories become transparent for the present life of the community.

The two stories of stilling of storms in Matt. 8:23–7 and 14:23–31 have been analysed by Bornkamm.[56] He has clearly shown their character of transparency for the present life of the Church. It is plain that in the disciples following Jesus into the boat, in the swamping by the *seismos* ("storm"),[57] in the request *kyrie sōson* ("save, Lord"), in the anxiety of the disciples or in their little faith, experiences of the community are reflected. It is clear that the evangelist is interested not simply in the miracle that happened in the past, but in the community's experience of the still ever helping presence of its Lord. But Bornkamm rightly observes, "In Matthew this characteristic of the story (i.e. as a real miracle) ... is not completely abandoned".[58] There remains a historical residue which the evangelist could easily have omitted: mention of the fourth watch of the night (14:25); the comment, which is even more exact than in Mark, that the boat was several furlongs away from the land (14:24). The "choral ending" in Matt. 8:27 also seems to be more appropriate in a miracle story than in a purely symbolic story. The stories of stilling of the storms were evidently proclaimed by the Matthean community as miracles of Jesus. And from its own experiences of the power of the Lord Jesus the community knew that this power was still at work in their midst. So again it is precisely the past event which is transparent for the present.

The position is similar with the healing miracles. Redaction criticism has shown that the Matthean interpretation is found on different levels. Again the past historical fact as such is itself important. Matthew interprets Jesus' miracles as the fulfilment of OT prophecies (8:17; 11:5f; 12:18–21). His filling out the Marcan miracle collection for the sake of a complete fulfilment of the Isa. 61:1 quotation at 11:5f[59] shows that the evangelist was at least partly interested in the factuality of the individual miracle stories. The frequent use of the title "Son of David" in the miracle stories (9:27; 12:23; 15:22; 20:30f) also indicates that Matthew interprets these as fulfilling the specific mission of Jesus which was meant for the people of Israel and which did not continue in this way in the post-Easter community.[60] But alongside that, the healing miracles were themselves transparent for the present. This transparency becomes clear at different points. I give only two of them.

(*a*) The Matthean understanding of faith: Matthew gives every indication of being familiar with the *pistis* ("faith") concept of hellenistic Christianity which used the word to paraphrase Christian existence as such: "John came ... and you did not believe him; but the tax-gatherers and the harlots believed him; ... You however did not repent and believe him" (21:32). In this redactional verse *pisteuō* ("I believe") is an all-encompassing term for describing their relationship to John the Baptist. The expression is of course taken from the believers' relationship to Christ and applied to John. The verse from the tradition, 18:6, also shows that Matthew, i.e. his readers and hearers, clearly understood the term without question as describing Christian existence. So when Matthew repeatedly orients the healings to the theme of "faith"[61] he is certainly speaking to the community about their faith, or their need of it. One might even wonder whether the frequent reference to little faith in Matthew's miracle stories (8:26; 14:31; cf. 16:8; 17:20) is perhaps aimed at a contemporary situation in the community; namely, that although it is a community of believers, miracles are sometimes absent. This experience would obviously be quite likely towards the end of the first century, as experiences of the Spirit generally receded.[62] Matt. 17:19ff would offer the clearest support for this interpretation. It would make good sense of Matthew's distinction between unbelief (e.g. that of the people at Nazareth, 13:58, or the Jews at 21:32) and little faith, which always refers to the disciples. The Christians, here represented by the disciples, are on the one hand believers – in that faith is the obvious characteristic of everyone who believes in the Lord and is the mark which distinguishes them from non-Christians, who are *apistoi* ("unbelievers"). On the other hand, these Christians are themselves unbelieving in the sense that they often lack that special faith which moves mountains and experiences miracles. In terms of the history of the tradition, Matthew's concept of *oligopistia* ("little faith") would then represent an attempt to reconcile by means of terminology two quite different understandings of faith current in hellenistic Christianity.[63] Existentially, the experience of, and reflection on, the cessation of the Spirit played a role. Be that as it may, Matthew seems to understand faith in the light of his present situation without giving it very clear conceptual expression.[64]

(*b*) The transfer of Jesus' authority to the community.[65] This trait is particularly clear in Matthew and again helps us to be more precise about the nature of faith in this Gospel. Matt. 7:22 presupposes in the community charismatic activity, of which the evangelist is evidently critical. But he is himself – at least so far as his basically positive attitude to miracles is concerned – not all that far from the charismatics he is attacking.[66] One might indeed understand the authority to perform miracles, which in 10:1 and 10:8[67] is given to the disciples with explicit reference to Jesus' miracles, as limited to the mission of the disciples during Jesus' own lifetime. But we have already seen that despite all its connection with the particular mission of Jesus to Israel the mission discourse nevertheless consciously goes beyond that historical situation. This is confirmed by other passages. In 14:28–31 Peter, whose own doubt and little faith here make him a model of Christians, participates in Jesus' authority to walk on the water. In 17:19ff, where the tradition's instruction of the disciples about doing miracles is considerably developed and made a matter of principle, it is assumed that miracles happen, or ought to happen, in Matthew's community. E. Schweizer[68] draws attention to Matt. 10:24f, where the disciples are "explicitly equated with their master who after the healing of the dumb man . . . called Beelzebul (cf. 9:34)". Particularly clear, however, is the transference to the whole community of the authority to forgive sins which Jesus exercises at the healing of the lame man (9:8). That Matthew's community practised forgiveness of sins, and considered this important, is clear not only from the community discourses in chap. 18, but also from the Matthean addition to the Last Supper liturgy at 26:28: "for the forgiveness of sins". This makes it probable that the redactor Matthew did in fact understand the authority to bind and loose promised to Peter (16:19), as applying to the whole community. Here, too, Peter for him is the "type" of a Christian;[69] the authority which is given to him is exercised by the whole community (18:15ff).[70]

Outside the miracle-stories, there is so much material showing the transparency of the concept of discipleship that we can only select a few observations to round off the picture.

1 Matthew avoids the word *apostolos* ("apostle"). He has it only in the heading given to the list of apostles in 10:2. It is applied there to the twelve which shows that the idea of the twelve apostles which Luke has developed into a theological conception, was evidently some kind of trend at this time.[71] In Acts, Luke clearly differentiates

between the twelve apostles who have a once for all historical function as witnesses of the life of Jesus and the resurrection, and the *mathētai* who in Acts represent the totality of believers (cf. for example 6:2; 9:1, 10, 26; 11:26; 16:1, etc.). This linguistic usage affects his Gospel as well (6:13, 17, 20; 19:37, 39; 24:9). In contrast Matthew consistently avoids the title apostle, even where he is speaking of the mission of the twelve.[72] Why? The reason may be as follows: the members of his community could identify with the *mathētai* but not with the *apostoloi* who had already become by that time figures of the past. Conversely, the word *mathētēs* is very well suited for teaching people to understand the essence of being a Christian as a relationship to the historical Jesus. *Apostolos* is more strongly coloured by the post-Easter function of the apostles.

2 The transparency of *mathētēs* is clear in Matthew's use of the verb *mathēteuō* ("I disciple"). It occurs three times in this Gospel and all of them are probably redactional: 13:52; 27:57; and 28:19. At 27:57 Matthew replaces Mark's *prosdechomenos tēn basileian* ("awaiting the kingdom") with *emathēteuthē tǭ Iēsou* ("he was discipled to Jesus"). We may take that as an interpretation of his source, Mark, not as a correction. Discipleship for Matthew consists in acceptance of the *basileia* ("kingdom"), i.e. of the good news from Jesus. In the same way the difficult passage in 13.52 relates *mathēteuein* ("to disciple") to the *basileia tōn ouranōn* ("kingdom of heaven"), i.e. to Jesus' teaching. The remaining difficult problems in this verse need not be attended to here. 28.19 should also be understood in a similar way. *Mathēteuō* ("I disciple") is here interpreted by "teaching them to observe what I have commanded you",[73] i.e. again by a reference to the teaching of the earthly Jesus.[74] That corresponds to the way in which Matthew profiles discipleship in his Gospel. Disciples are those who hear and understand the commands and teachings of Jesus,[75] and do God's will (12:50). At the same time, however, they are according to 28:20 those with whom the Lord with his authority is present always, even to the end of the world. What that might mean is explicated by Matthew in his miracle stories. In short, it is highly unlikely in the light of these passages that Matthew uses the verb *mathēteuō* in a quite different sense from the substantive *mathētēs*, as Strecker argues.[76] Rather, the verb *mathēteuō* functions as transparency to make discipleship in the gospel illuminate the evangelist's own day.

3 The transparency of the disciple concept in this Gospel is also

secured by other parallel concepts, for example *adelphos* ("brother"). In most cases the word is taken over by Matthew from his tradition and is only relatively seldom used by him redactionally (18:21, 35; 28:10?). Since it was current as a self-designation by Christians, the passages in which the word occurs gain a certain transparency automatically. At 12:46ff and 23:8 it is synonymous with *mathētēs*. Another parallel concept is the early term for disciples, *mikros* ("little one"),[77] which crops up in Matthew's tradition and is also probably understood by the evangelist as synonymous with *mathētēs*.[78]

III

We shall now pause for a moment and try to summarize what has emerged from our survey concerning the way the disciples are understood in the first Gospel.

1 The disciples of Jesus are transparent for the present situation. Behind them stands Matthew's community. *Mathētēs* is an ecclesiological term.[79]

The question whether the disciples represent the leaders or the members of the community has considerable significance for example for the interpretation of Matthew 18, but cannot be decided with certainty. In both feeding stories they seem to represent the leaders, but this restriction cannot be maintained in the stillings of the storms or the miracle story at 17:14ff. But that in itself shows that this distinction between leaders and community is in fact relatively unimportant for Matthew's understanding of discipleship. The parallel between *mikros* and *mathētēs* at 10:42[80] provides further support for interpreting chap. 18 in the same way and making no distinction between *mikroi* (members of the community) and *mathētai* addressed at 18:1. That means that community members who fulfil a leadership function are disciples in the same way as all other members. This would count against the common interpretation of Matthew 18 as instructions for appointed leaders.[81] Institutional problems seem to be not yet very significant for Matthew's community.[82]

Other problems arising from Matthew's discipleship transparency technique can here remain open – for example, the often discussed question whether we may conclude from the instructions to the disciples in Matthew that the Matthean community saw itself as still part of the Jewish federation of synagogues.[83] Another question that has recently been raised is whether the frequent redactional use of *poreuomai* ("I go") implies that in Matthew's church itinerant missionaries and prophets played a special role.[84] The answer to this question makes no difference to Matthew's basic conception and can here be left out of the discussion.

2   In the miracle stories we ascertained in each case a "historical residue". They are understood as historical events and the Lord Jesus is clearly understood as a figure in the past who fulfilled a unique mission in the history of salvation. But at the same time in the historical Jesus the risen Lord is present.[85] So transparency in the disciple concept means becoming contemporary with a figure of the past. The temporal distance is bridged, but evidently not in a way that simply dissolves the historical Jesus in the community's experiences of the Spirit. Rather, Matthew makes it clear that it is the power of the *earthly* Jesus that is efficacious in the community and calls for faith. The same result emerged from an investigation of Strecker's arguments for Matthew's historicizing of the disciple concept.[86] All that is essential is hearing, understanding and doing the words of the *earthly* Jesus. And precisely that is the essence of true discipleship in every age. Thus, characteristic for Matthew's concept of discipleship is the tendency to make the *past* – which Matthew emphasizes – transparent for the present.

Both aspects, the past and the transparency, seem to be correlated in Matthew in a quite definite way with Christology. The transparency of the disciple concept seems to be particularly important for the promise of salvation, i.e. for the indicative. Salvation in Matthew is essentially the continuing authority of the Lord in the community; it is receiving the efficacious forgiveness of sins which Jesus committed to the community's charge. Salvation is both the continuation in the community of miracles done in Jesus' name, which guarantee the nearness of the Kingdom of God, and also the experience in discipleship of the power of Jesus which overcomes all doubt and all cowardice. In Matthew the miracle stories themselves have a central function in announcing salvation. Without miracles proclamation of the gospel of the Kingdom of God is impossible. That is why Matthew has so consistently placed Jesus' miracles and his teaching alongside one another and emphasized both as equally important.[87] In my view it is impossible to speak of a devaluation of the miraculous in Matthew. Negatively, that means that it is not the kerygma of Jesus' death and resurrection which spells salvation. Positively, salvation is the abiding presence of Jesus in the community.[88] To express that, the transparency use of the disciple concept is necessary.

On the other hand, connecting being a disciple with the person of the earthly Jesus seems to be fundamental above all for the ethics of this Gospel, i.e. for the imperative. It has often been rightly emphasized that the evangelist has to defend himself, at least in part, against hellenistic Christian enthusiasts, as is apparent for example at the end of the Sermon on the Mount.[89] Against these he points to the commands of Jesus which the disciples heard; obedience to these constitutes the nature of true discipleship. Only by keeping his commands can true Christians be distinguished from false ones. Matthew has no institutional criterion for distinguishing them, such as is at least on the way in Luke. It corresponds to this lack of any such criterion that the separation can only take place at the last judgement. The relationship of discipleship to the historical Jesus is decisive for this basic conception. For Matthew historicizing is itself the presupposition for genuine transparency. For him true discipleship is at all times only possible as recourse to the historical Jesus.[90]

The result corresponds exactly with the report of a resurrection appearance which is transmitted only by Matt. 28:16-20. Since this pericope has recently been discussed at length, especially by G. Bornkamm and A. Vögtle,[91] we can be brief. It lacks important form-critical characteristics of an appearance story:[92] an exact description of the appearance of Jesus and the motif of recognition by the disciples are both absent. It is striking that the text ends not with Jesus' disappearance, but with a reference to his abiding presence. The motif of doubt does correspond to what is normally found in an appearance story, but there is no reference here to it being overcome. Since the combination of doubt and worship is also found at 14:31-3, it is probably the work of the redactor. The disciples' doubt is thus not overcome by Jesus' appearance, which is not itself important here. That reflects, as O. Michel was probably right in seeing, the problem of the Matthean community which could not settle its doubts by looking at the Easter experiences of their predecessors.[93] Rather, the disciples' doubt remains, as it were, unresolved in this pericope – in fact it is still found in the present (cf. 14:28ff). It is confronted by the power of the exalted one and by his word which is identical with the word of the earthly one. And that alone is evidently what matters for Matthew about being a Christian: the power of the exalted one and the word of the earthly one.

These two elements are both stressed in this pericope. On the one hand Matthew speaks of the continuing presence of Jesus in the community. G. Bornkamm has pointed out that unlike the pericope John 20:19-23, which is in many ways similar, there is here no talk of the Spirit.[94] That is true, though the formulation "I am with you" probably means in effect the same as what is said with the catch-word "Spirit". Matthew has made it clear in his miracle stories what he understands by the presence of the Lord. And it is notable that there are quite similar parallels of form in the Johannine Paraclete sayings (John 14:16, 17, 18, 23). Matthew himself at one point seizes hold of the same idea[95] of the presence of Jesus in his community back at 18:20, there in connection with the authority given to the community to exercise church discipline and to pray with the assurance of being answered. The closest theological parallel to Matt. 18:15–20 is presumably 1 Cor. 5:4f. When the hellenistic community in Corinth is assembled with the power (!) of the Lord Jesus, church discipline should be exercised. The theological parallels thus point us to hellenistic Christianity, as on the whole do the miracle stories which Matthew tells in his Gospel as illustrations. It is however significant that this text speaks of the presence of Jesus, rather than the presence of the Spirit.[96] In this way the evangelist again takes up everything that he has said in his Gospel about Jesus' power to perform miracles, and makes it transparent for the present and explains that it is valid now as it was then. Vögtle also has shown by another route that by referring to Jesus' authority in v. 18 the evangelist intends to fasten primarily on to the authority given to the earthly Jesus because this remains effective after his exaltation.[97] Finally Matthew intends with v. 20 to make the link with the one who was Immanuel for Israel (1:23) and rescues his people from their sins (1:21; cf. 9:8; 26:28). The one who is active in the community's experience of the Spirit is thus identical with the earthly Jesus.

On the other hand, Matthew speaks of keeping Jesus' commands and sees in that the essence of discipleship. Close parallels in respect of form with both the verb *tēreō* ("I keep") and the root *entell-* ("command") occur astonishingly again in John (14:15; cf. 14:16ff, 21; 15:10; 1 John 3:22). There, however, in magnificent and one-sided concentration, the commandment of Jesus refers only to the command to love the brethren. In contrast to that Matthew specifies and details *panta hosa* ("all things whatsoever").[98] It is a matter of the individual commands, not one of which shall pass away, until all things come to pass (5:18).[99] The aorist *eneteilamēn* ("I commanded") interprets the commands quite unambiguously as those of the earthly Jesus. Jesus is the only teacher of the community.[100] The proclamation of the disciples is identical with the commands of the earthly Jesus. That is probably part of the reason why the

Risen One meets the disciples in Galilee (28:16), because that is the place of his earthly activity, as the evangelist particularly emphasizes.[101]

Both in Matthew's understanding of the disciples and in his Christology we thus have an indicative and an imperative together. Jesus is the one to whom all power is given, the exalted one who is with his disciples even to the end of the world. To this corresponds discipleship, understood as participation in this authority as being secure under the protection of the exalted one. And Jesus is the earthly one, the great teacher of God's law. To this there corresponds discipleship as understanding and obeying the commands of the earthly Jesus. Both components stand together.[102] Their relationship does not seem to be clearly defined, either in the concept of the disciples, or in Matthew's conception of faith, or in Matthew's understanding of following. At any rate the relationship of the imperative to the indicative of salvation as something given is not made very clear in Matthew's conception of the Church. That is apparent for example in that the eschatologically coloured ecclesiological terminology, which expresses the priority of God's action for his people, is largely absent from Matthew. Expressions such as "true Israel" or *hagioi* ("saints") are absent. The ecclesiologically pregnant use of *klētos* ("called") and *eklektos* ("elect") is missing.[103] *Laos* ("people") is consistently applied to Israel[104] and only *ekklēsia* ("church") occurs twice in Matthew's tradition.[105] To this general lack of an eschatologically coloured understanding of the Church and the lack of correlation of indicative and imperative aspects in Matthew's understanding of the disciples, there corresponds a basic feature of his Christology: the indicative of salvation and the imperative of salvation seem no longer to be theologically related to one another in such a way as to make clear how in Matthew's theology the demand and the gift belong together. As the exalted one who is active in the community Jesus is giver; as the earthly teacher he makes demands. It is largely true to say that indicative and imperative are only connected in the person of Jesus because he himself is both giver and author of the demand. The fact that Matthew stressed so strongly the identity of the exalted and the earthly Jesus shows that he sensed this weakness in his theology, which is at the same time a weakness in his community's theology, and that he struggled to overcome it.

IV

This final section contains a few more traditio-historical consider-ations which arise from Matthew's understanding of discipleship and which help us to place Matthew in the development of early Christian theology. All that is possible here is a provisional sketch and a few very fragmentary and hypothetical pointers.

We have already indicated that the transparency of Matthew's concept of the disciples is in principle already present in the tradi-tion.[106] He himself has deepened this transparency and at a few points emphasized that it is in the disciples of the historical Jesus that the nature of the Church, including the Church of his own day, is visible. Of course the unity of the historical and the exalted Jesus which is fundamental for his conception, is also inherited from the tradition, even though Matthew has reflected more consciously on it than some of his predecessors. This is the christological basis of Christians being designated *mathētai*. So we can expect that Christians designated themselves as disciples of Jesus in churches where his words and teaching were handed on as applicable also for the present. We can expect the label *mathētai* where Christian communities recognized in the miracles of Jesus their own experiences with the Spirit and where they understood the words spoken to them by Christian prophets as a confrontation with Jesus, and consequently historic-ized them.[107] We cannot expect this designation in those communities where no great value was placed upon the life and teaching of Jesus.

However, it is striking that we do not seem to find the transparent use of *mathētēs* in the texts of the Q source.[108] That is striking because the believers' understanding of themselves as "disciples" would fit well in the theology of Q, and the related application of the word *akoloutheō* ("I follow") is found there.[109] But the lack of the *mathētēs* designation may be a coincidence, understandable because Q consists mainly in sayings and apophthegms; miracle stories are relatively rare.

We do however probably find evidence in the pre-Marcan com-munity. In Mark's controversy dialogues, which with Bultmann I would consider in their present form as largely community construc-tions,[110] Jesus often defends the behaviour of the disciples against the Pharisees (Mark 2:18, 23; 7:2; cf. 2:16). Behind these controversy dialogues one supposes there were communities in which the law was wholly or partly abolished on the basis of appeal to Jesus' authority. It is with this authority that the community defends its own freedom, i.e. in the text, the behaviour of the disciples.[111] These communities will have spoken Greek; there are no indications of an Aramaic original in these controversy dialogues.[112] The Pharisees are here depicted from a certain distance. The narrator is not disturbed by the improbability of Pharisees being present at a tax-collectors' party (Mark 2:15ff), or going for a walk in the cornfields on the sabbath (Mark 2:23ff). So there is good reason to place these controversy dialogues in hellenistic Jewish Christianity at no great distance from central Jewish territory. Also from the pre-Marcan communities come the two feeding stories where again experiences of the community are probably included.[113] The words and reports about following are also presumably transparent, insofar as the communities did at least use them in their own proclamation to strengthen and give a basis for their own call to discipleship. Other texts should be mentioned too: Mark 9:28f seems to presuppose that the disciples do miracles in the name of Jesus. Mark 6:7ff, which the pre-Marcan communities probably used in mission instruction, shows the role played by miracles in these communities' missionary work. One gets a similar picture from the mission legends in Acts where, as we shall see, the designation *mathētai* for Christians also possibly occurs. At any rate the transparent use of the disciple concept is at the root of pre-Marcan mission instruction. Mark 9:38ff contains debate with other Christian miracle-workers who do not belong to the circle of disciples, i.e. the community. Mark 10:28ff also probably mirrors the situation of the community. The same may perhaps be true of Mark 10:13ff, if this text reflects the practice of infant baptism, as is occasionally thought. But this can remain an open question here. At any rate the Christians of the pre-Marcan communities understood themselves to be disciples of Jesus. This suggestion is strengthened in that no other kind of ecclesiological conceptions are visible in these strata of the tradition.

The evidence of Acts perhaps fits in with this. The designation disciple is commonly used there to refer to the post-Easter communities. It corresponds to Luke's linguistic usage,[114] and a clear linguistic separation between tradition and redaction in Acts is probably not possible either with the word *mathētēs* or anywhere else.[115] It is however striking that the first time Christians are called *mathētai* occurs in the tradition about the hellenists at Jerusalem (Acts 6:1, 2, 7). It then comes repeatedly in the tradition of Paul's conversion in Acts 9 and again in the Peter traditions from Joppa (Acts 9:36, 38), in the Antioch tradition (Acts 11:26) and once in the "we" passages (21:4, 16). That gives all the passages where the word is possibly pre-redactional. Prior to 6:1ff the Christians are called *pisteusantes* ("those who had made an act of faith"). Now so far as this evidence can be assessed at all it supports the view that "disciples of Jesus" was a Christian self-designation above all in hellenistic Jewish Christianity outside Jerusalem. On grounds of content also it is probable that the Jerusalem Christians preferred to see themselves as God's holy and elect people of the end-time. It was because Jerusalem incorporated the totality of the people of God that some disciples may have left Galilee and moved to the holy city. The Christians of Galilee and Syria might accordingly have emphasized more strongly the link with the life and teaching of the historical Jesus and therefore have continued to apply the label *mathētai*, i.e. Jesus' school or group, to themselves. That they were first called Christians, i.e. adherents of Christ, in Antioch would be more intelligible if it was these hellenistic Jewish Christians who stressed the connection with Jesus. All this of course is no more than a proposal to be discussed, at best an arguable hypothesis. It can however be supplemented by the conclusion recently reached by H. W. Kuhn from another direction, that it is above all in Greek-speaking communities that one finds a piety based on continuity with the proclamation of the historical Jesus.[116]

The linguistic evidence does not contradict this. A widely held hypothesis sees the discipleship idea as coming into rabbinic Judaism from Hellenism.[117] The idea also crops up in the hellenistic *theioi andres* ("divine men") sphere, there too in the sense of following beyond the death of the master[118] or in the sense of following great teachers of the past. In contrast to this, rabbinic Judaism stressed the direct teacher–pupil relation. For the rabbinic principle of tradition it is important that a pupil really has heard the tradition direct from the rabbi. There are references to pupils in an indirect sense, but these occur relatively seldom.[119] This does not of course mean that the idea of discipleship to Jesus can be derived from the hellenistic background. It is quite clear that Judaism provided the model for it, whether rabbinic or perhaps zealot strands, and above all John the Baptist. But it is possible that the retention of the disciple label after Easter and among Christians who did not know Jesus himself makes particularly good sense on the basis of hellenistic linguistic tradition.

Mark's Gospel provides no material for our question because here the disciples are made to serve the christological conception of the messianic secret. It is, however, interesting to compare the Matthean conception with John. Even in the pre-Johannine tradition the disciple concept is at least partly transparent. This is apparent in John

13 where it seems likely that a foot-washing rite practised by the Johannine community provides the background.[120] It is apparent, too, in that the feeding of the five thousand occurs also in the pre-Johannine tradition. For John himself *mathētēs* ("disciple") and *akolouthein* ("to follow") are important.[121] In John 1:35ff the traditional stories about following are assimilated to the present situation when the disciples are won by the testimony of other disciples, not by Jesus' call, and where the christological definition of Christ's person plays such an extraordinarily large role (1:36, 41, 45, 49). But particularly interesting is the definition of the nature of discipleship in 13:35 and 15:8. When discipleship is defined here as bearing fruit and loving one's neighbour John comes into very close theological proximity with Matthew who describes the disciple as the one who does God's will (12:46ff). For him too the love command is the content of God's will and for him too the tradition's motif of bearing fruit is important for distinguishing between genuine and counterfeit Christianity (7:15ff, cf. 21:43; and John 15:2ff). There is no real likelihood of literary dependence; more likely a theological continuation by John and Matthew of related traditions. The differences between them are clear enough against the background of what they have in common. In John being a disciple is ultimately to be defined as being in Christ or connected to him (15:2–4). That of course allows him to express the indicative of salvation clearly. Only by being in Christ is there any fruit at all. The danger here is of this Christ becoming an ultimately uncheckable spiritual reality. Matthew is different. Precisely because he is faced with some kind of Christian spiritual enthusiasts he has built in a form of control. For him, to be a disciple means to be a disciple of the earthly Jesus. Having recourse to the history here operates as a protection against uncheckable enthusiasm. Nevertheless, the common basis of Johannine and Matthean theology, both of which probably have the roots of their ecclesiology in hellenistic Jewish Christianity, is clear. This is the more striking in that neither evangelist lays much weight on offices in their church, and in this respect they are a long way from early catholicism. The relationship between the two evangelists is the more significant in that they probably stem from about the same period and the same geographical area of Syria.

It is also significant that Ignatius of Antioch seems to have known both Gospels.[122] He is also one of the few[123] who is still familiar with the transferred use of the word *mathētēs*. Since for Ignatius only the martyr is Jesus' disciple in the full sense of the word, we may take it that where *mathētēs* designates the ordinary Christian this reflects a linguistic feature of the tradition.[124] Apart from Ignatius, none of the Apostolic Fathers knows the word *mathētēs* as a designation for Christians. Only in Justin does it occur again.[125] By then Matthew's specific aim in using the word *mathētēs*, namely to assert the connection with the earthly Jesus that being a Christian in every generation implies, was already overtaken by the way Christianity was developing. Guaranteeing the tradition by the ecclesiastical office had shown itself to be far more effective.

NOTES

1 See bibliography for all authors with dates attached.

2 Cf. K. Tagawa, "People and Community in the Gospel of Matthew", *NTS* 16 (1969/70) 149.

3 Hummel (1963) 154.

4 G. Barth (1963) 111. Cf. Hare (1967) especially 81ff.

5 Strecker (1962) 194.

6 Schulz (1967) 217.

7 W. Marxsen, *The Evangelist Mark* (1969) 141.

8 Strecker (1962) 206.

9 Hummel (1963) 60.

10 Strecker (1962) 191.

11 8 times in Matthew against 11 in Mark.

12 Cf. Bultmann (1963) 345; a different view is found in A. Schulz, *Nachfolgen und Nachahmen* (1962) 51ff. Schulz considers the identity of the disciples with the twelve to be pre-Marcan.

13 The same is true of Matt. 8:21. The parallel between *heis grammateus* ("one scribe") and *heteros tōn mathetōn* ("another of the disciples") does not mean that the *grammateus* is made one of the disciples. The following agree with this interpretation: Benoit (1961) 70; Bonnard (1970²) 118; Klostermann (1927²) 77; Strecker (1962) 191. For the contrary view, see McNeile (1915) 109; Grundmann (1968) 258. *Heteros* (another) is a "careless addition" (Klostermann) and does not imply that the person thus referred to belongs to the same species as the first named, cf. Luke 23:32 and the evidence given by Bauer under 1bB of his dictionary (ed. Arndt and Gingrich). Matt. 17:6 is the only passage where *mathētai* clearly does not mean the twelve but the three named at 17:1.

14 If anything can be inferred from Matt. 10:1 it is this: that Matthew inserts *mathētai* into Mark. Is he concerned to show that the authority which is there given to the twelve to heal and to exorcise is given to the disciples, i.e. to the whole community? But 10:2ff. inserts the names of the twelve and this can only refer to the historical twelve. However, the twelve are there called not *mathētai* but *apostoloi*. Is this a coincidence?

15 Strecker (1962) 99–122.

16 R. Walker (1967) especially 114ff.

17 There are different, not mutually exclusive, motifs which may explain the position of chaps. 8 and 9 in Matthew's outline. (1) The miracle stories come *after* the Sermon on the Mount because Jesus is being shown primarily as teacher and only then as Son of David and Servant of God healer. But cf. below, n. 102. (2) The Marcan material is perhaps being enriched by new material in Matt. 8–9 for three reasons: (a) to tighten up the composition, and bring together related miracle stories and material interpreted in similar terms; (b) the fulfilment of the Isa. 61:1 quotation in Matt. 11:5f is to be demonstrated in the biography of Jesus; (c) the authority given to the disciples at 10:1,8 is to be based on the authority of Jesus.

18 That tells against the thesis of Walker (1967) 77, that Mark 13:9–13 has been moved from its context in the eschatological discourse into the mission discourse because persecution by Israel "related to the sending (of the disciples) to Israel during Jesus' lifetime". Matthew's insertion in v. 18 of "and the Gentiles" shows that he does not intend to limit the applicability of the text to the lifetime of Jesus. Walker's presupposition that the mission to Israel and the mission to the Gentiles were strictly separate turns out to be read into the text. Despite Walker, the persecution by Israel belongs to the situation of the disciples in the end-time, as is shown by the retention of Mark 13:13 by Matthew. More probable reasons for Matthew's moving Mark 13:9–13 are the following: (1) The paragraph fits the theme of this chapter, "mission". (2) The relocation gives Matthew a chance to treat the theme of Christian enthusiasts and their false teaching, which he has already introduced at 7:15ff, under its eschatological aspect at 24:9ff. The passage 24:9–14 is certainly not a mere "resumé" (Klostermann [1927²] 193), or "repetition" (Filson [1960] 253), or "summary" (Stendahl [1962] 793), of Matt. 10:17ff. It is far too long to be that. Rather it is of fundamental significance for the evangelist.

19 Cf. E. Schweizer (1961) 59 on 10:32, 42.

20 On this see below, pp. 105ff.

21 Strecker's (1962) interpretation of *eis onoma mathētou* ("into name of a disciple") as "on appeal to the name" of a member of the twelve (191f) seems strained. Linguistically one would then expect *en onomati* ("in a name") instead of *eis onoma* ("into a name"). The parallel in v. 42 also supports taking *mikroi* ("little ones") and *mathētai* as synonymous. The difference in wording is because *eis onoma mikrou* ("into name of a little one") would have been difficult. *Mikroi*, however, is plainly to be related to the community, as is clear from 18:6, 10, 14.

22 B. Rigaux, *Témoignage de l'évangile de Matthieu* (1967) 205f, rightly speaks of a "glissement" (oscillation) in the discipleship discourse between history and "type". Walker (1967) 118 also speaks of the double function of the mission discourse which at the same time gives an "abiding word for mission and discipleship". But Walker tells us little about the relation of these two functions or the hermeneutical function of Matthew's kerygmatic sketch of history.

23 Cf. 28.20. That of course clashes with the statements which emphasize the mission of Jesus to Israel alone, and leads to a peculiar mixing of "his-

torical" statements and those which are valid for the present day. In the light of Matthew's understanding of miracle I would include 10:1, 7f among the latter. 10:9–15 is more difficult to interpret. But I see no compelling reason why this verse should not have contained a mission instruction which was still obligatory for Matthew. Even chap. 23 is in a sense a discourse still valid for the present, even though it verbalizes the judgement which is passed on Israel, by the sending of the earthly Jesus (and which is again and again made present by the Christian mission to the Jews! Cf. 23:34—24:2!). However, I cannot agree with Walker (1967) 68, that the discourse against the Pharisees is only "literary material which has lost its original life-setting ... within a ... controversy with 'Judaism', and in place of that receives a function in the written history of the gospel". The connections between 23:5,11f and 6:1ff, 18:4, 20:26f, for example, are too clear, and the agreement between the direction of vv. 8–10 and the 'most central concern of the Matthean theology is far too striking for vv. 2–11 to be understood in any other way than as addressed to the Matthean community. That then makes the scribes and Pharisees addressed in vv. 13ff into a negative contrasting picture to what Matthew has said positively in vv. 2–11. So it is not correct that chap. 23 is for Matthew only literary material. Certainly it has lost its original life-setting in polemic, but it has found a new life-setting as addressed to the community. Only so is the redactional introduction in 23:1 (Jesus speaks to the disciples too) intelligible. On this, see below.

24 See also F. Hahn (1965) 124f.

25 The difficulty with any theory of a consistently carried out salvation history periodizing in Matthew becomes again very clear if we ask when the replacement of Israel by the Church, i.e. by the Gentiles, is thought of as completed. In Jesus' death and resurrection? Matt. 28:11–20 would support that, but at least within Walker's scheme the mission to the Jews which also takes place after the death of Jesus and is clearly presupposed by Matthew, tells against it. Or in the destruction of Jerusalem in A.D. 70? This is emphasized by Walker (1967) throughout. Cf. especially 115.

26 Cf. the material in W. C. Allen, (1912) xxxiiif, and in Strecker (1962) 193f.

27 Strecker (1962) 194; cf. Schulz (1967) 218.

28 The alteration in Matt. 20:20f is presumably redactional and does not derive from an alternative tradition. The insertion of *proskuneō* ("I worship") supports this assumption. On the *basileia* ("kingdom") of Jesus, cf. 13:36ff, 16:28.

29 The disciples' *thambeisthai* ("to wonder") is missing in Matthew. It is difficult to unravel the composition of Mark 10:23–5. Both Luke and Matthew have smoothed it out by the obvious expedient of omitting Mark 10:24.

30 The disciples' fear and the crowd's astonishment are lacking, as they are however also in the Lucan parallel. Mark 10:32 belongs to the Marcan redaction which as is well known is treated quite freely by the authors of the larger Gospels. Cf. J. Schreiber, "Die Christologie des Markusevangeliums", *ZTK* 58 (1961) 154f. One reason for omitting Mark 10:32 may also have been that in Matthew's redaction fear is consistently understood as the expression of human unbelief and little faith, not as the expression of the disciples' failure to understand, as it is at Mark 9:32; 10:32; 16:8.

31 Here too Matthew like Luke has tightened up his composition of a complicated Marcan pericope. There is probably no intention of improving the disciples' image. On the contrary, since Mark 10:15 is inserted in the Matthean pericope and is formulated in the second person plural, the disciples themselves are challenged to conversion, otherwise they will not enter the kingdom of heaven (v. 3). That is quite strong, but corresponds to Matthew's conception of the community as a *corpus mixtum* (mixed body). The concept of disciple is thus to be understood here as a "type", not in a historicizing way.

32 It is true that in contrast to Mark, Jesus' blame is missing here. But the indignation which occasions it is found in v. 8. And in Matthew, unlike Mark, it is expressly the disciples who are indignant. If anything their image is worse here.

33 Redactional: 4:25; 8:1; 14:13; 19:2; 20:29. Contrary to Strecker (1962) 193 n. 10.

34 One cannot say that the image of the disciples is improved by the parallel formulation in Matthew, "... on the third day will he be raised; and they were greatly distressed." The great grief of the disciples follows directly after the prediction of the resurrection.

35 The argument of Strecker (1962) 193 n. 15, that on the basis of 24:3; 26:8 the disciples are the "only people who accompany Jesus" in the passion is curious. The anointing at Bethany is admittedly not yet the passion; in Mark too the disciples are self-evidently present up to the arrest, as in Matthew.

36 Cf. the material in Barth (1963) 119. It can be shown in some passages that the redactional blackening of Peter's character serves his function as a "type". Cf. Strecker (1962) 198ff.

37 So too Strecker (1962) 194.

38 Barth (1963) 106ff.

39 Barth (1963) 107f.

40 Matt. 9:37ff to 11:1 (in Luke spoken to the seventy); 13:10–23 (Mark is expanded); 13:36–52; 15:12ff (Mark expanded) 16:5ff (Mark); 16:33ff, cf. 20f (Mark expanded); 16:24ff; 17:10ff (Mark); 17:19ff (Mark expanded); 18; 19:23—20:19, cf. 20:17 (Mark expanded); 21:21ff (Mark); 24:1f, 3ff.

41 Cf. the contrast between Pharisees and disciples, Matt. 15:14,15.

42 Strecker (1962) 228ff.

43 The parables (chap. 13 *passim*); that Jesus used pictorial speech (16:12) or that he spoke about John the Baptist (17:13).

44 On Matthew's conception of faith see below under section II.

45 Barth (1963) 113.

46 Contrary to Barth, 113.

47 Substantially, because Matthew's conception of faith is not finally systematized; cf. below, section II.

48 Contrary to J. Dupont, *Les Béatitudes. Le problème littéraire. Le message doctrinal* (1954) 30f.

49 On the analysis of the text cf. Trilling (1959) 15f. Mark 3. 31–5 is tightened up by Matthew. In v. 49 Jesus now stretches out his hand over the disciples

and designates them as his brothers, sisters and mother because they do God's will. Is that stretching out of his hand to be understood symbolically as an indication of the authority of Jesus which protects the community?

50 Cf. above, n. 36.

51 H. J. Held (1963) 165ff.

52 Held, 187.

53 In the history of the tradition the eucharistic experience of the community presumably played, even in the early period, a big part in the formation and handing on of the feeding stories. Nevertheless the narrative of the healing is fully historicized as early as the pre-Marcan tradition, as is shown by its inclusion in the old pre-Marcan narrative sequence, feeding—crossing the lake —controversy dialogues—miracle; (on this cf. E. Schweizer, *The Good News According to Mark* (1970) 136–7. Mark has not destroyed this historicizing by his kerygmatic outline; the kerygma presupposes the history. In Matthew the experience which contributed to the original shaping of the pericope is even clearer, without the pericope losing its character of reporting history.

54 Matt. 15:36 shows that despite his abbreviating the story the redactor did not want to omit the fish. He has put them in here out of the omitted verse Mark 8:7. Matt. 14:19 also shows that the fish are important to the redactor. For the sake of mentioning them he is prepared to imply the awkward phrase "breaking fish".

55 In contrast to Mark, Matthew has both times given the number more precisely and probably heightened the miraculous character of the story. That shows that he did not understand the pericope simply as a presentation of the experiences of the community, but also as a miracle which really happened in the life of Jesus.

56 G. Bornkamm (1963) 52ff.

57 Illustrations of *seismos* ("storm"), which Bornkamm considers designates apocalyptic horrors, might be present at 5:11f; 23:32ff. The connection between persecution and eschaton is found in 10:22; 24:9. Cf. also how 24:7 (*seismos* = earthquake) occurs near to persecution and execution for the sake of faith in 24:9.

58 Bornkamm, 54.

59 Held (1963) 248; Schweizer (1970) 219f.

60 Cf. Strecker (1962) 118ff, Hummel (1963) 116ff, C. Burger, *Jesus als Davidssohn* (1970) 72ff.

61 Cf. Held (1963) 178ff, 193ff.

62 Cf. Bonnard (1970²) 259, 261.

63 We find both types of understanding of faith in pre-Pauline Christianity too. Cf. miracle faith in 1 Cor. 13:2, and for the other meaning the "general" understanding of faith found in the pre-Pauline connection of faith and the so-called faith formula or in the technical term *apistos* ("unbelieving") already in use (1 Cor. 6:6; 7:12ff; 10:27; 14:22ff; etc.).

64 At 21:32 the preceding parable of the Two Sons, and the interpretative phrase "he came ... in a way of righteousness", seem to imply that faith

123

means something like accepting the demand for righteousness which John (and Jesus) present. In the miracle stories where most of the occurrences of the stem *pisteu-* ("believe") are found, it means trusting in the unlimited power of Jesus. The two different nuances have different roots in the history of the tradition prior to Matthew. They cannot be completely harmonized.

The verb *akoloutheō* ("I follow") in the Matthean redaction also has similarly two layers which again cannot finally be conceptually harmonized. From the perspective of 11:28ff (where Jesus' yoke means law), and 19:16ff, the essence of discipleship is "obedience to the law" as interpreted by Jesus. (Barth [1963] 102 n. 1). At Matt. 8:18ff discipleship means rather "standing under the protection of the Lord". These two accents correspond to those notices in Matthew's conception of faith. The frequent connection of *akolouthein* ("to follow") with miracle stories is a striking feature of the Matthean redaction (4:25 [tradition]; 8:1; 8:10 [tradition]; 8:23; 9:27; 12:15; 14:13; 19:2; 20:29; 20:34 [tradition]). What is striking here is firstly that frequently it is the crowds who follow Jesus, and secondly that in the redactional passages without exception the experience of the miracle follows only after the mention of discipleship. Does Matthew mean that discipleship to Jesus leads to the experience of his power to do miracles? Is this statement intended for his own day? At least 8:23 is perhaps to be understood in this way.

65 Cf. on that Held (1963) 270ff.

66 Cf. also Schweizer (1970) 216ff.

67 Cf. 10:1 with 9:35.

68 Schweizer (1970) 220.

69 Strecker (1962) 201ff.

70 Against Schweizer (1961) 59, Matthew would not say that the whole community is the successor of Peter. For Matthew there was probably never a special period in which Peter had a special authority which the whole community then inherited. That would mean that the other disciples did not possess this authority during Peter's lifetime, which 18:18 makes impossible. If the Matthean community understands itself as the group of Jesus' disciples, then Peter, in the eyes of the evangelist, exercises no other authority than what was given to the disciple as such.

71 Cf. G. Klein, *Die Zwölf Apostel. Ursprung und Gehalt einer Idee* (1961) 202ff. But against Klein, cf. also Mark 6:7 where the idea of the twelve apostles is probably also presupposed in the verb *apostellō* ("I send"), and also Rev. 21:14 where again the idea of the twelve apostles as founders and representatives of the new people of God, the Church, is probably present.

72 Cf. the alteration of Mark 6:7 at Matt. 10:1 and the omission of Mark 6:30.

73 The baptismal command which at once follows is probably traditional, as Strecker (1962) 209 has rightly shown. Matthew's placing the tradition's baptismal command before the command which is to him far more important, to teach the nations to keep all that Jesus has commanded the disciples, is probably not conditioned by any strong emphasis on baptism in Matthew. The reason for it is rather that baptism stands at the beginning of Christian existence, whereas teaching and keeping the commands determine the whole

of a Christian's life following his baptism. Besides, v. 20b connects much better with v. 20 than with 19b.

74 The aorist *eneteilamēn* ("I commanded") there emphasizes that it is a matter of the commands of the earthly Jesus. Cf. G. Bornkamm (1964) 223f.

75 Cf. above, section I.

76 Strecker (1962) 192f. He points out that *mathēteuein* ("to disciple") is never said of a member of the twelve. Since there are only three occurrences of the word, however, that might be coincidence. Strecker himself establishes that *mathēteuein* and *mathētēs* agree in content. Against him G. Baumbach (1967) 891 formulates the matter correctly: *Mathēteuō* alludes not to some particular missionary practice of the community but to its own life. Hahn (1965) 121 n. 5 understands *mathēteuō* in a similar way, as does Schweizer (1970) 218.

77 Cf. O. Michel, "Diese Kleinen – eine Jüngerbezeichnung", *Theologische Studien und Kritiken*, 108 (1937/8) 401ff.

78 Cf. above n. 21, and on Matthew's redaction also Barth (1963) 121ff.

79 Similarly Bornkamm (1964) 221; Barth (1963) 111; Hummel (1963) 154; Bonnard (1970²) 416.

80 Cf. above, n. 21.

81 Contrary to J. Jeremias, *The Parables of Jesus* (ET 1963) 40; and ditto, art. *Kleis* ("key") in *TDNT* III, 752; G. D. Kilpatrick (1946) 127; R. Schnackenburg, *The Church in the New Testament* (ET 1965) 69ff; Trilling (1959) 100 (admittedly with reservations); Rigaux (n. 22) 210.

82 Against Strecker (1966) in this volume pp. 77ff. Strecker says correctly that the Church in Matthew is "representative of the ethical demand in history". That is right, in that the disciples have learnt from being with the historical Jesus and represent his interpretation of the law in their own day. But that has nothing to do with institutionalizing. Strecker is thinking here too much in Lucan categories. He himself describes Matt. 18:15ff correctly as eschatologically qualified penitential practice. But as E. Käsemann has taught us, eschatologically instituted church law is law instituted by the Spirit, not by an institution. That the tradition behind Matthew is marked by prophecy, as 10:40ff; 23:34 seem to show, tells in my opinion not for but against institutionalization.

83 So Lohmeyer–W. Schmauch (1958²) 335,341; Bonnard (1970) 333. Bornkamm, "End-expectation and Church in Matthew" (1963) 43; Hummel (1963) 31f; G. Kretschmar, "Ein Beitrag zur Frage nach dem Ursprung frühchristlicher Askese", *ZTK*, 61 (1964) 60. Haenchen (1951) 51f, 59; Trilling (1959) 94f. Cf. 13f, 70ff; and Hare (1967) 104f have rejected this hypothesis, in my view rightly, pointing out that most of the passages which support it belong to the tradition, or more exactly to a particular layer of tradition standing behind the Gospel.

84 This hypothesis is now supported by Schweizer (1970) 221ff, 229, taking up Kretzschmar (n. 83), 61 and Baumbach (n. 76) 890.

85 Held (1963) 262f rightly points to the *Kyrios* (Lord) title, the worship, the way human traits recede in Matthew's picture of Jesus, and the verbs *sōzō* ("I save") and *eleeō* ("I have mercy").

86 Cf. above, section I.

87 Cf. Matt. 4:23; 9:35; 10:7f; 19:2, and in addition 14:14 in comparison with Mark 6:34; also the way chaps. 5–7 and 8–9 are placed alongside each other, and 21:13f.

88 It is then of course correspondingly tragic for such a theology when miracles are absent, as was supposedly the case at Matt. 17.19ff.

89 Cf. Barth (1963) 159ff; Bornkamm (1964) 216; Schweizer (1970) 216ff, 225ff.

90 After all this I cannot help being rather doubtful about the occasionally argued view that Matthew is a Catholic Gospel within the NT. In my opinion the theologically closest relations to Matthew are the Free Churches such as the subsidiary movements of the Reformation and their tendency towards a loyal fulfilling of Jesus' law, and simultaneous emphasis upon the presence of the Lord's power in the community. A history of the interpretation of Matthew in the Free Churches, or a history of the Free Churches as a history of the interpretation of Matthew would be a worthwhile and much needed task.

91 Bornkamm (1964) 203ff; A. Vögtle (1964) 266ff.

92 Cf. Bornkamm, ibid., A. Vögtle, 279ff.

93 O. Michel (1950/1) 16ff (in this volume pp. 30ff); Barth (1963) 132.

94 Bornkamm (1964) 216.

95 It is the same idea, contrary to the view of Trilling (1959) 27f which I would like to interpret at 18:20 as the "static presence" of Jesus (comparable to Jahweh's name dwelling in the Temple), in contrast to his "dynamic presence" at 28:20 (comparable to Jahweh's presence in history). But the linguistic indications are probably too weak to support this thesis.

96 Contrary to Strecker (1962) 209 I am of the opinion that a pre-Matthean *formulation* cannot be demonstrated in 28:20b. But that the *idea* is pre-Matthean is plain from 18:20.

97 Vögtle (1964) 281ff. Cf. also Matt. 11:27.

98 Cf. however John 14:26: "And he will bring to your remembrance all that (*panta ha* all that ...) I have said to you." It is striking throughout how the corresponding motifs in Matt. 28:18–20 pile up in John 14:14–26. The common background of the two texts is clear, even if it is scarcely possible to re-construct an underlying tradition common to them. Cf. also Matt. 18:19 with John 14:14.

99 On the interpretation, see Schweizer (1970) 214f.

100 Baumbach (n. 76) 891. Cf. also Bornkamm (1971) 223ff; Strecker (1962) 212.

101 4:13 (probably not an early tradition!); 4:23; 21:11, etc. Cf. also Bonnard (1970[2]) 417.

102 In Matt. 28:18–20, however, the indicative (v. 18b and 20b) seems to frame the imperative (v. 19 and 20a). Did Matthew thus at least within the Christology intend a clear distribution of weight so that the indicative preceded the imperative? Or is he here bound by an earlier tradition (cf. Strecker [1962] 210)? Or did this tradition correspond to his own intention? Of course in his debate with the hellenistic charismatics Matthew stresses above

all Jesus' teaching, i.e. his interpretation of the law. Of course he places chaps. 5–7 before 8–9. And a certain tendency to make the parable material serve a moral purpose is unmistakable. But on the other hand it seems to me to be no coincidence that even before the Sermon on the Mount there is the summary of healings at 4:23–5, and that is not sufficiently considered.

103   Cf. Strecker (1962) 219 n.1.: *klētoi* ("called") and *eklektoi* ("chosen") are differentiated in Matt. 20:16 (alternative reading) and 22:14, the saying that many are called, few chosen. 22:14 shows clearly how these concepts which are normally used synonymously can be made to serve Matthew's conception of the Church as a mixed body. There are many *klētoi* – but then the word, which does not occur elsewhere in Matthew or the other Gospels, loses its eschatological dimension. There are few *eklektoi*, but then this word, which otherwise in Matthew is found only in the eschatological context of chap. 24, loses its reference to present historical reality.

104   Matthew's clear terminological distinction between *laos* ("people") and *ethnos* ("nation") is consistently carried through. Cf. 21:43. It is particularly striking how often in Matthew *laos* (mostly linked with the elders or high priests) occurs in the passion narrative to show the unity of the people with its leaders, and so the guilt of the whole people over the passion of Jesus. Cf. also Hummel (1963) 145f.

105   In 18:17 the word is clearly defined by the context. It refers to the assembly of an individual community. What in 16:18 the word meant for the evangelist can no longer be said with any certainty. Bornkamm (1964) 219ff, points to the connections between *ekklēsia* and hellenistic Jewish Christianity which might be significant for determining Matthew's position.

106   Cf. above, especially n. 53.

107   The expression "historicizing" here does of course invite misunderstanding. The community can only depict its own experiences as miracles of Jesus because it thereby depicts not a past thing which as past is isolated. It can only understand words spoken to it by the prophet as words of Jesus because Jesus is not seen as simply a figure who lived in the past. So it can only "historicize" because it does not see Jesus as the "historical Jesus" in the modern sense of the word.

108   Matt. 10:24f and parallels do not allow us to affirm with any certainty an ecclesiological background for Q. There is certainly no ecclesiological reference in the present text of Matthew on account of its context in the mission discourse, but Luke uses the saying at 6.40 in a *parabolē* ("parable") context, i.e. as a pure aphorism. In Luke 14:26, 27 I do not dare decide whether *mathētēs* is original against Matthew's *axios* ("worthy").

109   Thus certainly at Matt. 10:38 and parallel. Cf. D. Lührmann, *Die Redaktion der Logienquelle* (Neukirchen 1969), and already A. Harnack, *The Sayings of Jesus* (1907, ET 1908) 153.

110   Bultmann (ET 1963) 47f who speaks, however, of the Palestinian primitive community (What is that?).

111   Cf. Bultmann (1963) 48f. H. W. Kuhn's qualification thesis, now published as *Ältere Sammlungen im Markusevangelium* (Neukirchen 1971) was not available to me.

112 Of course individual elements of the controversy dialogues could go back to the Aramaic-speaking communities or to Jesus, especially the sayings, but in in my view not the controversy dialogues as such. Evidence for this includes the hellenistic coloured proverb in Mark 2:17a, and Mark 2:21f, which fairly certainly contains a Greek linguistic feature that cannot be expressed literally in a semitic language (cf. K. Beyer, *Semitische Syntax im Neuen Testament* 1 [Göttingen 1968²] 100 and 303), and Mark 2:25f where, however, the LXX is probably presupposed.

113 Cf. above, n. 53.

114 Cf. above, p. 108f.

115 H. Conzelmann, *Die Apostelgeschichte* (Tübingen 1963) on Acts 6:1.

116 H. W. Kuhn, "Der irdische Jesus bei Paulus als traditions geschichtliches und theologisches Problem", *ZTK* 67 (1971) especially 310.

117 K. H. Rengstorf's article on *manthanō* ("I learn") etc., *TWNT* IV, 438; A. Schulz (n. 12) 115ff.

118 cf. Rengstorf, ibid., 421; H. D. Betz, *Lukian von Samosata und das Neue Testament* (Berlin 1961) 108ff, esp. 109.

119 Evidence in Rengstorf (n. 117) 436f.

120 It need not be considered here whether this rite was nothing other than Christian baptism (so H. von Campenhausen, "Zur Auslegung von Joh. 13:6–10", in *Aus der Frühzeit des Christentums* [Tübingen 1963] 109ff), or some special rite.

121 Cf. Bornkamm (1964) 225.

122 This seems to me to be shown for Matthew above all by 3:15 and *Smyrn.* 1:1, despite the attempt of J. Smit Sibinga, "Ignatius and Matthew", *NovT* 8 (1966) 263ff, to argue that Ignatius is dependent on a pre-Matthean source, but *Smyrn.* 1:1 is dependent on the Matthean redaction. Admittedly H. Köster, *Synoptische Überlieferung bei den apostolischen Vätern* (Berlin 1957) 59, assumes that the contact with the Matthean redaction occurs within a kerygmatic formula. But this turns out to be linguistically heavily mixed up with Ignatius' own explanatory comment. So the supposition of literary dependence still seems to me more probable. For John and Ignatius, the strong contact in terminology and background is clear enough; literary relationships are possible. Cf. W. G. Kümmel, *Introduction to the NT* (ET Nashville and London 1975) 246.

123 Besides this there is also some sparse gnostic evidence. Cf. for example *Gos. Philip* 119;14; 129:1–3; or *Gos. Thomas,* logion 21. But generally *mathētēs* is used of the disciples of the historical Jesus in the Christian gnostic writings too.

124 Cf. for example *Magn.* 10:1; Polycarp 2:1. For *mathēteuō, Eph.* 10:1.

125 Neither, so far as I know, does the substantive occur without closer definition in Justin. *Mathētēs* is mostly used for disciples of the historical Jesus. It is related to the present at *Trypho* 35:2, though with the addition *didaskalias* ("of teaching"). The verb *mathēteuō* is more frequent: *Trypho* 39:2,5; *First Apology* 15:6; *Second Apology* 3(4):3.

8

Matthew's Church[*][1]

EDUARD SCHWEIZER

I *Syria the Home of the Evangelist*

A community in which the sabbath is still strictly kept or at least was kept for a long time, where the question of the law plays such an important role, and in which the Pharisees constitute the main discussion partners, even though the group of Jesus' disciples has long since separated from "their" (i.e. the Jewish) synagogues,[2] must be living in an area in which Judaism is dominant. That suggests at once Palestine or neighbouring Syria. Egypt[3] or even Babylon are not serious contenders, on the grounds that the existence of a largish Christian group alongside a Pharisaic scribal group is doubtful there. More important, Matthew knows Mark and the tradition which is also available to Luke (Q), so the evangelist is unlikely to come from a quite different part of the world from those. On the other hand, Jerusalem or the surrounding area is not likely either, even though the Pharisaic school of scribes from Jamnia is concentrated there.[4] The Greek language is admittedly possible in Palestine, but hardly to be expected, especially not quotations from the Greek Bible which differ from the original text.[5] A more decisive consideration is that non-Jews are evidently the majority in this community (21:43 etc.), and that even the fall of the holy city plays no great role, apart from the echo in 22:7.[6] What seems to me most important is the central role played by Peter, according to 16:16–19. That points to Syria![7] Around A.D. 44 Peter had to leave Jerusalem, as Acts 12 reports. From then on James plays the leading role in Jerusalem.[8] Both these conclusions are supported by Gal. 2:11f, according to which James in Jerusalem lays down through his emissaries instructions for Peter in Antioch. How the dispute with Paul finished is interestingly, and in contrast to Gal. 2:1ff, not told at Gal. 2:11ff. At any rate after this

[*] First published in *Matthäus und seine Gemeinde* by E. Schweizer (1974) 138–70. Translated by Robert Morgan.

129

incident Paul seems no longer to have used Antioch as a base for his mission.[9] This leads one to suppose that it was strongly under Petrine influence, whereas James had more power in Jerusalem and Paul in Asia Minor and the Greek communities. In contrast to Peter, however, James the brother of the Lord plays no role at all in Matthew.[10] Syria, or perhaps the neighbouring areas of Galilee, therefore remains the most probable supposition as the evangelist's home. What do we learn about the church in which he lives?

II *The Prophets*

1   The evangelist clearly sees the end of the Sermon on the Mount as giving a warning for the present against *false prophets* who present themselves with seemingly authoritative speech and acts of power.[11] It is of course at once clear that it is not their charismatic activity as such, nor the dogmatic content of their teaching which is repudiated, but their "lawlessness", which for Matthew means their behaviour which no longer consists in love.[12] Now the problem of false prophets played an extraordinarily large role in the whole of early Christianity. A solution was sought along very different routes. They were most frequently put down as in our passage by an examination of their overall ethical behaviour. (*Did.* 11:7–12 with very detailed instructions; *Hermas*, *Mandate* 11:7–16). Paul makes it more precise by asking whether they are really confessing Jesus as their Lord and so are of use to the community as a whole (1 Cor. 12:1–3, 7). Later on the criterion is the orthodoxy of their confession that Jesus has come in the flesh (1 John 4:2) or their position in the wider community (*Hermas*, *Mandate* 11:7–16). At the end of the second and the beginning of the third century their agreement with the apostle (*3 Cor.* 1:2–5; 3:34–8)[13] or the fulfilment of their prophecies (*Pseudo-Clementine Homilies* 2:6–11) was what counted. So right up into the third century this problem never quite died out. This shows that such prophetism remained a living force in the Church.

2   It is clear that Matthew by no means polemicizes against prophetic proclamation, exorcisms and acts of power, even though according to 7:22 the false prophets appeal to these. On the contrary. The fact that their emergence is so emphatically described as a sneaking in, as wolves in sheep's clothing, shows how like the other sheep's their actions are. There must therefore be proper prophets who behave in similar ways, the difference being of course that these proclaim and perform love for one's neighbour which is no longer

130

taught and practised by the false prophets. That the Matthean church indeed contained *prophets*[14] is confirmed by 23:34 and 10:41.[15] The first passage goes back to a Q saying found in a similar form at Luke 11:49.[16] Luke has undoubtedly kept the original formulation in saying that the wisdom of God is speaking and announces the sending of her messengers as an event still to come. It is a kind of damnation oracle in which before the beginning of history the wisdom of God announces her plan, but also the rejection of all her messengers by mankind. Mention of the "apostles" there alongside the "prophets" does of course probably go back to Luke himself.[17] Matthew's main alteration, however, as he changes the future tense into the present, is to reshape the sentence into a saying of Jesus.[18] So now Jesus as the personified wisdom of God explains to his contemporaries, "I am sending to you prophets and wise men and scribes", and prophesies at the same time their persecution. So alongside wise men and scribes (to be discussed below, III) prophets are a part of Matthew's community. They are to be thought of as itinerant prophets, as is clear from the second passage.

10:41 is a Matthean insertion between the promise to anyone who accepts the messengers of Jesus that he receives Jesus himself – indeed God who sent Jesus – and the other promise of reward for anyone who gives these messengers as little as a cup of cold water.[19] So both passages speak of Jesus sending prophets (along with other groups) to minister in his community. At 10:41 they appear as itinerant prophets who are to be refreshed. One may suppose that they are thought of as going through the countryside as Jesus did, understanding discipleship in this literal way, giving up house and possessions and dedicating themselves to his service.

3   But it is also apparent that these prophets *proclaim and act as charismatics*. The whole construction of chaps 5–11, which do not correspond with the Marcan outline, proves how important it is for the evangelist to show that Jesus' authority is continued in the preaching and mighty deeds of his disciples. Not only healings of sick persons and exorcisms, but even raising the dead are expressly promised to his disciples at 10:8, as they are reported of Jesus at 9:18–26. All these charismatic deeds should continue in the community as "deeds of Christ" and serve to answer all questions of doubt.[20]

4   There are further passages which point in the same direction. On the one hand with Jesus himself the deeds of power are strongly

emphasized, even though it is usually accepted that Matthew makes the teaching of Jesus central. But at 19:2 he can even put Jesus' "healing" in place of Mark 10:1 "teaching" (cf. Matt. 14:14). In what is a redactional note of the evangelist towards the end of the important composition of chaps. 5–11, it is Jesus' acts of power which most certainly ought to have led to repentance, and which therefore place the cities which repudiate Jesus under a worse judgement than what is coming to Tyre, Sidon and Sodom (11:20).[21] On the other hand it is particularly where charismatic authority is at issue that the disciples are linked closely with Jesus himself. That is true of the authority to forgive sins. When 9:8 speaks of authority given to "men" (instead of "the Son of Man", as at v. 6, formulated according to Mark 2:10), it is certain that Matthew has the community in view, where forgiveness of sins is still practised. The same goes for the authority over demons. At 10:24f the disciples are expressly equated with their master who has driven out demons and therefore caused Beelzebul to be rebuked, as the interpretation added by Matthew says. It is true finally for the authority to heal generally. The story of the epileptic boy is shortened so that everything is focused on the concluding saying that faith moves mountains, even if it is no larger than a mustard seed. Above all the phrase peculiar to Matthew, "nothing will be impossible for you" is taken up from the story itself; "it was impossible for them" (v. 16) is found also in Luke 9:40. What the disciples could then not yet achieve, namely the healing of the sick person, will now be possible for them if they act in faith in what Jesus has promised them. The time before Easter and the time after are indeed distinguished, but in such a way that even after Easter recourse must be had to Jesus' own earthly activity.

5   A further observation is less certain.[22] It is well known that right through the Gospel there are OT quotations which are introduced by a formula emphasizing fulfilment – the so-called "formula quotations".[23] Even if, as seems quite likely,[24] some of these quotations were already attached to the tradition prior to Matthew, that is hardly true of them all, and does not explain their spread throughout the Gospel. It is especially clear that at the centre of the whole book four quotations are added to summary descriptions of Jesus' activity and present him as the prophetic revealer of God's mysteries (13:13–16,[25] and 13:35) and charismatic healer (8:17 and 12:17–21). So in a similar way to the construction of chaps. 5–9, Jesus is here presented as the authoritative proclaimer and as a performer of

miracles. Most striking of all are the four passages of Scripture in chap. 2, followed by a fifth at 4:14–16.[26] It is of course not certain what these really aim to stress. But it is at once apparent that each quotation contains a place name. Above all 2:15 ("out of Egypt have I called my son") proves that what is being backed up is not the calling back of the son, which is not in fact related until vv. 19–21, but the geographical information "Egypt". So the five OT statements describe the places where Jesus spent some time, and depict his itinerary from Bethlehem through Rama to Egypt and from there back to Nazareth, and finally his moving residence to Capernaum. The fact that these are biblical statements does of course imply that this whole journey is a part of God's plan and stands under his protection. So: is the restless, itinerant life under God's direction meant to be depicted from the very beginning as a consoling and strengthening example for all itinerant prophets? The remaining three passages prove that the disciples' obedience is also a factor governing the choice of formula quotations. The last one (27:9f) underlines the depiction of the remorse and horrible judgement which threatens the unfaithful disciple. 1:22f and 21:5 by contrast stress conversely the genuine disciple's obedience.[27] In literal fulfilment of Scripture Joseph abstains from sexual relations so that Mary not only conceives but also gives birth as a virgin. So "he woke from sleep and did what the angel of the Lord commanded him." In an equally literal fulfilment of Scripture Jesus' disciples bring two animals and Jesus sits "upon them"[28] so that the saying in the prophet about ass and colt is observed exactly. So "they went away and did as Jesus had directed them."

With all due care one may therefore say that the OT passages which are especially emphasized present Jesus as a charismatic prophet and healer, whose life was right from the start homeless and insecure, without fixed residence and protection, but completely determined by God's leading, and so moving towards the goal willed by God. It is thus a model for the disciple whose obedience in following Jesus is understood quite literally.

III *The Scribes*

1   Together with prophets at 23:34 Matthew mentions *wise men and scribes*. Although since Ecclus. 19:20 and 21:11 wise men can in fact only be thought of as scribes,[29] there seems to be no parallel for putting the two designations together. The saying perhaps comes in this form from the tradition since the insertion of "apostle" in Luke

11:49 is probably redactional.[30] However 13:52 is to be understood, it clearly speaks of a scribe who has become a disciple in view of the Kingdom of heaven,[31] and the scribe at 8:19 at least wants to become a disciple of Jesus, if he is not one already.[32] Above all there is the saying about "binding and loosing" which is promised to Peter at 16:19 and to all the members of the community at 18:18.[33] It concerns the task of the scribe which is to ascertain, in a way that will remain valid at God's judgement, what the law or the current interpretation of the law considers is binding and what is no longer binding. So God's will, which Jesus interpreted in his proclamation and by his behaviour, must be interpreted afresh again and again with reference to the questions raised by new situations. We may distinguish here between the teaching authority which is given to Peter in a fundamental way and the disciplinary authority by which the community carries out the teaching at the practical level in individual cases.[34] But we should notice that Matthew designates both with exactly the same expressions. In fact they cannot be separated, or only insofar as the doctrinal formulation is always the basis for the action which dispenses or withholds forgiveness. It is therefore more common for a doctrinal decision once made to be applied at the practical level in a variety of concrete situations, than for the doctrinal statement to have to be formulated anew. But for Matthew both remain one and the same process even if it is to some degree possible to distinguish between its beginning and its end. That will have to be considered further in Section IV.

2   It is clear that this interpretation of the will of God is central for the Matthean community. This is shown by the linguistic usage of the expression "gospel". In two passages where Mark has the word Matthew omits it, leaving only a reference to Jesus or his name (16:25; 19:29). Twice, in the verses which frame the Sermon on the Mount, he adds "of the Kingdom" to "gospel", to connect it unambiguously with Jesus' proclamation of the Kingdom in this sermon (4:23; 9:35). Twice he formulates it more clearly, again in contrast to Mark, as "this gospel (of the kingdom)", referring in this way to the proclamation of Jesus that he had reported (24:14; 26:13). That can surely only mean that he wants to bind the post-Easter preaching, of which both these passages expressly speak, and of which the first two in effect do too, indissolubly to the preaching of the earthly Jesus. A "kerygma theology" in which the voice of the Spirit or the exalted Lord replaces that of Jesus of Nazareth is to Matthew highly suspect.[35] The ending to the whole Gospel corresponds to this.[36] The

exalted one is present as the earthly Jesus in the proclamation of his commands in the Church.

IV *Peter*

1 The *special position of Peter* must again be considered from this point of view.[37] He undoubtedly plays a special role in Matthew's church. It would otherwise be inexplicable why Matthew not only takes up the saying which blesses Peter but even places it at the centre of his Gospel. The promise that the whole Church is to be built on this foundation is so clearly theologically relevant that it is reasonable to ask whether Paul's saying that there is only one foundation which can be built upon, namely Christ (1 Cor. 3:11), is not polemic against this assertion. Peter is spoken of in that context,[38] and if Peter (as we supposed above) in fact came to the fore after a dispute in Antioch which did not turn out too well for Paul, then such a reference is not impossible. According to Matthew 16:19 he has authority to bind and loose. The church in which Matthew lives thus traces its knowledge about what Jesus commanded back to Peter. He not only communicated Jesus' new interpretation of the law to them; he also fitted it to the situations which arose after Easter. His authority is thus that of the apostolic proclamation seen as the basis of the Church's whole life. And the central interest of this proclamation is in Jesus' ethical instructions. But according to 18:18 the same authority is given to the whole community.[39] How are these two sides related?

2 It cannot be said that Peter is completely put in the foreground in this Gospel. Most striking is his absence in the angel's message which Mark 16:7 says is for "his disciples and Peter", whereas Matt. 28:7 has simply "his disciples". Again, at the discovery of the fig-tree miracle, Matt. 21:20 has "the disciples" in place of Peter (Mark 11:21).[40] His name is, however, probably inserted by Matthew at 15:15; 17:24–7; and 18:21.[41] All three cases are matters of halakhic instruction regulating ethical behaviour. It is admittedly plain in all these cases that Peter is speaking in the name of all the disciples. In 15:15 it is he who asks, but Jesus replies to the disciples in the second person plural. In the case of the temple tax and the practice of forgiveness the instruction again in effect applies to them all. And when Peter speaks at 19:27 he says, *"We* have left everything", and Jesus replies to them all. Even at Peter's confession where the special promise is directed to Peter alone, Jesus still turns again and again to them all (16: 20, 21, 24). At 26:35 it is again Peter who speaks, but

Matthew at once adds "and thus said all the disciples". In Gethsemane, Jesus speaks to Peter in the second person plural (26:40)
because by him he means in effect all disciples.

3   This confirms that Peter says and hears *in an exemplary way for
all disciples* what every disciple could say and hear.[42] It is probably
most strikingly clear, in that the first appearance to Peter (1 Cor.
15:5) does not appear at all in this Gospel where Peter is the
foundation of the whole Church. Even the faint echo of this in Mark
16:7 is removed. That stands in contrast to the special role which
Peter plays for the first time at Matt. 14:28f. This presents, again in
an exemplary way, what every disciple could experience: the courage
of faith which nevertheless at once turns to little faith when wind and
wave assail it, and which remains ultimately dependent on the
gracious help of its Lord.[43] So if there is a special place for Peter,
then at any rate this is not based on a special manifestation of the
Exalted One who – originally presumably from heaven – grants a
special commission. Rather it rests on the fact that Peter was a
witness of the earthly activity of Jesus, especially his ethical
instructions.

4   This corresponds to the *role of the twelve* in general. Like Mark,
Matthew also reports the call to discipleship which comes to Peter
and Andrew, the two sons of Zebedee, and the tax-collector.
Admittedly the tax-collector is no longer called Levi but is identified
with Matthew, one of the twelve (cf. 10:3). In addition, the call of the
twelve, evidently out of a large circle of followers (Mark 3:13–19) is
absent from Matthew, although he reports the list of names at the
beginning of the mission discourse (10:2–4). But this itself shows that
everything that is said and given to the twelve applies in principle to
all future disciples of Jesus. For the discourse passes silently over into
themes and statements which only apply to the post-Easter community.[44] That is of course why the discipleship stories are related,
because such discipleship continues to take place in the community.

5   The evidence is not easy to interpret. On the one hand the
twelve are emphasized almost to the exclusion of all others. There
seems to be no real discipleship outside this group. They are also
promised, in a saying of Jesus which is admittedly taken from the
tradition, that they will sit on twelve thrones in the coming kingdom
(19:28). On the other hand, everything that is said to them applies
in principle to every disciple of Jesus. It is again evident[45] that what

happened in the historical past of the time of Jesus is as important as it is to the evangelist because it is transparent: through it the period of the Church is disclosed. The special position of Peter and the twelve is that of the historical beginning to which, in Matthew's view, all succeeding generations of the Church are bound. True as it is that Jesus remains with his community even to the end of the age, this can nevertheless only be said when the earthly activity and proclamation of Jesus provide the norm. Peter and the twelve, as bearers of the tradition, constitute the connecting link for that. Even though the binding and loosing that happens in the community is the same that Peter exercises, nevertheless it cannot take place without recourse to his function in the tradition of laying the foundation. Since this applies in the first place to the tradition of doctrine, or is at any rate clearer and more marked there than in the disciplinary practice which follows from it, the promise in 16:19 shows more of that side and 18:18 more of the other side of the same event. Still, the model of Peter could also present and guarantee the freedom of the community in making its decisions.[46]

V *The Righteous*

In 10:41 righteous men appear alongside prophets as a special group of Jesus' followers. This combination is also characteristic of Judaism[47] and is found in Matthew as a description of OT figures (13:17; 23:29).[48] So it is impossible to distinguish sharply between righteous men and prophets. It is probably a somewhat wider concept, which includes prophets.[49] As a matter of fact Matthew elsewhere reckons on all Jesus' disciples being included among the righteous (13:43, 49; 25:37, 46). It seems that in the Judaism of Jesus' time the concept "righteous" was connected especially with the idea of obedience to the law, whereas works of love were rather designated as "pious".[50] The linguistic usage of Qumran where the community members designate themselves as righteous because they take fulfilling the commandments especially seriously fits this, and so does that of (*Ethiopic*) *Enoch* 81:7; 82:4, where it seems to designate a group that lives especially strictly according to the law.[51] In Dan.12:3 it is the wise who bring many to righteousness, namely to hold firm to God's law even in the midst of persecution – and this belongs to the same circle of ideas. The wise are those who know the Scripture. The second name of the Lord's brother, "James the just", handed down by Hegesippus could show that in Jewish Christian circles too a disciple who conspicuously strove to fulfil God's demands was so

137

named. The false prophets are characterized at Matt. 7:23 and 24:12 as those who have turned away from the law. The evangelist is no doubt thinking there of the law as interpreted by Jesus in the light of love of one's neighbour. It is thus possible that by the "righteous" Matthew is thinking of members of the community who by their conduct and doctrine exemplify life lived by God's commands. But that is uncertain.

VI *The Little Ones*

The most characteristic expression for the Matthean community, however, is "one of these little ones" used to describe the disciple. It is first found at 10:42 alongside the designation "prophets" and "righteous men" and is there evidently identical with the concept "disciple". It is not introduced by Matthew, as this passage makes clear; it comes from the tradition found also in Mark but which is pre-Marcan.[52] Matthew has taken it over and strongly emphasized it[53] in his "church order", as has been already shown above. One might wonder whether "the least of my brothers" in 25:40, 45 are not also disciples of Jesus, namely the itinerant missionaries who are either received or rejected by the nations of the world.[54] The fact that it is a judgement of the nations might count in favour of this idea.[55] And the oppressions listed here are substantially the same as those which according to 2 Cor. 11:23–7 are typical for the missionary apostle.[56] Above all, there is the formulation "one of these least" and the addition of "my brothers" in v. 40 which is comparable to the phrase used at 28:10. Finally there is also the fact that those who are condemned are not in the least aware of having ever met Jesus. So judgement is to take place on the grounds of people's attitude to the Christian missionaries to whom as is requested at 10:40–2 hospitality and care, perhaps even to the point of prison, has been shown – or else refused. This interpretation is not probable, at least not for the evangelist's own understanding. The superlative "these least" could go back to the underlying Aramaic and come from the same expression as the usual formula "these little ones". But Matthew is unlikely to have chosen a different phrase if he had meant the same as he means when elsewhere he uses the phrase "these little ones" so emphatically. He is most unlikely to have done so, since he was familiar with the superlative form of the same word[57] and could have used it if that is what he had wanted to say. There is also the difficulty that not even the righteous know that they have been confronted by Jesus himself in the form of his messengers. It is hard to believe that this comes from Matthew, who wrote 10:40.[58] Finally, the absence of the term "brother" in v. 45 suggests that really all of "these least" are intended, not only Christians or even Jesus' missionaries. It could perhaps be said that the one-sided emphasis on hospitality is not what we would expect from Matthew since in 10:14 he makes a redactional addition to say that what matters in people's reaction to the missionaries is accepting their word. Besides this, the limitation to Christians does not fit very well with love of one's enemies which he has earlier emphasized. So whatever 25:40, 45 may originally have meant, for Matthew himself[59] it is better to keep to the well-attested indubitable term for a disciple, "one of these little ones".

VII *The Question of the Ministry*

1   Matthew is in no doubt that the special position, historically speaking, of the twelve, particularly Peter, must be seen and preserved as the basis for the Church as such. But that does not necessarily mean that it has to be continued through a ministry. The fact that the authority given to Peter at 16:19 is in 18:18 promised to all members of the community suggests that the successor of Peter in this ministry is the community.[60] Much the same is true of everything that is said to the twelve in the mission discourse. What is true for them is true for all Jesus' messengers, in fact for all who have to expect hostility and persecution, and finally for everyone who confesses Jesus (10:32). The transparency of the past historical event for the later community enables the twelve, or from amongst them Peter, to say, do or suffer in a way that is exemplary for all who come after, whatever is said, done or suffered in the community.[61]

2   However, 23:8–12 forbids the community to use any titles of honour, especially rabbi, father and teacher.[62] That presupposes that there were members of the community who fulfilled functions which could justify claims to these titles. One must therefore presume the existence of such special ministries.[63] In point of fact any binding and loosing does presuppose a certain knowledge of Scripture or at least some knowledge of the Christian oral tradition. Those will in fact always have been a definite group of community members through which the ministry of teaching was mainly exercised. Neither of course will all members of the community ever have been itinerant prophets, nor will every disciple of Jesus have been given authority for charismatic healing. That is why Matthew can speak of scribes

and prophets as well. But the point is that he does all he can to counter what was presumably already a visible trend towards the development of an actual ministry whose members were then clearly to be distinguished from other Christians and had a certain status. Greatness is reserved for those who can subject themselves to others and serve them (23:11f). The baseline is and remains all those "little ones" that everyone is called on to serve. In 18:15–18 everyone is called upon to go after any wayward brother and be a pastor to him; everyone is involved on a par with everyone else when the community "binds" or "looses" him. Even where on occasion only two or three are gathered together, God himself will validate their request (18:19f). In the whole "church order" in chap. 18 there is not the slightest indication of a specially emphasized ministry to which certain things are reserved that not every community member can do.[64]

3   It is thus a community which seems to know neither elders nor bishops nor deacons.[65] This community resists the development of specific designations for those who perform particular duties, thus creating a ministry. It is at the same time a community which does not possess the whole range of spiritual gifts listed in 1 Cor. 12. It is in fact sceptical about a life too exclusively dependent on the Spirit that could loosen its connection with the word and work of the earthly Jesus. That is why binding and loosing are expressly mentioned whereas charismatic gifts are referred to only indirectly. So it is a community living somewhere in between Jewish Christianity and the Pauline church, somewhere in between Jerusalem and Asia Minor or Greece. If that is also geographically correct and we have to think of Antioch, it means too that it had strong connections with both Jerusalem, where Peter came from, and also with Paul's missionary area. So early Christianity cannot be simply split up into however many individual groups independent of each other.[66] But it is different from strict Jewish Christianity in that it neither demands a literal following of the law of Moses (however strongly it insists that in substance everything to the last jot and tittle should be fulfilled), nor is it interested in Jesus' relatives as leaders of the community, but rather recognizes the authority of Peter who is open towards the Gentile mission. It is also different from the Pauline communities in taking a thoroughly positive view of the law and is therefore also interested in Jesus' commands and his whole exemplary behaviour and is not prepared to let this recede behind a post-Easter proclamation. Love of neighbour and an ultimate

commitment that can renounce house, possessions and family, even marriage under certain circumstances, is central for it.[67] It is also a community in which the Old Testament lives on. The Deuteronomist and the Chronicler saw in the pitiful remnant community after the Exile "the people of God" and "the congregation of the Lord" for whom the covenant promises were still valid. That is how Matthew saw the community of Jesus. But whereas they thought of the holy remnant in a centripetal way, Matthew thought centrifugally of a flock from all nations. This has its roots in a period when Judaism and Jesus' disciples were not yet separated, though by the time Matthew wrote the separation had meanwhile become a fact. Like the group that lies behind the Book of Revelation, Matthew's community considers the prophets as the servants of God par excellence and allows them to work in its midst (Amos 3:7; Rev. 10:7; 11:18).[68]

VIII *From Jesus to the monastic movement of the Catholic Church*

1   This community has its earlier stages. The Q document contains a whole series of Jesus' sayings which call upon the disciple to leave house and family, to follow Jesus without any external security in sole trust in God, so as in this way to proclaim the coming Kingdom, heal the sick and drive out demons (Luke 9:57–62; 10:8–12; 12:22–31; 14:26; 16:13; 17:33). The Marcan tradition contains similar material. Such sayings would not have been transmitted orally for about three decades if there had not been groups of people who more or less literally followed them. Once written down or even become canonical, a saying can be interpreted anew, reinterpreted or spiritualized. But so long as it is being handed on only orally it gets reshaped as soon as it no longer corresponds to reality. The fact that these radical calls to discipleship are still found in our synoptic tradition points to a group who can be thought of as bearers of this tradition. There must always have been people who understood discipleship in a literal sense and gave up their possessions, and as itinerant prophets and charismatics proclaimed the Kingdom of God. Their doing without bag, staff and money (Matt. 10:9f) distinguishes them in this from the less radical itinerant preachers, the cynics.[69] There is no doubt that the call to discipleship goes back to Jesus.[70] This is presumably true also for a whole lot of the sayings listed above,[71] even if one reckons with the possibility of a certain radicalizing of the itinerant prophet movement after Jesus' death.[72]

2   What we see even behind these sayings and then quite clearly in the background of Matthew, was continued in the subsequent period too. One could point to Paul's catalogue (for example, 1 Cor. 6:4–10, cf.13:4), the more historically drawn depiction of his apostolic sufferings (2 Cor. 11:23–30) or the theological weight that he places on his renunciation of pay from the community (1 Cor. 9:12–18).[73] The typical characteristics of the Matthean community by contrast recur in the *Didache*, which also probably comes from Syria and is to be dated approximately in the last decade of the first century. Its dependence upon Matthew or his tradition is unmistakable. That is plain from the now strongly popularized statements out of the Sermon on the Mount, which appear straightaway at the beginning; also the Matthean baptismal formula with its three-fold name; the Lord's Prayer; the demand for perfection which is also characteristic of Qumran; and the warning against the false prophets of "lawlessness", where sheep become wolves (*Did.* 7:1; 8:2; 6:2; 16:3f). Here too faith is in the first instance obedience and a passionate expectation of the Lord's coming on the clouds of heaven (chap. 16). *Did.* 10:7 and 11:7 testify explicitly to itinerant prophets who speak in the Spirit and to whom full freedom for this is to be given. They are dependent upon the hospitality of the community because they are wanderers without money or possessions (11:4–12). They follow in everything "the Lord's way of life" (11:8). They presumably also practice sexual abstinence, perhaps even living together with wives ascetically. That is probably the point of the phrase about the "earthly mystery of the Church" which they carry out and which is to be defended so long as they do not teach others to do it (11:11).[74] It is not surprising to find that the problem of false prophets emerges here too. It is solved in a thoroughly sane way. Anyone who wants too obviously or too long to live off the hospitality of the community is a false prophet (11:8f; 12:2).

The teachers appear to be closely connected with the prophets as is the case as early as Acts 13:1, if they are to be strictly distinguished from them at all (*Did.* 13:2; 15:1f). Teachers are also itinerant, though evidently in a way that leads one to expect a longer period of residence in this case (11:1f; 13:2).[75] The "apostle" in 11:3–7 is clearly identical with the itinerant prophet, despite the phrase "apostles and prophets". More importantly, "bishops and deacons" are spoken of here. The trend which can be seen as early as Matthew has developed further. Prophets begin to disappear (13:4); in their place bishops and deacons are to come forward (15:1f). They still have to be expressly recommended by the author, but they are already a separate group with a particular designation. But this recommendation still shows that the community does not yet consider them a fully-fledged substitute for the prophet, who is here clearly introduced as a proclaimer gripped by the power of the Spirit.[76]

3   Although the petering out of such prophetic itinerant preaching is visible here, this does not mean the end of the movement. In the second century Papias still knows itinerant "disciples of the Lord" on whose authority he still places far more reliance than on written authority.[77] The *Gospel of Thomas*, some of whose sayings tend towards asceticism, probably also belongs in this sphere, even if much of it has already been spiritualized, because it was no longer practical. This work also probably belongs in the Syrian, now East Syrian church, which for two centuries maintained a type of church with its own peculiar character. Indigenous Jewish Christianity and Encratite newcomer are here united.[78] But the clearest case is a passage in the Pseudo-Clementine letters to virgins.[79] According to this passage there were still in the third century men and women who lived together in strict sexual abstinence. They walked through the country, alone or in groups, and visited believers, drove out demons, called the brethren together, and proclaimed the gospel to them, without using elaborate speeches, but trusting only in the Spirit. Finally we have to consider the apocryphal *Acts of the Apostles* which depict the apostles as itinerant prophets who heal the sick and drive out demons. But here a reinterpretation is already apparent. Whereas for the prophets in the Pseudo-Clementines the old motif of a literal following of Jesus is decisive, we have here a motif with quite different roots coming in. It is the idea of a "heavenly" life which in spiritual exuberance can leave the earth and its limits behind.[80] A self-description of this group has been found in the Nag Hammadi documents discovered in Egypt (*Apocalypse of Peter* VII/3 79. 19–30; cf. 71:14f; 75:15ff; 83:12ff;—third century A.D.? ET ed. J. M. Robinson, *The Nag Hammadi Library in English*). It depicts "these little ones" (Matt. 18:6) who are seen by God, will not let themselves be called bishop or deacon, and do not rush to take the top places at table (Matt. 23:6–10). They repudiate possessions and sexual relations and evidently value highly Spirit-inspired revelations.

We thus see in Syria an independent Christianity of poor itinerants who live in passionate expectation of the Coming One and therefore often renounce marriage, wine and meat. Like Matthew they reckon seriously with evil, including evil in the community, and understand their Christianity more as a "way" than as teaching; or to put it better, they understand teaching as guidance for pilgrimage along this "way". It is interpreted totally as cutting loose from the world in imitation of the unmarried, poor and itinerant Jesus.

4   Until quite recently we had only indirect testimony to this kind of Christianity. The newly discovered *Apocalypse of Peter*[81] from Nag Hammadi, however, seems to be the self-description of such a group which clearly appeals to certain statements in Matthew. In quite Matthean terminology they call themselves "these little ones who are seen (by God)" and they polemicize against those who "let themselves be called bishop and also deacons, as if they had received authority from God, who recline at table after the law of the places of honour."[82] At the same time the ideal of poverty and chastity is maintained, for p. 71, 14f polemicizes expressly against "people who love possessions", and 75:15ff against those who "serve their desires" by "loving the created things of matter". The form of the *Apocalypse*, which begins with vision and audition, shows that there is an element of prophecy and enthusiasm here. Since the document proceeds to attack Hermas, most probably the *Shepherd of Hermas*, and various gnostic assertions, it can hardly be dated before the end of the second century or the third. It is thus direct evidence for the later influence of Matthean formulations in a Christianity which is similar to the Syrian type described above.

5   Much of this Christianity which seems to have remained typical for Syria flowed subsequently into the monastic movement. It is easy to see that this one-sided understanding is in many respects dangerous. Just as proclamation can never consist simply in the repetition of "teachable" statements of Jesus, neither can pure imitation itself really be discipleship. The motive for an action which externally looks just the same could be quite different from that of its model. That is clear in the distinction, found as early as *Did.* 6:2, between the perfect who bear the whole yoke of the Lord, and those who just do what they can. It is true that the statement, "if you want to be perfect . . ." is also found at Matt. 19:21. But as 5:48 shows, it is here presupposed that every disciple of Jesus is perfect, even if the concrete demands faced by each may be different. The *Didache* by contrast makes a clear value difference between two groups of disciples. This of course contributed to this particular kind of piety being taken up into the Catholic Church. It is the model for distinguishing between the *consilia evangelica* (evangelical counsels)

which are valid for monks and the *praecepta* (commands) which are valid for all.

On the other hand, however, it must be recognized what powerful and fruitful renunciation and commitment have flowed on down the centuries from this stream of Christian thought and life. Questionable though an uncritical understanding of discipleship as imitation of Christ is, nevertheless a teaching and practice of discipleship to Jesus which bears clear witness to the fact that without it there is no access to the truth of Christian proclamation or to the entire activity of Jesus, is an urgent requirement. Jesus used no clearly defined christological titles which could be simply taken note of and accepted; he formulated no dogmatic statements which could be simply repeated and adopted, but spoke in parables. This shows exactly that only those who let themselves be moved and sent on the "way" can understand what Jesus is speaking about. He professed no method of salvation which could be set up and simply imitated; he did not allow himself to be put into any Zealotic, Sadducean, Pharisaic or any other definable mould. This again shows exactly that only those who allow themselves to be called by him to follow after him and to be for ever open for new meetings with him, can understand what kind of a life Jesus presents him with. Not that Matthew ever forgets the absolute priority of Jesus. His action is not on the same level as that of his followers. This is done "for him" only insofar as they find in what happened with Jesus the possibility of following (20:28). To use once again an old image:[83] a little boy trots behind his father who cuts a path through the impenetrable jungle with his bush knife. By his own feeble powers the boy could not have done that himself, so he is doing something quite different from his father in front, but he nevertheless follows exactly in his footsteps. That is how followers walk in the way that Jesus has opened up for them. That is certainly not all that the NT has to say on the subject. Paul and John and their communities have differently accentuated statements to make. But it does say something of great importance, and it was fed into the life of the whole Church.

NOTES

1 Cf. Schweizer (1970) esp. 226–30 and the discussion of the literature there.

2 Schweizer (1974) 9–12.

3 So S. G. F. Brandon, *The Fall of Jerusalem and the Christian Church* (London 1951) 221–4; more recently, Tilborg (1972); against this, already Davies (1964) 318.

4 Davies (1964) 256–315.

5 Cf. e.g. 1:23; 12:21.

6 23:38 and 24:2 are taken from the tradition. Davies (1964) 298f thinks that the fall of Jerusalem is an important concern of Matthew, but connects this event with the anti-Pharisaic polemic (so too Hare [1967] 94–6), 23:34–6 is of course connected with the woes even in Q, and vv. 37–9 were probably connected with those verses prior to Matthew (Schweizer [1976] *ad loc.*). In any case that only shows that Pharisaism was a discussion partner, not that Palestine was the evangelist's setting. According to Hare (1967) 125–9 (cf. 62–5) even the references to persecutions point to the Diaspora rather than to Palestine. C. W. F. Smith, "The Mixed State of the Church in Matthew's Gospel", *JBL* 82 (1963) 167f also decides in favour of Syria, with the surprising argument that the exodus of the Qumran community to Damascus could have also caused in Jesus' community an all too radical observance of the law, against which Matthew protests.

7 So too Kahmann in Didier (1972) 277f. Despite Matthew's tendency to combine the list of disciples and the call tradition (9:9), and his emphasis upon Peter by his *prōtos* ("first") at 10:2 (Hoffmann [1974] 108–10) this first call alone would probably not suffice, if Peter did not play a special role in the evangelist's community.

8 Acts (12:17); 21:18. In Gal. 2:9 he is put first (not in Gal. 1:19).

9 In contrast to the so-called first missionary journey (Acts 13–14), subsequently only a short visit there is mentioned, at Acts 18:22f. In his own letters Paul never mentions Antioch again (after Gal. 2:11). That does not of course mean a lasting hostility with Peter or with this community, which 1 Cor. 1:12f, 3:22 tells against, even if 1 Cor. 3:11 was formulated to counter Petrine claims (Matt. 16:18) cf. n.38. On the contrary, Peter probably stands closer to Paul than to James. Matt. 16:18 might even be aimed against James (Davies [1964] 339 and n. 2).

10 He is mentioned only at Matt. 13:55 (= Mark 6:3). With Frankemölle, (1974) 323 n. 71, it may be pointed out that the triadic baptismal formula (Matt. 28:19) also appears at *Did.* 7:1; Ignatius, *Magn.* 13:2; *Odes Sol.* 23:20. These too point to Syria.

11 Since after the conclusion proper to the Sermon on the Mount at 7:12 (Schweizer [1974] 47) everything else is characterized by 7:15 as an appendix giving a warning, contemporaries of Matthew are certainly intended. Cf. Schweizer (1974) 45, and Minear (1974) 80–6, though Minear gets into difficulties with v. 21 because he thinks the section refers exclusively to leaders of the community.

12 The possibility that 24:10–12 (and 7:15) are pre-Matthean tradition (so H. Koester, *Synoptische Überlieferung bei den apostolischen Vätern* [Berlin 1957] 183f, cf.189, 239f) must be considered, although the vocabulary statistics tell against this (Lambrecht in Didier [1972] 320 n. 29). The catchwords "lawlessness" and "love" appear also at 2 Thess 2:3–8 in the pictures of the end. *Life of Adam* 29b in Paris MS 5327 (K. Berger, *Die Gesetzauslegung Jesu* I [Neukirchen 1972] 246) provides with its reference to love growing cold and unrighteousness increasing in the final period an impressive parallel from Jewish apocalyptic, provided it is not itself influenced by the NT. The "wolves" too belong to the eschatological events according to Acts 20:29. More importantly, the same catchwords appear at *Did.* 16:3f. Since signs and portents also are mentioned at *Did.* 16:6, it is only the state-

ments peculiar to Matthew that are taken up from Matt. 24. May therefore both have used an apocalyptic fragment as a common source? There are indeed, apart from the coming of the Son of Man on the clouds of heaven (slightly closer to the Septuagint in Matt. 24:30 than in Mark 13:26) also echoes of Matt. 24:42 (parallel in Mark 13:35) and Matt. 24:44 (Q) and Luke 12:35 (?Q). Besides, A. Sand, "Die Polemik gegen die 'Gesetzlosigkeit' im Evangelium nach Matthäus und bei Paulus", *BZ* 14 (1970) 118–25 has shown how widespread the motif of lawlessness was and the very different meanings it has in Matthew and Paul. *Did.* 1:3–5 is a special case, where sayings from the Sermon on the Mount occur, mostly depending on Matthew, but occasionally on Luke. Köster, 240, assigns it to an earlier redactor. Beyond this there are in *Did.* 1:2; 2:2f; 5:1; 11:7, echoes of Matthean passages which have a usually not very different Marcan parallel to them, and at *Did.* 13:1f, one with an underlying Q text. Material peculiar to Matthew can perhaps be found also at *Did.* 7:1f; 8:1f; 9:5; 10:5; 14:2. *Did.* 3:7 is similar to the Matthean form of this beatitude, but even more similar to Ps. 37:11 (LXX 36:11) which is utilized there. Unless all these texts came from a perhaps already overgrown tradition of Matthew, the *Didache* must have combined Marcan material, Q tradition and different kinds of material peculiar to Matthew independently, and thus duplicated the evangelist's own procedure. Since, furthermore, passages like Matt. 7:6, 15; 24:10–12, 30f, are redactional insertions into Q or Marcan contexts, we must suppose that for all these passages the author of the *Didache* possessed Matthew or an extract from it, though allowance must be made for changes resulting from the oral usage in his own community. These changes could be in part influenced by the OT, Jewish apocalyptic ideas, or other sayings of Jesus.

13 Cf. M. Testuz, *Papyrus Bodmer* X–XII (Geneva 1959) 30, 42, 44, = *Acts of Paul*, in Hennecke-Schneemelcher-Wilson, *New Testament Apocrypha*, vol. 2, (London 1965) 322ff, 374, 377.

14 Minear (1974) 76–8 even makes it his first thesis that the disciples are in principle seen much more as prophets than as apostles.

15 The models are no doubt the OT prophets who are mentioned thirty-five times (Cothenet [1972] 283).

16 On this see Suggs (1970) 13–28, 58–60.

17 O. J. F. Seitz, "The Commission of Prophets and 'Apostles'", in *Studia Evangelica* IV (Berlin 1968) 239, argues for its originality with a reference to 1 Kings 14:6 (LXX *apostolos*, "messenger").

18 Cf. Schweizer (1974) 54ff.

19 Cf. D. Lührmann, *Die Redaktion der Logienquelle* (Neukirchen 1969) 111. The history of the tradition of this saying is not easy to illuminate. I am convinced that Mark 9:41, 42 originally stood together as positive and negative formulation, and that both spoke of behaviour towards "one of these little ones". That is the only way to avoid breaking the chain of catchwords in Mark 9:37–50 which connects the end of each unit of meaning with the beginning of the next: "In my (your) name", vv. 37f (or 37/41?); "one of these little ones", vv. 41f; "cause to stumble", vv. 42f; "fire", vv. 48f; "salt", vv. 49f. The occurrence of the catchphrase "one of these little ones" in Matt. 10:42 is thus also easy to understand. Matthew has taken the saying about behaviour towards missionaries and put it

into the discourse on mission (10:42) and has used the fundamental equation of messenger Jesus and God (Mark 9:37b) as an introduction (10:40). Cf. Schweizer (1974) 109.

20 Cf. Schweizer (1974) 20–2.

21 Cf. also 12:28, 31f, and on this Schweizer (1974) 23 n. 58.

22 In reply to Cothenet (1972) 291, as long ago as Schweizer, *Beiträge* (1970) 60, and *NTS* (1970) 222, I claimed no more than some probability for these conclusions. I also noted that in Matthew teaching authority is directly emphasized whereas the reference to "charismatic" activity is often only indirect (*Beiträge*, 70).

23 The relevant literature is listed in Schweizer (1970) 221 n. 1, and 229f (McConnell, Gärtner, Gundry, Lindars, Perrin, Rothfuchs). Cf. the survey in Martin (1968) 132–6; and D. M. Smith, *The Use of the Old Testament in the New, and other Essays* (Duke, Durham, N.C. 1972) 43ff. Segbroeck in Didier (1972) 107–30, Hartman in Didier (1972) 131–52; Dupont *Les Béatitudes* III (Paris 1973) 517. We must agree with Stendahl (1969) vi–ix against Strecker (1966²) 13, 82–4, 162, that in a few cases the OT quotation is unthinkable without the context, so cannot be a source for Matthew's train of thought. For the same reason one must with Gärtner (1954) against Stendahl (1959) be careful about finding in Matthew a parallel to the methods of the Qumran Habakkuk commentary (1Qp Hab), and recognize that individual points in the life of Jesus are interpreted, rather than his whole activity being paralleled with the history of Israel (Hummel [1963] 129–32). The idea here is not that obscure passages in the text only now find their correct interpretation, but that in God's definitive act what was then only announced is now completed. Gundry has shown that the text form which agrees exactly with neither the LXX nor the Hebrew does not derive from a catechetical tradition taken up only by Matthew, but (apart from Mark and a few Matthean additions which follow the LXX) is one that is found broadly elsewhere in the NT. In his revised edition Stendahl himself formulates his thesis far more cautiously than in the first edition.

24 It is clear at 21:7 that the quotations influence the context. But 27:3–10 shows that this has happened over a lengthy pre-Matthean development (Descamps in Didier [1972] 388–90; P. Benoît, *Exégèse et Théologie* I [Paris 1961] 348–52; Schweizer [1976] *ad loc.*). On the other hand in 2:23 the indisputable fact that Jesus came from Nazareth has led to the discovery of a "quotation", also presumably at the pre-Matthean stage, since he probably accepts it as a saying which really can be found in the OT. In chap. 2 there are three sayings expressly marked out as formula quotations, one each at the end of sections 3, 4 and 5 (vv. 15, 18, 23). Section 1 is concluded with a longer quotation containing an abbreviated introductory formula (v. 6). Towards the end of section 2 the gifts of the Magi are described by an OT formula, which Hartman (in Didier [1972] 139] for example considers comes from Isa. 60:6 (on all this cf. now M. Hengel and H. Merkel, "Die Magier aus dem Osten und die Flucht nach Ägypten (Mt 2)", in *Orientierung an Jesus*, Festschrift J. Schmid, ed. P. Hoffmann [Freiburg 1973] 140f). It is striking here that 2:15 appears neither at the first mention of the name "Egypt" (v. 13) nor when the journey back is mentioned (v. 21), but as the close of the section vv. 13–15 (on this cf. Stendahl, in this volume, p. 15).

Certainty is impossible, but it perhaps follows that vv. 15 and 18 (cf. Hartman [1972] 137–41) were already linked with the story of flight and rescue in pre-Matthean scribal work and concluded sections 3 and 4, whereas the two first scriptural references grew together later (perhaps when the flight was connected with the Magi tradition). 2:23 (together with 26:56!) is the only passage which refers to the "prophets" in the plural and (as in 2:5) without the participle ("who say so"). Did the evangelist himself insert this and take the sentence as a real quotation? (Judg. 13:5, 7)? Cf. Zuckschwerdt on Matt. 2:23b; 3:1.7, where all the material is worked through; his explanation of *Nazōraios* ("Nazarene") as Kĕtib – Qĕre from *nasir and qadoš* (3.2.5) is surely impossible since there was no text with vowels available at the time. (Cf. J. A. Sanders, "NAZŌRAIOS in Matt. 2:23", *JBL* 84 [1965] 169–72, and E. Schweizer [1963] 51–5). That would then mean that an emphatic introductory formula was used in the tradition too, though this does not exclude the possibility that Matthew has modified it or himself inserted it in other passages. (On this cf. R. Pesch, "Der Gottessohn im matthäischen Evangelienprolog (Matt. 1–2)", *Biblica* 48 [1967] 395–420). Cf. also Schweizer (1974) 41 n. 147. Against this C. T. Davies, "Tradition and Redaction in Matt. 1:18—2:23", *JBL* 90 (1971) 404–21 cf. 420, considers all the scriptural quotations to be Matthean redaction.

25 J. Gnilka, "Das Verstockungsproblem nach Matthäus 13:13–15", in *Antijudaismus im Neuen Testament?* ed. W. P. Eckert, N. P. Levinson, M. Stöhr (Munich 1967) 119–28, considers this passage to be post-Matthean; it is the only formula quotation on Jesus' own lips and corresponds exactly to the LXX.

26 The attribution of 4:14–16 to this first group is most questionable. Rothfuchs (1969) 101–3, has pointed out that apart from the prologue (chaps. 1–2) and two quotations which certainly stem from the tradition (21:4f, cf. John 12:15; 27:9f cf. n.24) there are five quotations which are all latched on to the evangelist's summary – like observations, and are except for 13:35 expressly traced back to Isaiah. (This only happens otherwise outside the formula quotations: 3:3; 15:7; = Mark 1:2; 7:6.) They appear in the chapters which Matthew has constructed most independently. Rothfuchs takes this to mean that the quotation in chaps. 1 and 2 may have already existed in the tradition and that Matthew used the following five to characterize Jesus' activity. But even if that were correct, he has still taken up again as a conclusion in 4:14–17 what he has taken over in chap. 2: Jesus who is led by God is the same person who later appears as charismatic leader and healer (Segbroeck in Didier [1972] 125f). So there is no real difference of substance from the division proposed here.

27 On this, R. Pesch, "Eine alttestamentliche Ausführungsformel im Matthäusevangelium", *BZ* 10 (1966) 220–45; 11 (1967) 79–95. That is inexplicable only if we posit an exegetical method proper to Judaism which concentrates only on the literal sense (Stanley, "Etudes matthéennes. L'entré messianique à Jérusalem", *Sciences Ecclésiastiques* 6 [1954] 93–106).

28 In fact Matthew does not really see what he describes (Dupont, *Les Béatitudes* III [Paris, 1973] 540).

29 More details in U. Wilckens, *TDNT*, VII. 505, 23ff.

30 Cf. also Cothenet (1972) 294–7. It is possible, but unlikely that Matthew himself

has inserted this, in which case he contrasted the "wise men and scribes" sent by Jesus with the "scribes and Pharisees" (v. 29).

31 Or, as Trilling (1964) 145, prefers: who "is instructed about the kingdom of heaven". Cf. Walker (1967) 23f. According to Bacon (1930) 131f, 13:51f is the evangelist's self-portrait. Similarly Strecker (1966) 37–9. Gerhardsson (1966) sees even the temptation story as this kind of early Christian midrash (79–83), though the parallel he suggests with "Hear O Israel ..." (Deut. 6:5, 71–9) is not convincing. Cf. Schweizer (1974) 45 n. 169.

32 Walker (1967) 27f. Cf. Schweizer (1974) 12, n. 19. Davies (1964) 106. "Another of the disciples" (8:21) presupposes that the scribe is himself also a disciple. But against this, he addresses Jesus as "teacher", whereas at v. 21 the disciple follows Matthean usage and calls him "Lord". So the right interpretation is, "another, one of the disciples". V. 21 is therefore without the resolution of v. 19, "I will follow you", and the addition of "first" presupposes as self-evident that discipleship will subsequently take place.

33 Cf. 23:13 and Hoffmann (1974) 98f. On the rabbinic (and Qumran) terminology cf. Davies (1964) 225; Kretzer (1971) 246–9; Kahmann, (1972) 274–6; critically Hoffmann (1974) 101 n. 29; and see below Section IV.3. Emerton, "Binding and Loosing – Forgiving and Retaining", *JTS* 13 (1962) 325–51, tries to find from Isa. 22:22 a common Aramaic basis for Matt. 16:19 and John 20:23 (where *kratein* ("to retain" is ungreek). His derivation of the term "bind" is difficult, so one must at any rate assume the influence of the rabbinic double expression.

34 Cf. Bornkamm's essay in this volume. The neuter of the pronoun in 18:18 ("whatever") counts against this, since it does not suggest members of the community (Argyle [1963] *ad loc.*).

35 We owe this insight to P. Stuhlmacher, *Das paulinische Evangelium* 1, (Göttingen 1968) 241f. One should also remember that in Matthew the Jewish scribes are contrasted not with the disciples but with Jesus. He alone is the fount of all new *halakah* (Tilborg [1972] 128). The Church does indeed continue the function of Jesus, but it cannot be understood as a "Christus prolongatus" (cf. Via [1958] 279). To say that the words of the earthly Jesus are only a literary fiction for preaching Christ as the exalted Lord of the community (Frankemölle [1974] 268) seems to me to be at least highly misleading. Matthew insists on testing the post-Easter proclamation by reference to that of the earthly Jesus which he takes over unreflectingly as historical. Cf. also Luz, in this volume p. 109.

36 On this see especially Vögtle (1964); and Baumbach (1967) 889–93. In place of proclaiming verbs (*kērussein*, "to proclaim"; *euangelizein*, "to proclaim good tidings"; *martyrein*, "to witness") we find teaching verbs (*mathēteuein*, "to disciple"; *tērein*, "to keep"); and verbs implying movement (*poreuesthai*, "to go").

37 Cf. Schweizer (1974) 43.

38 Whereas in 1 Cor. 1:12 Paul, Apollos, and Cephas are mentioned together, the positive account in 3:4–11 is restricted to the relationship between Paul and Apollos. Cephas does not crop up again as a third person until v. 22. That excludes any hostility or theological split – Gal. 2:14–16 argues on the basis of a common conviction between Paul and Peter, too. But it does not preclude a certain tension which formulations proceeding from the community rather than from Peter himself might have strengthened. However, we know far too little here to say

anything with certainty (cf. n. 9). There is also the possibility of dependence upon shared traditions, as K. Kertelge proposes, in "Apokalypsis Jesou Christou (Gal. 1:12)", in *Neues Testament und Kirche*, Festschrift Schnackenburg (1974) 276–9. It could then be a matter of the apostolic consciousness of mission shared by early Christian itinerant missionaries.

39 There is no doubt that this was Matthew's understanding (despite Benoit [1962³] *ad loc.*) because vv. 19f expressly promise the "two or three" who are gathered in Jesus' name, the presence of Jesus now and so God's fulfilling everything that is asked in agreement. That cannot be separated from the authority promised in v. 18, since vv. 10–14, like vv. 1–9 apply to all members of the community. There is no need even for the ten times prescribed for the Jewish liturgy (Schlatter [1963] 558; F. Hahn, "Der urchristliche Gottesdienst", in *Jahrbuch für Liturgie und Homologie*, 12 [1967] 19 = Stuttgarter Bibelstudien 41 [1970] 42). Kretzer (1971) 252 also sees that the authority is "in principle" given to all; it is naturally possible (see below 7.2) that in practice there are scribes who normally exercise it (ibid.). Similarly, J. Radermakers, *Au fil de l'Évangile selon saint Matthieu* (Louvain 1972) 247f. Bonnard (1962) 275, thinks (with Aquinas) of the local community, perhaps that it votes for or against applying an already existing disciplinary regulation (thus Hill, [1972] *ad loc.*). It is no longer clear but it is improbable that it was understood differenty at an earlier stage (v. 18 is formulated in the plural, vv. 15–17 in the singular: Trilling, [1964³] 157, assumes a redactional construction of Matthew, on account of *hosa an*, "whatever ..."). It is widely accepted that 16:19 is the earlier saying (Trilling [1964³] 156–8; [1972] 30–2), contrary to e.g. W. Pesch (1966) 42 n. 11.

40 Jesus' rebuke after Peter's confession (Matt. 16:23) is made even stronger: the foundation-stone of the Church becomes a stone of stumbling (cf. B. Lindars, *New Testament Apologetic* [London 1961] 181–3; Kahmann [1972] 262, 270–2 also points out the parallelism in the picture of Peter in 14:28–31; 16:18–23; 17:24–7).

41 Cf. Hummel (1963) 59f. In Mark 7:17 the disciples ask Jesus what he meant by the saying about what comes out of the mouth and defiles a person. In the parallel passage Matt. 15:12 the disciples draw attention to the Pharisees, and Jesus replies with the saying about plants not planted by the Father and the blind leading the blind. In 15:15 Peter then takes up the question of Mark 7:17 (cf. Schweizer [1974] 26 n. 71). 17:24–7 is material special to Matthew; the question of temple tax is under discussion. At 18:21 Peter asks how often one must forgive, thus making possible the link with v. 22 (= Luke 17:4), since the preceding saying Luke 17:3 had already been used by Matthew at 18:15.

42 So too Kahmann (1972) 272; Hoffmann (1974) 106–10. A pericope like 17:24–7 shows too how strongly Peter is seen as the disciple taught by Jesus. Cf. also Schweizer (1974) 113 n. 13.

43 G. Braumann, "Der sinkende Petrus. Matt. 14:28–31", *TZ* 22 (1966) 403–14 understands the episode in the light of the situation of the community where miracles are failing to happen and little faith, care and fear are creeping in.

44 B. Rigaux, *Témoignage de l'évangile de Matthieu* (Bruges 1967) 205; R. Schnackenburg, "Die Kirche in der Welt", *BZ* 11 (1967) 4f; F. W. Beare, "The Mission of the Disciples and the Mission Charge, Matthew 10 and

Parallels", *JBL* 89 (1970) 3f. Kingsbury (1976) 31–6 stresses against Strecker and Walker that Matthew knows only the two epochs, promise and fulfilment. Like Jesus, the disciples are described from the post-Easter perspective. So they are not idealized (Schweizer [1974] 25 n. 67), but their knowledge is that of the post-Easter community.

45 Cf. Schweizer (1974) 65–8 and 21 n. 52. So it is wrong to disallow any historical understanding, as Frankemölle (1974) does. It is things that Matthew considers historical facts which become transparent. Cf. Luz, in this volume pp. 98–105, or in fact 118f.

46 Trilling (1970) 43.

47 G. Schrenk in *TDNT* II, 186, 23f.

48 This is stressed by Cothenet (1972) 293. He is no doubt correct that Matthew sees the prophets in the Jesus community as parallel to those of the OT, as 22:6 (or even better 22:3f, cf. Schweizer [1974] 118) together with 21:35f proves. But that does not mean that only their commission and the status this gives (Cothenet, 292f) are emphasized.

49 Käsemann, "The Beginnings of Christian Theology", in *NT Questions of Today* (ET 1969) 91 is probably wrong to think directly of local leaders (prophets) and church members (righteous ones), since the righteous ones are evidently thought of as itinerant and again distinguished from the "disciple" in 10:42 (against Cothenet [1972] 297f too). Minear (1974) 78f also sees in the prophets the local leaders.

50 Evidence in J. Dupont, *Les Béatitudes* III (1973) 364f.

51 In other parts of the book those who survive the last judgement are called righteous. On the Matthean understanding of righteousness see Schweizer (1974) 51.

52 It *could* therefore go back to Jesus himself. The absence of rabbinic parallels (Frankemölle [1974] 186) and the virtual equivalence of "little" and "humble" in the LXX (ibid. 186f) does not constitute evidence against this. The context is a stronger argument (ibid. 186), since it does not suggest an early Jesus saying But I do not see here purely Matthean redaction (ibid. 187f); cf. n. 19. Also Luz, above p. 110.

53 18:6, 10, 14; cf. Schweizer (1974) 106.

54 J. R. Michaels, "Apostolic Hardship and Righteous Gentiles. A Study of Matthew 25: 31–46", *JBL* 34 (1965) 27–37; L. Cope, "Matthew XXV: 31–46" *NovT* 11 (1969) esp. 38–44; S. Légasse, *Jésus et l'enfant* (Paris 1969) 51–100; J. Broer, "Das Gericht des Menschensohnes über die Völker", *Bibel und Leben* 11 (1970), 273–95 esp. 293–5; J. Lambrecht (1972) 324–40; J. Manek, "Mit wem identifiziert sich Jesus", in Festschrift Moule (1973) 18–25 (the corporate understanding of the Son of Man is untenable though); further references in Grundmann (1968) 527 n. 12. Feuillet, "La synthèse eschatologique de Saint Matthieu", *RB* 57 (1950) 181–3, and Légasse 95 assume that Matthew presupposes that after the conclusion of the world mission there will only be Christians.

55 Lambrecht (1972) 334 emphasizes that the nations previously appear either as those to be evangelized (24:14) or as persecutors of the disciples (24:9) who at the coming of the Son of Man will be able only to mourn (24:30).

56 That might explain why unlike the usual Jewish specifications of works of love (cf. Grundmann [1968] 526f) there is no mention of funeral processions and lamentations whereas visiting those in prison is included.

57 *Ho mikroteros* ("the smallest") (11:11; 13:32) instead of *ho elachistos* ("the least"). Lambrecht (1972) 337 solves the problem by saying the designation "little ones" does not apply to all disciples but only to the itinerant missionaries. But Matthew could not very well say "my little brothers" since all believers are brothers; and he would have to write "my least ones" to stress a special group amongst the brothers. But that probably breaks down on account of chap. 18 where the "little ones" represent the disciples in general (against Lambrecht, 338, who sees both groups distinguished by their poverty).

58 It is also conceivable that a whole people will receive grace at the judgement because some of them have accepted the Christian message, but it cannot be said of the same people that they have done everything for Jesus' messengers and also that they have known nothing about Jesus' coming.

59 Vocabulary statistics reveal some clearly Matthean words alongside non-Matthean formulations: Lambrecht (1972) 331f. But he thinks it is Matthew who has introduced the reference to the missionaries whereas (Jesus') original description was meant in the usual sense (332f, 338).

60 Cf. Cullmann, *Peter, Disciple – Apostle – Martyr* (London 1962²) 209–17. Trilling, (1970) 40f rightly emphasizes that Matthew has no particular interest in apostleship but instead restyles the apostle into a disciple and model of being a Christian in general.

61 Hoffman (1974) 108–10.

62 This can hardly be understood as polemic against the teacher of righteousness at Qumran (Spicq, "Une allusion au docteur de justice dans Matthieu XXIII. 10?", *RB* 66 [1959] 395). On the other hand the typically Greek expression in the third part intends expressly to exclude all titles of honour, including those which stem from a non-Jewish milieu (Frankemölle [1974] 101).

63 Rightly emphasized in Trilling (1970) 31f. Frankemölle (1973) sees behind this section the real ministries of the Matthean church.

64 Cf. Luz, above p. 110. From this point of view the position of this chapter in the Gospel as a whole is also important. Cf. Schweizer (1974) 106 (including n. 1).

65 I do of course agree with Cothenet (1972) 306, that the argument from silence is never absolutely certain. I also agree with him and Trilling (1970) that the ministry of teacher was in fact exercised (cf. above, p. 139f.). But it should not be overlooked that wherever the twelve are made transparent to disclose the period of the evangelist, the totality of the disciples stands behind them, not particular office-bearers. If offices in this sense existed there would have been indications in chap. 18 that institution into a ministry open only to particular church members gave one this special authority and right. Note also that even Peter lacks any legitimation through ordination such as would be necessary for a rabbinic teacher (Hummel [1963] 60–3), although he remains "the first" (Trilling [1964³] 159; Kahmann [1972] 278).

66 The importance of Peter shows that this community did not emerge independently of Jerusalem, e.g. under the direct influence of a Galilean mission. Just as the

Pauline letters show that there was only one early community of any importance, so too does Matthew show that the church standing behind it was largely rooted in the early church in Jerusalem. Galilean influence is possible, if Q belongs there. But it would from the start exist alongside that of Jerusalem which is represented by Peter. It is more probable that from the beginning "Jerusalem" took many forms because the Hellenists were active there and clearly became decisive for the formation of the church in Syria.

67 The hard word about eunuchs (19:12) cannot easily be softened to apply only to those who have divorced their wives for impurity, preventing them from remarrying (Quesnell, "Made themselves Eunuchs for the Kingdom of Heaven (Matt. 19:12)", *CBQ* 30 [1968] 335).

68 This view has been nicely worked out by Frankemölle (1974) 246, 326f, etc. Bacon (1930) 361 understood our Gospel as a book for itinerant "gospellers". Baumbach (1967) 890f, 893 also stresses that Matthew understands the life of faith above all as being on the move, as a "way".

69 On this, G. Theissen, 'Wanderradikalismus', *ZTK* 70 (1973) 245–71, esp. 245–52, 258f (ET forthcoming in *The Miracle Stories of the Early Christian Tradition*); adumbrated by G. Kretschmar, "Ein Beitrag zur Frage nach dem Ursprung frühchristlicher Askese", *ZTK* 61 (1964) 27–67; and P. Hoffmann, *Studien zur Theologie der Logienquelle* (1972) 312–34. Cf. also n. 73 below.

70 Jesus calls disciples in a quite different way from what was normal in Judaism. It was besides not a question of teaching about scriptural interpretation, and no disciple expected to become a Son of Man himself, whereas the rabbi pupil expected to become a rabbi himself. But neither are these sayings community formations since apart from Rev. 14:4 discipleship is expressed only in relation to the earthly Jesus (even in sayings which emerged only after Easter). The only model is 1 Kings 19. 19–21. On this see E. Schweizer, *Lordship and Discipleship* (ET 1960) 13; M. Hengel, *The Charismatic Leader and his Followers* (ET 1981) 16–37, 50–66.

71 Theissen (see n. 69) 257, suggests that probably more sayings may be "suspected" of authenticity than some modern sceptics like to think. W. Pesch, "Zur Exegese, von Matt. 6:19–21 und Luke 12:33–4", *Biblica* 41 (1960), 366–8 stresses the much more radical renunciation of security in Jesus than in Qumran.

72 K. M. Fischer, "Asketische Radikalisierung der Nachfolge Jesu", in *Theologische Versuche* IV (Berlin 1972) shows that for the pericope about the rich man.

73 Cf. G. Dautzenberg, "Der Verzicht auf das apostolische Unterhaltsrecht", *Biblica* 50 (1969) 216.

74 G. Bornkamm in *TDNT* IV, 824, 40ff. H. Schlier, *Religionsgeschichtliche Untersuchungen zu den Ignatiusbriefen* (Giessen 1929) 92 (referring to Irenaeus, *Adv. Haer.* I. 6, 4); J. Daniélou, *The Theology of Jewish Christianity* (ET 1964) 351–6. J. P. Audet, *La Didaché* (Paris 1958) 452 sees here only symbolic actions. Cf. H. Sasse in *TDNT* III, 897, 35ff.

75 Admittedly 11:1f does not contain the title, only a verbal paraphrase, perhaps because the actual "teacher" is a settled minister.

76 More detail in Schweizer, *Church Order in the NT* (ET 1961) §15. Bonnard (1963) 9f, like L. Goppelt, *Christentum und Judentum in ersten und zweiten Jahrhundert* (1954) 178–85, sees Matthew and *Did.* as closely related in time and place.

77 Eusebius, *Hist. eccl.* 3. 39.4. Is it coincidence that the catchword "follow" appears here? Admittedly it is following the "old" in this case.

78 More detail in G. Quispel, *Makarius, Das Thomasevangelium und das Lied von der Perle* (Supplements to *NovT* 15, 1967) 5–38, 110 (cf. also 47:74); further A. F. J. Klijn, "Christianity in Edessa and the Gospel of Thomas", *NovT* 14 (1972) 70–7; G. Theissen (n. 69) 269 n. 68.

79 G. Kretschmar (n. 69, 32–9) has drawn attention to this and should be consulted on the whole of this section VIII.

80 It is in general striking how rarely new miracles by Jesus appear in the post-canonical, especially gnostic, literature, whereas new miracles by apostles are frequent. The reason for this is presumably in part that the layer of tradition that in the name of Jesus promises God's help to anyone who follows him in literal imitation (especially in doing exorcisms and the dangers of the itinerant life – e.g. from poisonous snakes) is to be distinguished from the other layer that promises the believer a connection with the heavenly Lord and his Spirit, i.e. here on earth the realization of heavenly life with angel languages, visions and the like.

81 Cod. VII/3. I quote from the German translation which the Berlin working group on coptic-gnostic writings has kindly made available to me prior to publication.

82 P. 71, 19–30. Cf. Matt. 18:10; 23:8–11.

83 E. Schweizer, *Lordship and Discipleship* (ET 1960) 11.

Select Bibliography

A Commentaries

Albright, W. F., and Mann, C. S., *Matthew*, Anchor Bible 26. New York: Doubleday, 1971.

Allen, W. C., *A Critical and Exegetical Commentary on the Gospel according to S. Matthew*, ICC, Edinburgh: T. & T. Clark, 1912.

Argyle, A. W., *The Gospel According to Matthew*. CBC. Cambridge: CUP, 1963.

Beare, F. W., *The Gospel According to Matthew*, San Francisco: Harper, and Oxford: Blackwell, 1981.

Benoit, P., *L'Évangile selon S. Matthieu*. Paris: Cerf, 1950.

Bonnard, P., *L'Évangile selon saint Matthieu*. Neuchatel: Delachaux et Niestlé, 1963[1], 1970[2].

Fenton J. C., *The Gospel of St Matthew*. Pelican. Harmondsworth: Penguin, 1963.

Green, H. B., *The Gospel according to Matthew*. New Clarendon Bible. Oxford: OUP, 1975.

Grundmann, W., *Das Evangelium nach Matthäus*. Theologischer Handkommentar I. Berlin: Evangelische Verlagsanstalt, 1968[1], 1972[3].

Gundry, R. H., *Matthew, A Commentary on his Literary and Theological Art*. Grand Rapids: Eerdmanns, 1982.

Hill, D., *The Gospel of Matthew*. New Century Bible. London: Oliphants, 1972.

Klostermann, E., *Das Matthäusevangelium*. Handbuch zum NT. Tübingen: Mohr, 1927[2] and 1938[3].

Lagrange, M.-J., *Évangile selon Saint Matthieu*. Paris: Gabalda, 1927.

Lohmeyer, E., *Das Evangelium des Matthäus* (ed. W. Schmauch), KEK. Göttingen: Vandenhoeck u. Ruprecht, 1956.

McNeile, A. H., *The Gospel According to St Matthew*. London: Macmillan, 1915.

Schlatter, A., *Der Evangelist Matthäus*. Stuttgart: Calwer, 1929[1], 1963[6].

Schmid, J., *Das Evangelium nach Matthäus*. Regensburg: Pustet, 1965.

Schniewind, J., *Das Evangelium nach Matthäus*. NTD. Göttingen: Vandenhoeck u. Ruprecht, 1956.

Schweizer, E., *Das Evangelium nach Matthäus*. NTD. Göttingen: Vandenhoeck u. Ruprecht, 1973; ET *The Good News According to Matthew*. Atlanta: John Knox, 1975, and London: SPCK, 1976.

Wellhausen, J., *Das Evangelium Matthaei*. Berlin, 1914[2].

B Articles and Books

Bacon, B. W., *Studies in Matthew*. New York: Holt, 1930.

156

Banks, R. J., "Matthew's Understanding of the Law: Authenticity and Interpretation in Matthew 5:17–20", *JBL* 93 (1974) 226–42.

Barth, G., "Matthew's Understanding of the Law", in G. Bornkamm, G. Barth and H. J. Held, *Tradition and Interpretation in Matthew*. ET London: SCM, 1963.

Baumbach, G., "Die Mission im Matthäusevangelium". *TLZ* 92 (1967) 889–93.

Blair, E. P., *Jesus in the Gospel of Matthew*. New York: Abingdon, 1960.

Bornkamm, G., "The Stilling of the Storm in Matthew" and "End Expectation and Church in Matthew", in G. Bornkamm, G. Barth and H. J. Held, *Tradition and Interpretation in Matthew*. ET London: SCM, 1963¹, 1983².

—"The Risen Lord and the Earthly Jesus: Matthew 28:16–20" in *The Future of our Religious Past*, ed. J. M. Robinson (ET London: SCM, 1971) 203–29, rep. in *Tradition and Interpretation in Matthew*. ET London: SCM, 1983².

—"The Authority to 'Bind' and 'Loose' in the Church in Matthew's Gospel: the Problem of Sources in Matthew's Gospel", ET in *Jesus and Man's Hope* I, ed. D. G. Miller (Pittsburgh: Pittsburgh Theological Seminary, 1970) 37–50.

Brown R., Donfried, K. P., and Reumann, J. (ed.), *Peter in the New Testament*. Minneapolis: Augsburg; New York: Paulist Press; London: Chapman, 1973.

—*The Birth of the Messiah*. New York: Doubleday, 1977.

Brown, S., "The Matthean Community and the Gentile Mission". *NovT* 22 (1980) 193–221.

Bultmann, R., *The History of the Synoptic Tradition*. ET Oxford: Blackwell, 1963.

Burnett, F. W., *The Testament of Jesus-Sophia. A Redaction-Critical Study of the Eschatological Discourse in Matthew*. Washington: University Press of America, 1979.

Butler, B. C., *The Originality of St. Matthew*. Cambridge: CUP, 1951.

Clark, K. W., "The Gentile Bias in Matthew". *JBL* 66 (1947) 165–72.

Cope, O. L., *Matthew: A Scribe Trained for the Kingdom of Heaven*. Washington: Catholic Biblical Association, 1976.

Cothenet, E., "Les prophètes chrétiens dans l'Evangile selon Matthieu", in M. Didier (ed.), *L'Evangile selon Matthieu*, 281–308.

Dahl, N. A., "Die Passionsgeschichte bei Matthäus", *NTS* 2 (1955–6) 17–32. ET "The Passion Narrative in Matthew", in *Jesus in the Memory of the Early Church: Essays by Nils Alstrup Dahl* (Minneapolis: Augsburg, 1976) 37–51.

Davies, W. D., *The Setting of the Sermon on the Mount*. Cambridge: CUP, 1964.

Didier, M. (ed.), *L'Evangile selon Matthieu. Rédaction et Théologie*. Gembloux: Duculot, 1972.

Dobschütz, E. von, "Matthäus als Rabbi und Katechet". *ZNW* 27 (1928) 338–48.

Ellis, P. F., *Matthew: his Mind and his Message*. Collegeville: Liturgical Press, 1974.

Farmer, W. R., *The Synoptic Problem*. New York and London: Macmillan, 1964.

Frankemölle, H., *Jahwebund und Kirche Jesu. Studien zur Form – und Traditionsgeschichte des Evangeliums nach Matthäus*. Münster: Aschendorff, 1974.

Gaechter, P., *Die Literarische Kunst im Matthäus-Evangelium*. Stuttgart: KBW, 1965.

Gärtner, B., "The Habakkuk Commentary (DSH) and the Gospel of Matthew", *Studia Theologica* 8 (1954) 1–24.

Garland, D. E. *The Intention of Matthew 23*. Leiden: Brill, 1979.

Gaston, L., "The Messiah of Israel as Teacher of the Gentiles". *Interpretation* 29 (1975) 25–40.

Gerhardsson, B., *The Testing of God's Son* (*Mt 4:1–11 and Par.*). Lund: CWK Gleerup, 1966.

—*The Mighty Acts of Jesus according to Matthew*. Lund: CWK Gleerup, 1979.

Goulder, M. D., *Midrash and Lection in Matthew*. London: SPCK, 1974.

Guelich, R. A., *The Sermon on the Mount: a Foundation for Understanding*. Waco, Texas: Word, 1982.

Gundry, R. H., *The Use of the Old Testament in St. Matthew's Gospel*. Leiden: Brill, 1967.

Hahn, F., *Mission in the New Testament*. ET London: SCM, 1965.

Hare, D. R. A., *The Theme of Jewish Persecution of Christians in the Gospel according to St Matthew*. Cambridge: CUP, 1967.

Hartman, L., "Scriptural Exegesis in the Gospel of Matthew and the Problem of Communication", in M. Didier (ed.), *L'Evangile selon Matthieu*, 131–52.

Held, H. J., "Matthew as Interpreter of the Miracle Stories", in G. Bornkamm, G. Barth and H. J. Held, *Tradition and Interpretation in Matthew*.

Hickling, C. J. A., "Conflicting Motives in the Redaction of Matthew: Some considerations on the Sermon on the Mount and Matthew 18:15–20", in E. A. Livingstone (ed.), *Studia Evangelica VII* Berlin: Akademie Verlag, 1982) 247–60.

Hill, D., "Son and Servant: An Essay on Matthean Christology", *Journal for the Study of the New Testament* 6 (1980), 2–16.

Hoffmann, P., "Der Petrus-Primat im Matthäusevangelium", in J. Gnilka (ed.), *Neues Testament und Kirche*, Festschrift R. Schnackenburg. (Freiburg: Herder, 1974) 94–114.

Hubbard, B. J., *The Matthean Redaction of a Primitive Apostolic Commissioning: An Exegesis of Matthew 28:16–20*. Missoula: SBL, 1974.

Hummel R., *Die Auseinandersetzung zwischen Kirche und Judentum im Matthäusevangelium*. Munich: Kaiser, 1963[1], 1966[2].

Johnson, M. D., "Reflections on a Wisdom Approach to Matthew's Christology", *CBQ* 36 (1974) 44–74.

Kahmann, J., "Die Verheissung an Petrus. Mt 16:18–19 im Zusammenhang des Matthäusevangelium", in M. Didier (ed.), *L'Evangile selon Matthieu*.

Käsemann, E., "The Beginnings of Christian Theology", in E. Käsemann, *New Testament Questions of Today* (London: SCM, 1969) 82–107.

Kilpatrick, G. D., *The Origins of the Gospel according to St Matthew.* Oxford: OUP, 1946.

Kingsbury, J. D., *The Parables of Jesus in Matthew 13.* Richmond: John Knox; London: SPCK, 1969.

—"The Composition and Christology of Matt 28:16–20", *JBL* 93 (1974) 573–84.

—*Matthew: Structure, Christology and Kingdom.* Philadelphia: Fortress, 1975; London: SPCK, 1976.

—"The Figure of Peter in Matthew's Gospel as a Theological Problem", *JBL* 98 (1979) 67–83.

Krentz, E., "The Extent of Matthew's Prologue", *JBL* 83 (1964) 409–14.

Künzel, G., *Studien zum Gemeindeverständnis des Matthäus-Evangeliums*, Stuttgart: Calwer, 1978.

Lambrecht, J., "The Parousia Discourse: Composition and Content in Mt. XXIV–XXV", in M. Didier (ed.), *L'Evangile selon Matthieu*, 309–42.

Lange, J., *Das Erscheinen des Auferstandenen im Evangelium nach Matthäus.* Würzburg: Echter, 1973.

—(ed.), *Das Matthäus-Evangelium*, Wege der Forschung 525. Darmstadt: Wissenschaftliche Buchgesellschaft, 1980.

Légasse, S., " 'L'antijudaïsme' dans l'Evangile selon Matthieu", in M. Didier (ed.), *L'Evangile selon Matthieu.*

Luz, U., "Die Erfüllung des Gesetzes bei Matthäus (5, 17–20)", *ZTK* 75 (1978) 398–435.

—"Die Jünger im Matthäusevangelium", *ZNW* 62 (1971) 141–71.

Martin, R. P., "St Matthew's Gospel in Recent Study", *ExpTim* 80 (1968–9) 132–6.

Massaux, E., *Influence de L'Evangile de saint Matthieu sur la littérature chrétienne avant saint Irenée.* Louvain: Publications Universitaires, 1950.

Meier, J. P., *Law and History in Matthew's Gospel.* Rome: Biblical Institute Press, 1976.

—*The Vision of Matthew: Christ, Church and Morality in the First Gospel.* New York: Paulist Press, 1979.

—"John the Baptist in Matthew's Gospel", *JBL* 99 (1980) 383–405.

Michel, O., "Der Abschluss des Matthäusevangeliums", *Evangelische Theologie* 10 (1950–1) 16–26.

Minear, P. S., "False Prophecy and Hypocrisy in the Gospel of Matthew", in J. Gnilka (ed.), *Neues Testament und Kirche.* Festschrift R. Schnackenburg (Freiburg: Herder, 1974) 76–93.

—"The Disciples and the Crowds in the Gospel of Matthew", *Anglican Theological Review* Supplementary Series III (1974) 28–44.

Moule, C. F. D., "St Matthew's Gospel: Some Neglected Features", *Studia Evangelica II* (Berlin 1964) 91–9; rep. in C. F. D. Moule, *Essays in New Testament Interpretation* (Cambridge: CUP, 1982) 67–74.

Neirynck, F., "La redaction Matthéenne et la structure du premier évangile" in I. de la Potterie (ed.), *De Jésus aux Evangiles* (Gembloux: Duculot,

1967) 41–73; rep. in *Evangelica: Collected Essays by F. Neirynck* (Leuven: Peeters and the University Press, 1982) 3–36.

Nepper-Christensen, P., *Das Matthäusevangelium – ein judenchristliches Evangelium?* Aarhus: Universitetsforlaget, 1958.

Nolan, B., *The Royal Son of God: The Christology of Matthew 1–2*. Göttingen: Vandenhoeck u. Ruprecht; Fribourg Suisse; Editions Universitaires, 1979.

Pesch, W., *Matthäus, der Seelsorger*. Stuttgart: KBW, 1966.

Przybylski, B., *Righteousness in Matthew and his World of Thought*, Cambridge: CUP, 1980.

Rist, J. M., *On the Independence of Matthew and Mark*. Cambridge: CUP, 1978.

Rohde, J., *Rediscovering the Teaching of the Evangelists*. ET London: SCM, 1968.

Rothfuchs, W., *Die Erfullungszitate des Matthäus-Evangeliums*, Stuttgart: Kohlhammer, 1969.

Sand, A., *Das Gesetz und die Propheten: Untersuchungen zur Theologie des Evangeliums nach Matthäus*. Regensburg: Pustet, 1974.

Schlatter, A., *Die Kirche des Matthäus*. Gutersloh, 1930.

Schweizer, E., "Observance of the Law and Charismatic Activity in Matthew", *NTS* 16 (1970) 213–30.

—*Church Order in the New Testament*. ET London: SCM, 1961.

—*Neotestamentica*. Zürich: Zwingli, 1963.

—*Beiträge zur Theologie des Neuen Testaments*. Zurich: Zwingli, 1970.

—*Matthäus und seine Gemeinde*. Stuttgart: KBW, 1974. (The essay translated here is taken from this volume.)

Senior, D. P., *The Passion Narrative According to Matthew*. Leuven: University Press, 1975.

Segbroeck, F. van, "Les citations d'accomplissement dans l'Evangile selon Matthieu d'après trois ouvrages récents" in M. Didier (ed.), *L'Evangile selon Matthieu*, 107–30.

Slingerland, H. D., "The Transjordanian Origin of St Matthew's Gospel", *Journal for the Study of the New Testament* 3 (1979) 18–28.

Soares Prabhu, G. M., *The Formula Quotations in the Infancy Narrative of Matthew*. Rome: Pontifical Biblical Institute, 1976.

Stanton, G. N., "5 Ezra and Matthean Christianity in the Second Century", *JTS* 28 (1977) 67–83.

—"Matthew 11:28–30: Comfortable Words?", *ExpTim* 94 (1982) 3–9.

—"The Origin and Purpose of Matthew's Gospel: Matthean Scholarship from 1945–1980", *Aufstieg und Niedergang der Römischen Welt* II, 25, 3, ed. H. Temporini und W. Haase. Berlin: de Gruyter, 1983.

—"Matthew as a Creative Interpreter of the Sayings of Jesus", in P. Stuhlmacher (ed.), *Das Evangelium und die Evangelien*. Tübingen: Mohr, 1983.

Stendahl, K., *The School of Matthew and its Use of the Old Testament*. Lund and Copenhagen, 1954[1]; Philadelphia: Fortress 1968[2].

—"Quis et Unde? An Analysis of Mt 1–2", in W. Eltester (ed.), *Judentum, Urchristentum: Kirche*, Festschrift J. Jeremias (Berlin: Topelmann, 1960) 94–105.

Strecker, G., *Der Weg der Gerechtigkeit*. Gottingen: Vandenhoeck u. Ruprecht, 1962¹, 1966², 1971³.

—"Das Geschichtsverständnis des Matthäus", *Evangelische Theologie* 26 (1966) 57–74; rep. in J. Lange (ed.), *Wege der Forschung*. ET in *JAAR* 35 (1967) 219–30.

Suggs, M. J., *Wisdom, Christology and Law in Matthew's Gospel*. Cambridge, Mass.: Harvard University Press, 1970.

Thompson, W. G., *Matthew's Advice to a Divided Community: Matthew 17:22—18:35*. Rome: Pontifical Biblical Institute, 1970.

—"An Historical Perspective in the Gospel of Matthew", *JBL* 93 (1974) 243–62.

Tilborg, S. van, *The Jewish Leaders in Matthew*. Leiden: Brill, 1972.

Trilling, W., *Das Wahre Israel*. Leipzig: St Benno 1961²; Munich: Kosel, 1964³.

—"Amt und Amtverständnis bei Matthäus", in A. Descamps and A. de Halleux (ed.), *Mélanges bibliques en hommage au R. P. Béda Rigaux* (Gembloux: Duculot, 1970) 29–44.

—"Zum Petrusamt im Neuen Testament", *Theologische Quartalschrift* 151, (1971) 110–33.

Via, D. O., "The Church as the Body of Christ in the Gospel of Matthew", *SJT* 11 (1958), 271–86.

Viviano, B. T., "Where was the Gospel according to Matthew Written?", *CBQ* 41 (1979) 533–46.

Vögtle, A., "Das christologische und ekklesiologische Anliegen von Mt 28, 18–20", in F. L. Cross (ed.), *Studia Evangelica II* (Berlin: Akademie Verlag, 1964) 266–94.

Walker, R., *Die Heilsgeschichte im ersten Evangelium*. Göttingen: Vandenhoeck u. Ruprecht, 1967.

Zumstein, J., *La Condition du croyant dans l'évangile selon Matthieu*. Fribourg, Göttingen: Vandenhoeck u. Ruprecht, 1977.

Index of Matthean References

162

Index

Select Index of Subjects